Batsford Chess Library

Beating the French
Gary Lane

An Owl Book
Henry Holt and Company
New York

To Regula, Samuel and Benjamin Zutter

Henry Holt and Company, Inc.
Publishers since 1866
115 West 18th Street
New York, New York 10011

Henry Holt® is a registered
trademark of Henry Holt and Company, Inc.

Library of Congress Catalog Card Number: 93-80864

ISBN 0-8050-3292-4 (An Owl Book: pbk.)

First American Edition—1994

Printed in the United Kingdom
All first editions are printed on acid-free paper.∞

10   9   8   7   6   5   4   3   2   1

Adviser: R. D. Keene, GM, OBE
Technical Editor: Graham Burgess

Contents

Symbols

+	Check
++	Double check
#	Checkmate
± (∓)	Slight advantage to White (Black)
± (∓)	Clear advantage to White (Black)
+− (−+)	Winning advantage to White (Black)
=	Level position
!	Good move
?	Bad move
!!	Outstanding move
??	Blunder
!?	Interesting move
?!	Dubious move
Ch	Championship
Wch	World Championship
Z	Zonal
IZ	Interzonal
C	Candidates
OL	Olympiad
corr.	Postal game

Introduction

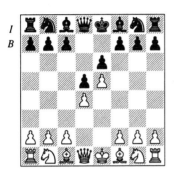

I
B

A Brief History

The surge of popularity in the Advance French during recent years has seen it become one of the most challenging openings available. The question of how to respond to the French Defence has in the past concentrated on 3 ♘c3 and 3 ♘d2, with a mass of theoretical analysis to absorb. Consequently, attention has turned to the lesser known Advance, with a wealth of promising new ideas being contributed by such world-class players as Anand, Nunn and Short. This book aims to present the common variations with an emphasis on the most popular lines and allow the reader to create a repertoire suited to his or her style.

It has a fine pedigree with early devotees such as Jaenisch and Paulsen. It was a frequent choice of Aron Nimzowitsch who transformed the understanding of the line. Since the 1930s its popularity has fluctuated as players began to follow fashion by exhaustively analysing the Tarrasch and Winawer variations. In the 1980s and 1990s the reversal of fortunes has been accomplished by shedding the unfair image as a gambit line to concentrate on adventurous, reliable systems that are still being explored.

Ideas in the Advance French

1) The Centre

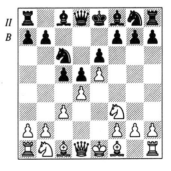

II
B

This is the critical position of the Advance French. Black has developed so as to put pressure on d4. The 'Nimzowitsch' pawn centre (d4, e5 for White, e6, d5 for Black) requires White to support d4 and be ready to meet ...f6. White's space advantage affords him the luxury of choosing between positional and tactical continuations; thus White can sometimes instigate a kingside attack, or can otherwise try to restrict Black's forces further.

The current trend is 6 a3, which is discussed in Chapter 1. The idea is that b4 will gain greater space and rule out the prospect of a queenside pawn advance by Black. In tournament practice Black tends to adopt a direct plan of putting pressure on d4 and controlling the c-file with his queen's rook. A less positive response can see Black's game deteriorate due to the lack of active squares for his minor pieces.

The following position is typical:

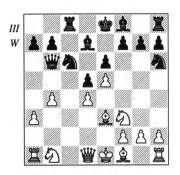

Now White plays 10 &d3 ♘g4 11 0-0 &e7 12 ♘bd2 ♘xe3 13 fxe3 0-0

14 ♘b3 f6?! 15 exf6 &xf6 16 ♘c5 ♖cd8 17 ♘e5 &xe5 18 &xh7+ shattering Black's defences. See the note to Black's 11th move in Game 13.

A number of games examine the consequences of Black preventing b4 with 6...c4, followed by queenside castling. This leads to a long manoeuvring game where White has a slight edge thanks to his space advantage. Black often tries to obtain counterplay by a rapid pawn push on the kingside. The usual problem with this is that lack of co-ordination amongst Black's cramped minor pieces results in White either picking off the pawns themselves or else using the vacant squares in their wake to infiltrate Black's camp. It is also possible for White to launch a queenside attack. This can be achieved with the b4 thrust which, if taken, enables the queen's rook to enter the fray on the b-file; if ignored, then a4 will help to reduce Black's activity severely. The following position demonstrates that knowledge of a standard idea in this line can have a dramatic effect.

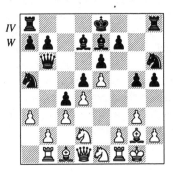

White now plays 14 ♗h1! 0-0-0 15 ♘g2 g4 16 ♘e3 ♖dg8 17 b4 ♘c6 18 a4 h4 19 ♘dxc4! and White has excellent prospects. See Game 5. Thus Black cannot completely ignore White's attacking prospects by merely launching a pawn storm.

Therefore an early ...f6 to contest the centre is sometimes considered the antidote. However, this move leaves e6 weak and backward, and White can then focus on controlling the e-file. In return Black has more freedom to find better posts for his pieces, resulting in a double-edged game. See Games 7 and 8.

White's most ambitious approach is the Milner-Barry Gambit. 6 ♗d3, placing the bishop on its most active square, is regarded as an extremely aggressive continuation. It is renowned for numerous tactical possibilities with White sacrificing his d- and e-pawns for active play. Black often has trouble neutralizing White's lead in development, since the black queen is constantly hounded. The following position shows a key point of the gambit; the e- and d-files are open *(see following diagram):*

Now White can convert his lead in development into a mating combination: 17 g3 ♕g5 18 ♕xd5+! exd5 19 ♗b6+ axb6 20 ♖e8 mate. The complete game can seen in the note to Black's 12th move in Game 14.

There are various ways for Black to shield his exposed queen; note how many variations there are in

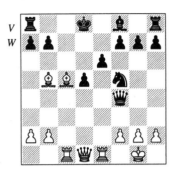

Chapter 2! In view of the defensive problems experienced when both pawns are taken, Black will often settle just for the d-pawn, when White has to rely on positional advantages as a form of compensation rather than a direct attack. See Game 16. It is worth taking an interest in the bizarre 9 ♘g5 featured in Game 14, note to White's 9th move.

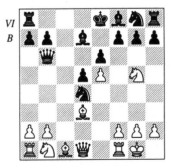

A move that has largely been explored in Scandinavian postal games, it has tremendous surprise value and there is still a lot of scope for new ideas. The initial point is to provoke Black into weakening his kingside pawn structure while trying

to make use of the open lines to launch an attack.

Chapter 3 deals with 6 ♗e2, which is a solid and reliable line. White will develop steadily while keeping d4 securely guarded. Black relies on queenside expansion to add tension to the position. The following position demonstrates the type of slight edge for which White is aiming:

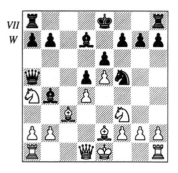

Now 12 a3! ♗xc3+ 13 ♘xc3 0-0 14 0-0 ♖ac8 15 b4 with advantage to White – see line 'b' in the note to Black's 11th move in Game 17.

2) Black Avoids 5...♕b6

The desire to follow an independent path has prompted research into a variety of alternatives. The common approach is 5...♗d7 which is discussed in Chapter 4 and often transposes to established lines. It has the benefit of not committing the queen until White has declared a plan of action. Sometimes Black follows up with ...f6. The task for White is to

maintain a pawn on e5 and then seek to exploit the resultant space advantage.

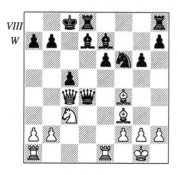

An idea of White's attacking possibilities can be gauged from Romanishin-Ivanchuk, Irkutsk 1986. White won in fine style with 18 ♘b5!! ♗xb5 19 ♗xb7+ 1-0. The note to Black's 9th move in Game 20 illustrates the game.

The standard response is 6 ♗e2, in the knowledge that 6...♕b6 would transpose to a poor line that is demonstrated in section 4 of this introduction. Instead, Black follows a plan of ...♘ge7-f5 while White counters with ♘a3-c2 before trying to make progress on the kingside. See Games 21, 22 and 23. Also possible is 6 a3 which is less convincing with the queen on d8 but is perfectly feasible. The disadvantage is that ...♕c7 will put pressure on e5; Black follows up by ...f6 or the manoeuvre ...♘e7-c8-b6, having saved a tempo with his queen.

Chapter 5 examines an early knight sortie with ...♘ge7. Play is similar to the previous chapter although White has the option of ♗d3. A likely continuation is ...♘f5 to increase pressure on d4. White can reply with ♘a3-c2 and ♗d3 which can be seen in Game 31. A more active course of action is to be found in Game 30 by responding with ♗d3 and g4 to oust the knight on f5, followed by a kingside attack.

After 5...♘h6 White can follow the illustrative game in Chapter 6 with 6 dxc5 or transpose to other lines. It represents one of Black's most fashionable defences and the relative lack of theory has encouraged a growing band of followers.

3) Exchange of Light-Squared Bishops

These lines feature Black resolving to exchange White's king's bishop. However, while this is positionally desirable, it involves a loss of time which allows White to seize the initiative. One of the most popular is the Wade Variation, which involves the manoeuvre ...♗c8-d7-b5.

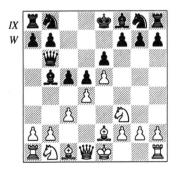

The most radical way to invite complications is to play c4 which is discussed in detail in Chapter 9. If Black routinely exchanges on c4 then White can cause disruption with the pawn thrust d5. Thus after 7 c4 ♗xc4 8 ♗xc4 dxc4 9 d5 ♘e7 10 dxe6 fxe6 11 0-0 ♕c6 12 ♕e2 ♘f5 13 ♕xc4 ♗e7 14 ♘c3 0-0 15 ♗g5 ♕a6 16 ♘b5 ♗xg5 17 ♘xg5 ♘d4 18 ♕xc5 ♘xb5 19 a4 White will take on b5 when the extra pawn should secure victory. See the note to Black's 8th move in Game 39. For those preferring a more positional approach, Game 40 examines 7 dxc5 ♗xc5 8 0-0 ♗xe2 9 ♕xe2 ♕a6 10 ♕c2 ♘d7 11 a4 which also gives White good prospects.

It is also possible to try to exchange bishops with 3...b6, planning ...♗a6. This was once considered to be one of the main defences, but the modern treatment 4 ♗b5+, which has been championed by Anand, has forcibly demonstrated that White can pose Black numerous problems. The point is that 4...♗d7 is answered strongly by 5 ♗d3 when the uncompleted fianchetto is a potential weakness. The main alternative 4...c6 5 ♗a4 gives White sufficient time to exploit his territorial advantage, especially as there is little pressure on d4. See Game 41.

Chapter 11 features a rare move: 3...♗d7, aiming to continue with 4...a6 and 5...♗b5. Black's positional aims are laudable, but this is no help to his lagging development.

4) White exchanges on c5

The burden on White to maintain the chain of pawns c3, d4 and e5 has led Black to tempt fate by avoiding an exchange of pawns in the centre for as long as possible. While the aim may be to reduce White's options, very often the opposite is the case. Thus there are cases when White can break up the pawn structure by taking on c5, generally followed by b4 intending to limit Black's activity further:

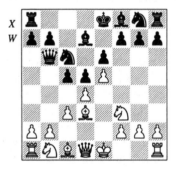

Now White plays 7 dxc5! ♗xc5 8 0-0 f6 9 b4 ♗e7 10 ♗f4 fxe5 11 ♘xe5 ♘xe5 12 ♗xe5 ♘f6 13 ♘d2 and the outpost on e5 gives White the advantage. See the note to Black's 6th move in Game 14 for details.

The exchange on c5 can also occur when Black has temporarily blocked the bishop's route to c5 by playing ...♘ge7. Consider the following example:

This position (*see following diagram*) is from Euwe-Kramer, Zaandem 1946. White now gained an

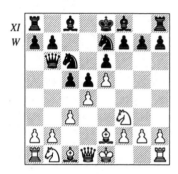

advantage with 7 dxc5! ♕c7 (or 7...♕xc5 8 b4 ♕b6 9 b5 ±) 8 ♘d4 ♘xe5? 9 ♘b5 ♕xc5 10 ♕d4 +−. The example is from the note to Black's 6th move in Game 17.

5) White Deviations

5 ♗e3, which is examined in Chapter 7, represents White's soundest way to avoid well-known lines. It has the benefit of keeping the option of ♘e2 which allows White to adopt a set-up different from that which is usually associated with the opening. The d4 pawn is well supported, freeing White's hands to attack on the kingside. It has only recently been subjected to serious attention at tournament level and so the theory of the line is still evolving.

Chapter 8 deals with various miscellaneous ideas for White. These offer independent lines which require little knowledge of theory to play. 4 ♕g4 is an aggressive line that attempts to disrupt Black's development by targeting g7. However, while the activity of White's queen can prove useful, Black can gain counterplay by undermining White's pawn centre.

By omitting 4 c3 in favour of 4 ♘f3 (like 4 ♕g4, an idea pioneered by Nimzowitsch) White aims to accelerate his development. The consequence of this may be that White must gambit the d4-pawn, in return for a firm grip on the e5 square and piece play. With best play White should restore material equality after a while, when the chances ought to be equal.

4 dxc5 is an interesting line. White continues by quietly developing and maintaining support of e5. It offers Black some chances to go wrong but is considered relatively harmless.

6) General Strategy and Suggested Repertoires

For those interested in creating a repertoire with the Advance French, the following alternatives might be considered.

Firstly, for players who wish to build up methodically:

1) Meet 5...♕b6 by either 6 a3 (Chapter 1) or 6 ♗e2 (Chapter 3), and answer 5...♗d7 by 6 ♗e2 (Chapter 4).

2) The Wade variation can be met by 7 dxc5.

3) The recommendation 4 ♗b5+ is suitable for all players to seek an advantage in Chapter 9.

Secondly, for more aggressive players who delight in complications:

1) The games contained in Chapter 2 should provide suitable inspiration.

2) Meeting 5...♗d7 by 6 ♗d3 will usually transpose to a Milner-Barry Gambit, but consideration should also be given to 6 dxc5 (see Game 29).

3) The Wade variation is well met by 7 c4.

However, in order to obtain a feel for the characteristic middlegame positions which arise from the Advance French, the reader is recommended to play through each illustrative game.

1 Modern Variation

The Modern Variation was originally inspired by Paulsen. However, it is only in recent decades that its popularity has expanded to the point where it is considered the main line. The idea of 6 a3 is to gain space on the queenside. This forces Black to resolve c5-d4 pawn tension, which can then allow White to develop his light-squared bishop to its optimum square. The variation has been championed by such players as Fedorowicz, Korchnoi and Tal.

Game 1
Sveshnikov-Timman
Tilburg 1992

1	e4	e6
2	d4	d5
3	e5	c5
4	c3	♘c6
5	♘f3	♕b6
6	a3 *(1)*	

White's plan is to continue with 7 b4 and take the pressure off the centre by removing the tension on d4.

| 6 | ... | c4 |

With this move Black pinpoints b3 as a weakness. The next stage

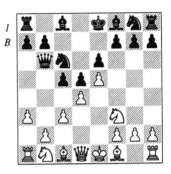

usually consists of a long manoeuvring phase. White aims to control the kingside by advancing his pawns, while Black takes charge on the opposite flank.

The main alternatives 6...♘h6, 6...a5 and 6...♗d7 are examined later in this chapter.

The rarer continuations do not merit detailed coverage:

a) 6...f6?! and now:

a1) 7 exf6 ♘xf6 8 ♗e2 (8 b4 cxd4 9 cxd4 ♗d6 10 ♗b2 0-0 11 ♗e2 a6 12 0-0 ♘e4 13 ♘bd2 = Mestel-Comay, Tel Aviv 1977) 8...♗e7 9 b4 c4 10 0-0 0-0 11 ♗g5 a5 = Corvi-Santis, Rome 1990.

a2) 7 ♗d3! ♗d7 (7...cxd4 8 cxd4 ♗d7 9 b4 ± Nilsson-Thorbergsson,

Munich 1958) 8 0-0 (8 b4!?) 8...fxe5 9 dxe5 0-0-0 10 ♕c2 ♘ge7 11 ♗xh7 g6 12 ♗xg6 ♘xg6 13 ♕xg6 ♗e7 and Black has active play in compensation for the sacrificed pawns; M.Schlosser-McDonald, Oakham 1988.

b) 6...♘ge7 7 dxc5! ♕xc5 (or 7...♕c7 8 ♘d4! ♕xe5+ 9 ♗e2 ± *ECO*) 8 ♗d3 ♘g6 9 ♕e2 ♗e7 10 0-0 0-0 11 g3 ♕b6 12 ♗e3 ♕c7 13 ♗d4 ♗d7 14 ♘bd2 ♘xd4 14 cxd4 ♖ac8 16 h4 f5 17 exf6 gxf6 18 h5 ♘h8 19 ♘h4 ♘f7 20 ♘f5 ± Hloušek-Mišta, Olomouc 1977.

7 ♘bd2   ♗d7

7...♘ge7? would be a disaster after 8 ♗xc4! (Xie-Akhsharumova, Thessaloniki OL 1988) 8...dxc4 9 ♘xc4 intending ♘d6+ winning.

8 b3!?

This is unusual, but the opportunity to free the position has presented itself since Black has avoided the more common move-order 7...♘a5. Now 8 ♗e2 would transpose to the next illustrative game, but Sveshnikov reveals a different approach.

8 ...   cxb3
9 ♘xb3   ♘a5

The preparatory move 9...♖c8 should be considered as a possible improvement.

10 ♘xa5   ♕xa5
11 ♗d2   ♕a4
12 ♕b1! *(2)*

A delicate switch which results in

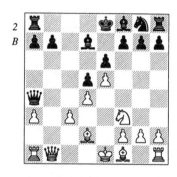

the queen adopting a more positive role. The pawn on b7 is attacked, while ♗d3 will prove to be bothersome if Black envisages castling kingside.

12 ...   ♗c6

Black may try to reinforce his control over c4 with 12...b5. However, this can be undermined by 13 ♗d3 intending ♗c2 and a4.

In Prié-Apicella, Paris 1990, White's unusually placed queen proved its worth after 12...b6 13 ♗d3 ♘e7 14 0-0 ♖c8 15 ♘e1 g6 16 ♘c2 ♗g7 17 ♘e3 ♕c6 18 a4 ♕c7 19 c4 ♗c6 20 cxd5 ♘xd5 21 ♘xd5 ♗xd5 22 ♗b5+ ♔f8 23 ♖c1 ♕d8 24 ♕b4+ ♔g8 25 ♖xc8 ♕xc8 26 ♕e7 ♗f8 27 ♕xa7 ♕d8 28 ♖c1 h5 29 ♖c7 ♖h7 30 ♕xb6 ♕h4 31 h3 ♕e4 32 ♗f1 g5 32 ♖c8 1-0.

13 ♗d3   ♘e7
14 0-0   h6?!

Timman prefers 14...♘c8 with the idea of ...♘b6 and and ...♖d8 with decent chances. However, White can play the aggressive 15 ♗xh7 g6 16

16 ♗xg6 fxg6 17 ♕xg6+ ♔d7 18 ♕f6 ♖g8 19 ♘g5 forcing 19...♖xg5, and White is better according to Sveshnikov.

15	♖c1	♘c8
16	c4	dxc4?

In a difficult position Black walks into a crafty trap. Necessary was 16...♘b6, after which White would still be better placed: 17 cxd5 exd5 (17...♘xd5 18 ♖c4 ♕b5 19 ♖b4 +−) 18 e6! with the advantage.

17	♖xc4	♕b5
18	♕xb5	♗xb5 (3)

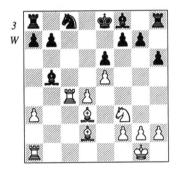

3
W

19   ♖xc8+

White engineers a won ending.

19	...	♖xc8
20	♗xb5+	♔d8
21	♔f1	♔c7
22	♖c1+	♔b8
23	♖xc8+	♔xc8
24	♗e8	

White can demonstrate his superiority by pursuing the kingside pawns and consequently wrecking their structure.

24	...	f6
25	a4	♗e7
26	♗f7	♔d7
27	d5!	exd5
28	e6+	1-0

Game 2
Sveshnikov-Eingorn
Palma de Mallorca 1989

1	e4	e6
2	d4	d5
3	e5	c5
4	c3	♘c6
5	♘f3	♕b6

5...f6 which aims to undermine the pawn chain, but Nimzowitsch demonstrated the way to handle this idea: 6 ♗b5! ♗d7 (6...a6!? 7 ♗xc6+ bxc6 8 0-0 cxd4 9 cxd4 c5 10 exf6 gxf6 11 ♖e1 ±) 7 0-0 ♕b6 (7...♘xe5? 8 ♘xe5 ♗xb5 9 ♕h5+ ♔e7 11 ♕f7+ ♔d6 12 dxc5+ ♔xe5 13 ♖e1+ ♔f5 14 ♕h5+ g5 14 g4#; 7...f5?! 8 c4! a6 9 ♗xc6 bxc6 10 ♘c3 cxd4 11 ♘xd4 ± Maudsley-Wise, British Junior Ch 1970) 8 ♗xc6 bxc6 9 exf6 ♘xf6 (9...gxf6 10 ♘e5!) 10 ♘e5 ♗d6 11 dxc5 ♗xc5 12 ♗g5 ♕d8 13 ♗xf6 ♕xf6 14 ♕h5+! g6 15 ♕e2 ♖d8 16 ♘d2 0-0 17 ♖ae1 ♖fe8 18 ♔h1 ♗d6 19 f4 c5 (Nimzowitsch-Levenfish, Karlsbad 1911) 20 ♕a6! ±.

In Vasiukov-Velimirović, Vršac 1989, an attempt to stifle White's attacking ambitions with 5...f5?! failed after 6 ♗e2 c4 7 b3 cxb3 8 axb3 ♗e7 9 h4 ♘h6 10 ♗xh6 gxh6 11 ♕c1

♕b6 12 ♕xh6 ♕xb3 13 ♕g7 ♖f8 14
0-0 ♕c2 15 ♗d1 ♕b2 16 ♘g5 ♔d8
17 ♘xh7 ♖e8 18 ♗h5 ♗d7 19 ♘a3
♗xh4 20 ♗xe8 ♗xe8 21 ♘f8 1-0.

6 a3   c4
7 ♘bd2   ♘a5

Without doubt the safest choice at
Black's disposal.

Attempts to destabilize the centre
are not so good, for example 7...f6!?
8 ♗e2 (8 g3!? fxe5 9 ♘xe5 ♘f6 10
f4!± Cooley-Brown, Middlesex 1985)
and now *(4)*:

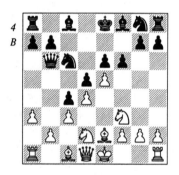

a) 8...fxe5 9 ♘xe5 ♘f6 (after
9...♘xe5 10 dxe5 ♘h6 11 ♘xc4!
dxc4 12 ♗xh6 ♗d7 13 ♗g5 ♕xb2
14 0-0 ♕xc3 15 ♗h5+ g6 16 ♕b1
White is better according to Pähtz)
10 f4 ♗d6 11 ♘df3! (11 ♗h5+ g6
12 ♗f3 0-0 13 ♕e2 ♗e7 14 0-0
♘xe5 15 fxe5 ♘e8 16 ♗g4 ♖xf1+
17 ♔xf1 ♗d7 18 g3 ♘g7 19 h4
♖f8+ 20 ♔g2 ♕d8 21 ♘f3 ± Prié-
Wintzer, Lugano 1989) 11...0-0 12
0-0 ♗d7 13 ♘xd7 ♘xd7 14 g3 ♘f6
15 ♔g2 ♘e4 16 ♗xc4! ♘xc3 17

bxc3 dxc4 18 ♕e2 ♖fe8 19 ♕xc4 +−
Kharlov-Guedon, Torcy 1991.

b) 8...♗d7 9 0-0 and now:

b1) 9...0-0-0 10 b3! cxb3 11
♘xb3 ♕c7 12 ♖b1 ♗e8 13 ♗f4 h6
14 c4 ± Sveshnikov-Meshkov, Podolsk 1990.

b2) 9...♘a5 10 ♖e1 ♘e7 11 ♗f1
♘g6 12 h4! fxe5 13 h5 e4 14 hxg6
exf3 15 ♘xf3 ♘b3 16 ♘e5! ♘xa1
17 ♘f7 hxg6 18 ♘xh8 ♕b3 19 ♕f3
0-0-0 20 ♗g5 ♖e8 21 ♖xa1 +− Khar-
lov-Edelman, Maringa 1991.

8 ♗e2

There is little to be gained from
trying 8 b3?! cxb3 9 ♖b1 ♗d7 10
♗d3 ♗a4 11 c4 dxc4 12 ♘xc4 ♘xc4
13 ♗xc4 ♖c8 14 ♗xb3 ♗xb3 15
♖xb3 ♕a6 16 ♗d2 h6 17 ♕e2
♕xe2+ 18 ♔xe2 b6 19 a4 ♘e7 20 a5
♘d5 with at least equality; Emodi-
Glek, Budapest 1989.

8 ...   ♗d7
9 0-0   ♘e7 *(5)*

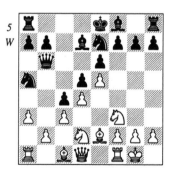

Black has tried a number of
other moves:

a) 9...h6 and now:

a1) 10 a4 ♘e7 11 ♕e1 g5 12 ♔h1 ♘g6 13 g3 ♗e7 14 ♗d1 h5 15 ♗c2 0-0-0 16 ♕d1 g4 17 ♘e1 ♗c6 18 ♘g2 ♖dg8 19 ♖e1 ♕d8 20 ♘f1 ♕f8 21 ♔g1 ♗d7 22 ♕e2 ♕g7 23 ♗d2 ♗d8 24 ♖eb1 ♗c7 25 ♘f4 ♘e7 26 ♘g2 ♖f8 27 ♖e1 ♔b8 28 ♗e3 ♘g6 ½-½ Vasiukov-Kuzmin, Moscow 1991.

a2) 10 ♖b1 0-0-0 11 b3 ♘xb3 12 ♘xb3 cxb3 13 c4 dxc4 14 ♗xc4 ♘e7 15 ♕d3 ♗c6 16 ♖xb3 ♕c7 17 ♗e3 ♔b8 18 ♖fb1 ♔a8 19 ♘d2 ½-½ Kjeldsen-Jensen, Lyngby 1989.

b) 9...0-0-0 and now:

b1) 10 ♖b1 f5 11 b3 cxb3 12 c4 ♗a4 13 cxd5 exd5 14 ♘g5 ♘h6 15 ♗b2 ♗e7 16 f4 ♔b8 17 ♗c3 ♘c4 18 ♘xc4 dxc4 19 ♗xc4 ♕c6 20 ♗xb3 ♕xc3 21 ♗xa4 ♕e3+ 22 ♔h1 ♖xd4 23 ♕b3 ♕xb3 24 ♗xb3 ♘g4 25 ♘e6 ♖d2 26 ♘xg7 ♘f2+ 27 ♖xf2 ♖xf2 28 ♗d5 ♖d8 29 ♗f3 ♖b2?? 30 ♖xb2 1-0 Westerinen-Tisdall, Gausdal 1992.

b2) 10 ♖e1 ♘h6 11 ♘f1 ♘f5 12 ♘e3 h6 13 ♖f1 ♗e7 14 ♘e1 ♘xe3 15 ♗xe3 f5 16 exf6 gxf6 17 ♖b1 ♗e8 18 ♗h5 ♗xh5 19 ♕xh5 ♗xa3 20 ♘f3 ♗e7 21 ♖fe1 ♕d6 22 ♘h4 ♘c6 23 ♘g6 ♖h7 24 ♗f4 ♕d7 25 ♕g4 e5 26 ♕xd7+ ♖xd7 27 dxe5 fxe5 28 ♘xe5 ♘xe5 29 ♖xe5 ♗d6 30 ♖e8+ ♔c7 31 ♗e3 a6 ½-½ Mukhametov-Naumkin, Leningrad 1991.

c) 9...f6 10 ♖b1 0-0-0 11 ♖e1 ♘e7 12 ♗f1 ♘g6 13 b3 cxb3 14 c4

fxe5 15 c5 ♕c7 16 ♘xe5 ♘xe5 17 ♖xe5 ♗xc5 18 ♘xb3 ♗d6 19 ♘xa5 ♕xa5 20 ♗d2 ♕c7 21 ♖e3 ♔b8 22 ♖eb3 ♔a8 23 ♖xb7 ♕xb7 24 ♖xb7 ♔xb7 25 ♗b4 ± Anand-Prasad, New Delhi 1987.

10 ♖e1

This is a safe continuation that offers White a small advantage with which to play for a win. The alternatives are:

a) 10 g3 ♘b3 (10...♘ec6 11 ♖b1 ♗e7 12 ♘e1 0-0-0 13 ♘?? ♔b8 14 ♘f4 ♔a8 15 ♗f3 ♗c8 16 ♖e1 ♗g5 17 b4 cxb3 18 ♘xb3 h6 19 ♘d3 with an unclear position; Nikolenko-Ristović, Moscow 1991) 11 ♘xb3 ♗a4 12 ♕d2 ♗xb3 13 ♘h4 ♘g6 14 ♘g2 ♘e7 15 h4 ♘c6 16 ♘e3 h5 17 f4 0-0-0 18 ♔h2 f5 19 exf6 gxf6 20 ♗f3 = Morales-Bellón, Palma 1991.

b) 10 ♘g5 h6 11 ♘h3 0-0-0 12 ♘f4 f5 13 exf6 gxf6 14 ♗f3 ♕d6 15 ♘h5 e5 16 ♖e1 e4 17 ♗e2 f5 18 a4 ♗e8 19 b4 ♗xh5 20 ♗xh5 ♘ac6 21 b5 ♘a5 22 g3 ♘g8 23 ♗a3 ♕d7 24 f4 ♘f6 25 ♗xf8 ♖dxf8 26 ♘f1 ♖hg8 27 ♘e3 ♔c7 28 ♖a2 ♖g7 29 ♔h1 ♖fg8 30 ♖g1 ♔b6 31 ♕e2 ♕e6 32 ♕d1 ♕d7 33 ♕e2 ♕e6 ½-½ Grošar-Bareev, Bled/Rogaška Slatina 1991.

10 ...   ♕c6

The queen makes room for the king's knight to shuffle along to b6. Such a slow process is possible due to the lack of feasible pawn breaks.

Black has also tried alternatives,

but has received little reward for the endeavour:

a) 10...♘c8 11 ♕c2 h6 12 a4 a6 13 ♗d1 ♘a7 14 h4 ♖c8 15 h5 ♗e7 16 ♖e3 ♔d8 17 ♕b1 ♘7c6 18 ♕a2 g5 19 ♘h2 f5 20 exf6 ♗xf6 21 ♘g4 ♗g7 22 ♖b1 e5 23 b4 cxb3 24 ♘xb3 ♘xb3 25 ♖xb3 ♕c7 26 ♘xe5 ± Sinowjew-Piskov, Dortmund 1992.

b) 10....♘g6 11 g3 ♗e7 12 h4 f5 13 h5 ♘f8 14 ♖b1 g5 15 b4 cxb3 16 c4 with an unclear position; Motwani-I.Gurevich, Hastings 1991.

c) 10...h6 and now:

c1) 11 ♕c2 0-0-0 12 ♖b1 ♔b8 13 ♘f1 ♕b3 14 ♕xb3 ♘xb3 15 ♗f4 ♘c8 16 ♘g3 ½-½ Sveshnikov-Nikolenko, USSR 1991.

c2) 11 ♖b1 ♘c8 12 ♘f1 ♕b3 13 ♕xb3 ♘xb3 14 ♗f4 ♗a4 15 ♘g3 b5 16 ♘h5 ♘b6 17 g4! ± Sveshnikov-Luce, Berlin 1989.

11 ♕c2   ♘c8
12 ♘g5

The best way to break down Black's fortress is to provoke concessions as part of a patient manoeuvring game.

12 ...   h6
13 ♘h3   ♘b6
14 ♘f4   0-0-0!

Black rightly judges that his king will be safer on the queenside. Now a standard misjudgment is that the kingside pawns need only to be pushed forward to force White to take defensive measures. In reality, such schemes are invariably flawed;

the pawns are easily picked off as it is difficult for Black to mobilize forces in their support.

15 ♘h5   ♕c7
16 a4

White has no desire to allow 16...♗a4, dislodging his queen.

16 ...   ♗c6
17 ♗d1   ♔b8
18 ♖e3! *(6)*

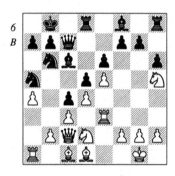

With this useful move White prepares to torment Black's kingside pawns. The long-term plan is to exploit the resulting weaknesses by rapidly transferring the queenside pieces to the other flank.

18 ...   ♖c8
19 ♖g3   g6
20 ♘f6   ♘d7
21 ♘xd7+   ♕xd7
22 ♖f3

Sveshnikov suggests 22 h4! as a way to pursue the initiative. This is similar to the actual game but saves time in view of the fact that the rook soon returns to g3.

22	...	♖c7
23	♕b1	♕e8
24	h4	h5

Now 24...♗e7 25 ♖h3 (25 h5 gxh5 with an unclear position) 25...h5 26 ♘f3 intending ♗g5 gives White the g5 square as a jumping-off point for invading Black's position.

25	♖g3	♗d7
26	♘f3	♘b3!

This simplifying exchange makes White's task of steadily claiming more space rather less smooth. It is necessary to hold on to the important dark-squared bishop but the drawback is that a4 is now under attack.

27	♗xb3	cxb3
28	a5	♗b5
29	♗g5	♗e2
30	♗f6?! *(7)*	

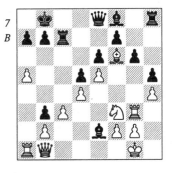

7
B

At this stage a finesse is required to present Black with more problems by temporarily shifting attention to the loose pawn on b3: 30 ♘d2 ♕b5 31 ♖e3 ♗c4 32 ♕d1 with a slight advantage according to Sveshnikov.

30	...	♖g8
31	♘g5	♗h6
32	♘h3	♗g4
33	♗g5	♗xh3
34	♖xh3	♗xg5
35	hxg5	♕d8
36	♖g3	♖c6
37	♕f1	♖a6
38	♕b5	♖e8!

The other rook comes across to the queenside to add to the defence. This ensures equality.

39	c4	dxc4
40	♖c3	♖c6
41	♖xc4	♖xc4
42	♕xc4	♕xg5
43	a6	

A blunt attack with 43 ♖c1?! actually manages to allow Black to contemplate trying to win the game after 43...♕d8! 44 a6 ♖e7!, when d4 will come under pressure.

43	...	♖c8
44	♕xb3	♖c1+
45	♖xc1	♕xc1+
46	♔h2	♕f4+

½-½

Game 3
Haba-Knaak
Halle 1987

1	e4	e6
2	d4	d5
3	e5	c5
4	c3	♘c6
5	♘f3	♕b6
6	a3	c4

7 ♘bd2

The rare alternatives are as follows:

a) 7 ♘g5 (suggested by Ciocaltea) 7...♗d7 8 ♕h5 ♘h6 9 ♘h3 g6!. Keres evaluated the position as slightly favourable to Black.

b) 7 b4 a5 8 ♗b2 axb4 9 axb4 ♖xa1 10 ♗xa1 ♕a6 11 ♘bd2 ♗xb4! 12 cxb4 ♘xb4 (intending ...♕xa1) 13 ♗c3 ♘a2 followed by ...♘e7-c6 and ...b5-b4 is Keres' recommendation to gain Black an advantage.

c) 7 ♗e2 ♗d7 8 0-0 f6?! (or 8...♘ge7 9 ♘bd2 ♘a5, transposing into Game 2, Sveshnikov-Eingorn) 9 ♘bd2 fxe5 10 ♘xe5 ♘xe5 11 dxe5 0-0-0 12 a4 ♘e7 13 b3 cxb3 14 ♘xb3 ± Bastrikov-Zurakhov, USSR 1955.

| 7 | ... | ♘a5 |
| **8** | **♖b1** | |

A popular idea that prepares a future b3 or b4.

8	...	♗d7
9	♗e2	♘e7
10	♘f1 (8)	

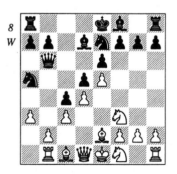

With this useful move White is cleverly trying to save a tempo. Normally White will castle, but then he must play ♖e1 in order to free f1 for the knight to transfer to the kingside. By playing ♘f1 first, White saves the tempo with the rook.

After the routine 10 0-0 Black may play:

a) 10...h6 11 ♖e1 (11 g3 0-0-0 12 ♘h4 ♔b8 {12...f5 13 exf6 gxf6 14 ♗g4 e5? 15 b3! cxb3 16 ♘xb3 f5 17 ♗h3 ♗a4 18 ♘xa5! ± Zaitsev-Farago, Szolnok 1975} 13 ♗h5 g6 13 ♗e2 ♕c7 15 ♘g2 ♗c6! = was Timman-Liberzon, Venice 1974) 11...♗c6 12 ♘f1 ♕b3 13 ♗f4 ♗a4 (13...♕xd1 14 ♗xd1 intending g4 and ♘g3 ±) 14 ♕c1 ♕b6 15 ♘3d2! ♘g6 16 ♗e3 ♘h4 (Sveshnikov-Eingorn, USSR Ch 1985) 17 ♗g4!? with equal chances.

b) 10...♘b3? 11 ♗xc4! ♘xd2 12 ♘xd2 dxc4 13 ♘xc4 followed by ♘d6+ and ♘f7 +−.

c) 10...♗c6 11 b4 cxb3 12 c4 dxc4 13 ♗xc4 h6 =.

d) 10...♘g6 11 ♖e1 ♗e7 12 g3 ♕c7 13 ♗f1 ♗c6 14 h4 ♕d7 15 h5 = Tischbierek-Vogt, Halle 1987.

e) 10...♘ec6 11 ♕c2 ♗e7 12 b4 cxb3 13 ♘xb3 ♘xb3 14 ♖xb3 ♕c7 15 c4 ♘a5 16 ♖c3 ♖c8 17 c5 ♗c6 18 ♘g5 ♕d8 19 ♖g3 ♗xg5 20 ♗xg5 ♕d7 21 ♗d2 ± Bartolome-Goldschmidt, Acasusso 1991.

f) 10...♕c7 11 ♘g5 h6 12 ♘h3 0-0-0 13 ♘f4 ♔b8 (13...g6!?) 14

♘h5 with an unclear game; Zaitsev-Vasiukov, Moscow 1969.

10 ...   f6

Black follows the traditional theme of striking at the centre in an effort to open up the position. In Sveshnikov-Eingorn, Sochi 1985, Black managed to defuse the situation by opting for an ending: 10...♕b3!? 11 ♗f4 ♗a4 12 ♕xb3 ♗xb3 13 ♘e3 ♘g6 14 ♗g3 h5 15 h4 ♗e7 16 ♘g5 ♗d8 17 ♘h3 ♘c6 18 ♘f4 ♘xf4 19 ♗xf4 ♘e7 20 ♗g5 ♘g6 21 ♗xd8 ♖xd8 22 g3 ♗a4 23 ♔d2 ♔d7 24 ♖af1 ♘e7 25 ♘g2 ♖h6 26 ♘f4 =.

11   h4   0-0-0
12   h5   ♘ec6
13   ♗f4

White is reluctant to release the tension with 13 exf6 gxf6 as Black can attempt to force through ...e5 with bright prospects.

13   ...   fxe5
14   ♘xe5   ♘xe5
15   ♗xe5   ♘c6

If 14...♗d6, then White maintains his territorial gains with 15 f4!.

16   ♗g3   e5?! *(9)*

Without a supporting pawn on f6, this gallant gesture lacks conviction. The quieter 16...♗e7 is a steadier option, although 17 ♘e3 and ♘g4 keeps a hold on the important e5 square.

17   dxe5   ♗c5

Not 17...d4? 18 ♘d2 with a winning game.

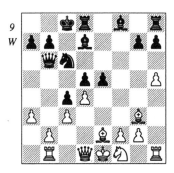

18   b4   cxb3
19   ♖xb3   ♕a5
20   ♘d2   ♖he8

It is difficult for Black to justify his pawn sacrifice, for example 20...d4 (20...♖de8 21 c4!) 21 0-0 d3 (21...♗e6 22 ♖b5 ♕xa3 23 ♘b1 +−) 22 e6 (22 ♗g4 ♖he8 23 e6 ♖xe6!? ±) 22...dxe2 (22...♗xe6 23 ♗g4 ♗d7 24 c4 +−) 23 exd7+ ♖xd7 24 ♕xe2 ± (Haba).

21   0-0   ♘xe5
22   ♕b1!   ♕c7 *(10)*

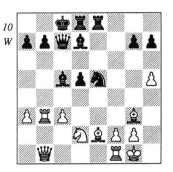

A practical choice, as it is the obvious way to defend b7. Other treatments invite complications but White emerges on top:

a) 22...h6 23 ♖xb7 ♗b6 24 ♘b3 ♕xa3 25 ♘c5! ♕xc5 (25...♗xc5 26 ♖b8+ ♔c7 27 ♗xe5+ ♖xe5 28 ♕b7+ and 29 ♖xd8) 26 ♗a6 ♗b5 27 ♕f5+ and White wins.

b) 22...♘c6 23 ♖xb7 ♗b6 24 ♘b3 ♕xa3 25 ♖xd7 ♖xd7 26 ♗g4 ±.

23   c4   ♗a4?!

This leads to a speedy débâcle. Black has slightly more chance of surviving after 23...d4 24 ♘e4 b6 (24...♗f8 25 ♗h4 ♗e7 26 ♗xe7 ♖xe7 27 ♖xb7 +−) 25 ♘xc5 ♕xc5 26 ♕xh7 ±.

24   cxd5   ♖xd5

Grabbbing the exchange also does not enable Black to defend: 24...♗xb3 25 ♘xb3 ♖xd5 26 ♖c1 b6 27 ♕e4 ♕d6 28 ♘xc5 ♖xc5 (28...bxc5 29 f4 +−) 29 ♖d1 ♕c6 30 ♕xh7 ±.

25   ♘e4   ♗xb3
26   ♕xb3   ♖ed8

There is no redemption for Black:

a) 26...♖d4 27 ♕b5 ♖xe4 28 ♕xe8+ ♕d8 29 ♗g4+ +−.

b) 26...♕a5 27 ♖c1 ♔b8 28 ♗c4 ♖d4 29 ♗a6! ♕xa6 (29...♗b6 30 ♕f7 +−) 30 ♘xc5 ♕b6 (30...♕c6 31 ♗xe5+ ♖xe5 32 ♘a6+ +−) 31 ♕f7 ♕b5 32 ♘e6 +−.

27   ♗c4   ♖d4
28   ♗e6+   ♔b8
29   ♘xc5   ♕xc5
30   ♕e3   1-0

Game 4
Degraeve-Delmont
Belfort 1992/93

1	e4	e6
2	d4	d5
3	e5	c5
4	c3	♘c6
5	♘f3	♕b6
6	a3	c4
7	♘bd2	

White can experiment with 7 h4, aiming to increase his control of the kingside while keeping options open as to where to position the king's bishop. It is relatively unknown, although Black tends to secure equality by forming a defence based upon an early ...f6.

a) 7...♗d7 8 h5 and now:

a1) 8...f6 9 ♕e2 ♘a5 (9...fxe5 10 ♘xe5 ♘xe5 11 dxe5 ♗c5 =) 10 ♗f4 ♘b3 11 ♖a2 0-0-0 12 g4 ♘h6 13 ♗h3 ♘f7 14 0-0 g5! 15 ♗e3 ♗e7 16 exf6 ♗xf6 17 ♘e5 ♖hf8 18 ♘xd7 ♖xd7 19 ♘d2 ♘xd2 20 ♕xd2 ♕d6 21 ♖aa1 = Djurić-Vaganian, Bled/Rogaška Slatina 1991.

a2) 7...♗d7 8 h5 h6 9 ♘h4 ♘a5 10 ♘d2 0-0-0 11 ♖b1 ± Khomiakov-Kabadze, Budapest 1992.

b) 7...f6 8 exf6 (8 ♕e2) 8...♘xf6 9 ♘bd2 ♗d6 10 b3 cxb3 11 ♕xb3 ♕xb3 12 ♘xb3 0-0 = Miljanić-Müller, Budapest 1989.

c) 7...♘a5 8 g3 transposes to Game 6, Sveshnikov-Eingorn, Sochi 1986.

7	...	♞a5
8	♗e2	♗d7
9	h4!? *(11)*	

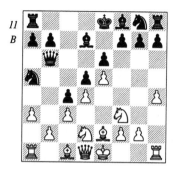

The closed nature of the position allows White a certain amount of room for creativity. Normally when advancing his h-pawn, White has in mind the possibility of continuing with g3 and ♗h3. In this case, the purpose is to stifle Black's kingside play with h5.

9 ... h5

A reflex move which blocks White's intended push, but gives up the g5 square for future operations.

10	♖b1	♞e7
11	♞f1	

This device to save time can be recognised from the game Haba-Knaak. White delays a decision about castling whilst the knight can leap to g3 or e3.

11	...	♞b3
12	♗g5	

The drawback of ...h5 is clear; the bishop can take up an active post.

12	...	♗a4
13	♞e3	♞c6 *(12)*

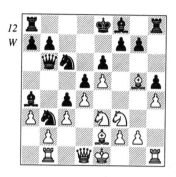

14 ♔f1

A preliminary measure to lessen the influence of a possible discovered attack on the queen. Now 14...♕a6 can be met with ♕e1 followed by g3 and ♔g2 with a complex middlegame.

14 ... ♗xa3!?

An interesting, if not completely sound, continuation. Black offers two pieces for the rook, which is dangerous due to the threat of the queenside pawns romping to the eighth rank.

15	bxa3	♞d2+
16	♕xd2	♕xb1+
17	♞e1	♕a1
18	f4!	

White has no choice but to relinquish his a-pawn, so opts for a lightning assault on the black king: Note that 18 ♞c2 ♗xc2 leaves White passive, while the a-pawn drops anyway.

18	...	♛xa3
19	f5	♞a5

The straightforward 19...b5!? is a suggestion by Jadoul to try to create a passed pawn which will distract White from his campaign. Now the knight is added to the task of hassling the queen but more importantly it takes away another defensive piece.

20	♗f3	♞b3
21	♛f2	♞c1
22	♖h3	♛xc3
23	fxe6	fxe6 (13)

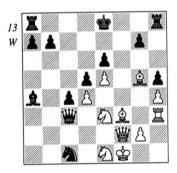

13
W

24 ♞xd5!

It is hardly surprising that with the black king shielded by a thin line of pawns there is an opportunity for a tactical explosion. The knight is taboo due to 24...exd5 25 ♗xh5+ ♖xh5 26 ♖xc3.

24	...	♛a5
25	♞c3	♞d3
26	♞xd3	♛xc3
27	♞e1	♛b4
28	♗e4	

The culmination of White's attack: the two bishops are about to snare the hapless king.

28	...	♖f8
29	♖f3	♚d7
30	♗xb7	

Also crushing is 30 ♖f7+ ♖xf7 (30...♚e8 31 ♗g6) 31 ♛xf7+ ♚c8 32 ♛g8+ ♚c7 33 ♛xa8 +–.

30	...	♖xf3
31	♗xf3	♖f8
32	d5	♛b6
33	dxe6+	♚c7
34	♗e3	♛xe6
35	♗xa7	c3
36	♛c5+	1-0

Game 5
Yilmaz-Manni
Budapest 1992

1	e4	e6
2	d4	d5
3	e5	c5
4	c3	♞c6
5	♞f3	♛b6
6	a3	c4
7	g3	

White declares his intention to develop the bishop on h3. The idea is to reduce the effectiveness of Black's basic plan (...f6 to break up the pawn chain) by targeting the potentially weak point e6.

7	...	♗d7
8	♗h3 (14)	h6

One of the most ambitious defences; Black simply envisages an

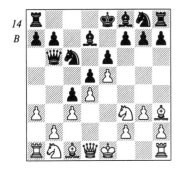

14
B

avalanche of pawns to smother White's kingside. This line requires careful handling by White who needs to employ an unusual manoeuvre to thwart the problem. 8...♗e7 is also worth consideration. For example:

a) 9 ♘bd2 and now:

a1) 9...0-0-0 10 ♘f1 f5?! 11 exf6 ♘xf6 12 ♘e3 e5 13 ♗xd7+ ♖xd7 14 dxe5 ♘e4 15 e6 ± Jezek-Lundquist, corr. 1956/59.

a2) 9...♘a5 10 0-0 (10 ♖b1 ♖c8?! 11 0-0 h5 12 ♘e1 g6? 13 ♘g2 ± Walther-Frank, Amsterdam 1954) 10...h5 11 ♘e1 (11 ♖b1 0-0-0 12 ♘e1 g5 13 ♗g2 ♘h6 14 ♗h1 ♘f5 15 ♘g2 with an unclear position; Bosboom-Brenninkmeijer, Holland 1992) 11...g5 (11...0-0-0 12 ♘g2 g6 13 ♘e3 ♘h6 ± Vitolinš-Zelinsky, Latvian Ch 1978) and now:

a21) 12 ♘c2 ♗a4 13 ♖b1 g4 ∓ Blatny-Drvota, Děčin 1978.

a22) 12 f4 g4 13 ♗g2 ♘h6 14 ♕e2 ♘f5 ∓ Storm-Casper, Děčin 1978.

b) 9 0-0 0-0-0 10 ♘bd2 (10 ♘e1 g5 11 f4 gxf4 12 gxf4 f5 ± Makropoulos-Gavrilakis, Greek Ch 1976) 10...♘a5 11 ♘e1 g5 12 f4! gxf4 13 gxf4 h5 14 ♘g2 ♘h6 15 ♘e3 ♖dg8+ 16 ♔h1 ♘g4!? 17 ♘xg4 hxg4 18 ♗xg4 f5 19 exf6 ♗xf6 20 ♖g1 ♕d6 21 ♘f3 ♘b3 22 ♖b1 ♗e8 23 ♕e2 ♖xg4 24 ♖xg4 ♗h5 25 ♕g2! ♗xg4 26 ♕xg4 ♘a5 27 f5! +− Ciocaltea-Heim, Romania 1979.

9	♘bd2	♘a5
10	0-0	g5
11	♖b1	♗e7

In the game Silman-Kushnir, Lone Pine 1975, Black preferred to activate her king's knight: 11...♘ge7 12 ♗g2 0-0-0 13 h4?! (13 ♘e1!?) 13...g4 14 ♘e1 h5 15 ♗h1 ♘f5 16 ♘g2 ♗h6 17 ♖e1 f6 18 ♘f1 ♖df8 19 exf6 ♖xf6 20 ♗xh6 ♖8xh6 21 ♘1e3 ♘d6 22 ♘f4 ♖xf4! 23 gxf4 ♕d8 24 f5 ♕xh4 25 fxe6 ♗xe6 26 ♘g2 ♕f6 27 ♕d2 ♗f5 28 ♖ad1 ♗e4 29 ♕f4 ♕g7 30 ♘h4 ♖f6 31 ♕h2 ♕g5 32 ♗g2 ♘c6 33 ♖e3 ♘e7 34 ♖1e1 ♘7f5 35 ♗xe4 ♘xe4 36 ♖xe4 dxe4 37 ♕e5 ♘xh4 0-1.

12	♘e1	h5
13	♗g2	♘h6 (15)
14	♗h1	

An essential move if White is to create dynamic play. In practical tournament play, White often becomes congested and Black can steadily build up his forces behind the pawn shield. The difference here is that White embarks on a clever

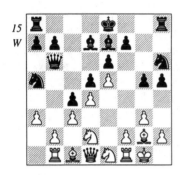

15
W

manoeuvre to transfer the e1 knight to a more prominent post.

14	...	0-0-0
15	♘g2	g4
16	♘e3	♖dg8

Simple development, adding another rook to the offensive. However, the next step (...h4) carries no immediate threat, so White can now follow up his minor-piece manoeuvre with queenside counterplay.

17	b4	♘c6
18	a4	h4
19	♘dxc4!	

A scintillating sacrifice. The knight is given up in order to penetrate into the heart of Black's camp. The attack will gather momentum as the queenside pawns roll forward.

19	...	dxc4
20	♘xc4	♕c7
21	♗f4	♘d8
22	♘d6+	♗xd6
23	exd6	♕c4

Upon 23...♕b8 White's pawn avalanche crashes through with 24 b5 and c4-c5-c6.

24	♕d2	♘f5 (16)

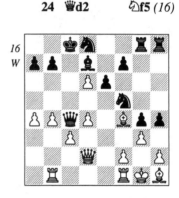

16
W

25 b5!

All of a sudden, the queen is on the verge of being trapped by 26 ♖b4, forcing Black to take evasive measures.

25	...	a5
26	bxa6	♕xa6
27	c4	

The pair of bishops directed towards the opposing king will enhance their influence once the c- and d-pawns advance. It is too late for Black to switch his kingside forces to the other flank to create a defensive barrier.

27	...	♘xd6
28	d5	e5
29	♗xe5	♖h5
30	♗f4	♗f5
31	♖bc1	

There is no respite for Black, as White energetically maintains the pressure.

31	...	♗e4
32	♗xe4	♘xe4

33	♕d4	♘d6
34	c5	♘e8
35	c6	

The reward for having faith with the speculative 19 ♘dxc4 is the c-pawn reaching the sixth rank with a vengeance.

35	...	bxc6
36	dxc6	♘xc6
37	♖fd1	♔b7
38	♕d7+	♔a8
39	♖xc6	1-0

Game 6
Sveshnikov-Eingorn
Sochi 1986

1	e4	e6
2	d4	d5
3	e5	c5
4	c3	♘c6
5	♘f3	♕b6
6	a3	c4
7	g3	♗d7
8	h4	

Since Black may have in mind a pawn storm commencing with ...g5, White takes immediate steps to prevent such activity.

8	...	♘a5
9	♘bd2	♕c6!? *(17)*

A sortie to disrupt White's plan of kingside expansion. Black prepares to offer the trade of queens and, should White avoid the exchange, infiltrate the opposition's camp.

A number of other moves have been tried:

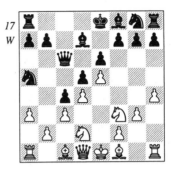

a) 9...h5 and now:

a1) 10 ♘g5!? ♘e7 11 ♕f3 ♘f5 12 ♗h3 g6 13 ♗xf5! gxf5 14 ♕e2 ♗a4 15 ♘df3 ♘b3 16 ♖b1 ♘xc1 17 ♖xc1 ± Degraeve-I.Sokolov, Baguio City 1987.

a2) 10 ♗h3 ♘h6 11 0-0 ♗e7 12 ♘e1 g6 13 ♘g2 0-0-0 14 ♖b1 ♔b8 15 ♘f3! ♕b3 16 ♕e2 ♗a4 17 ♗g5 ♗xg5 18 ♘xg5 ♕c2 19 ♕f3 ♘b3 20 ♕f4! ± Sax-Ree, Amsterdam 1979.

b) 9...h6 10 ♗h3 (10 h5 ♘e7 11 ♗h3 ♘b3? 12 ♘xb3 ♗a4 13 ♘fd2 ♘c6 14 0-0 ♘a5 15 f4 ♘xb3 16 ♘xb3 ♗xb3 17 ♕e2 ± was Bronstein-Mestel, London rapid 1976) 10...0-0-0 11 0-0 ♘e7 12 ♖b1 ♔b8 13 ♘e1 ♘f5 14 ♘g2 ♗e7 15 ♕f3 ♗c8 16 h5 ♖hf8 17 ♘f4 ± Sax-Knaak, Szirak 1985.

c) 9...0-0-0 10 ♗h3 f5 (more accurate than 10...♔b8?! 11 0-0 h6 12 h5 ♘e7 13 ♖e1 g6 14 ♘h2 gxh5 15 ♕xh5 ♗e8 16 ♕f3 ± Hodgson-Lee, London 1977) 11 0-0 ♘h6 12 ♘e1 ♘f7 13 ♘g2 g5 14 hxg5 ♘xg5 15 ♘f4 ♘xh3+ 16 ♘xh3 ♗e7 17 ♖b1

罩dg8 18 公f3 ∓ Klinger-Portisch, Dubai OL 1986.

d) 9...公e7 10 h5 h6 11 公h4 0-0-0 12 鱼h3 f6 13 f4 罩g8 14 豐g4 f5 15 豐e2 g5 16 hxg6 公xg6 17 公g2 鱼e7 18 公f3 公b3 19 罩b1 公xc1 20 罩xc1 罩g7 21 當f2 = Prié-Ree, France-Netherlands 1990.

10 公g5

It is natural that White is keen to make room for the queen to escape Black's attentions.

After 10 鱼h3?! (10 鱼e2 gives White a slight plus) 10...豐a4 11 豐e2? 豐c2 12 0-0 公b3 Black is better.

10	...	h6
11	公h3	豐a4
12	豐f3!	

Sveshnikov suggests that the ending after 12 鱼e2 豐xd1+ 13 鱼xd1 slightly favours White. However, the text declares more aggressive intentions.

12	...	豐c2
13	公f4	

The knight is heading for the central post e3 to oust the queen.

13	...	公e7
14	公g2	豐h7?!

An interesting idea to bring the queen to the defence of the kingside and enforce ...g5. It would, however, be more precise to preserve control of b3 in order to keep the queenside closed: 14...鱼a4 (14...公f5 15 公e3 ±) 15 公e3 豐h7 16 鱼h3 公b3 17 公xb3 鱼xb3 when White has a slight edge.

15	b4!	cxb3 *(18)*

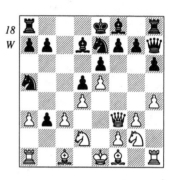

16 鱼d3

As the knight has not been obliged to occupy e3, White's thematic pawn sacrifice allows him to gain time by attacking the enemy queen. The main point is that as Black has transferred the queen to the kingside, White now signals the attack on the opposite flank. As usual with the advance of the b-pawn, the priority is not necessarily to recapture on b3 but to open up the position with c4.

16	...	豐g8
17	罩b1	鱼a4
18	公e3	罩c8

If 18...b5 then 19 c4! bxc4 10 公dxc4 is strong due to the d-pawn being pinned.

19	c4	dxc4
20	公dxc4	公xc4
21	公xc4	公d5

The flurry of tactics fails to make an impression: after 21...罩xc4 22 鱼xc4 鱼c6 23 豐xb3! 鱼xh1 24 f3 the bishop is blocked and White will demolish the queenside.

22	♗d2	♗e7
23	0-0?!	

As the king is quite safe in the centre, Sveshnikov recommends dislodging Black's most active piece: 23 ♘e3 ♗c6 24 ♗e4 with the superior chances. Now Black can create some counterplay by utilizing the power of his dormant queen.

23	...	g5!
24	h5	♕g7
25	♘e3	♗c6
26	♘xd5	♗xd5
27	♗e4 *(19)*	

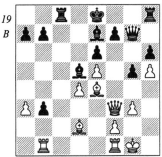

19
B

27	...	g4

Black will not readily allow a bishop exchange, as the blockade of d5 is soon undermined by 27...♖d8 28 ♗xd5 ♖xd5 29 ♖xb3 b6 30 ♖b5!.

28	♕e2	♗c4
29	♗d3	♗d5
30	♗b5+	♖c6?!

A valiant attempt to create counterplay by offering the exchange in return for control of the h1-a8 diagonal. 30...♗c6 31 ♗xc6+ bxc6 32 ♖xb3 is better for White, but the more restrained 30...♔d8!? deserved consideration.

31	♗xc6+	bxc6
32	♖xb3!	♗xb3
33	♖b1	0-0

On 33...♗d5 comes 34 ♖b8+ ♗d8 35 ♗a5 (35 ♖xd8+? ♔xd8 36 ♕a6 f5 37 ♗a5+ ♔e7 ∓) 35...0-0 36 ♗xd8 ±.

34	♖xb3	♖d8
35	♗a5	♖e8
36	♕e4	♖c8
37	♗d2!	

Black can no longer adequately defend his shattered queenside pawn structure.

37	...	♗d8
38	♖b7	♗b6
39	♗e3	♖d8
40	a4	♔h8
41	♕xc6	♕h7
42	a5	♗xa5
43	♖xa7	1-0

Game 7
Sax-Uhlmann
Sarajevo 1982

1	e4	e6
2	d4	d5
3	e5	c5
4	c3	♘c6
5	♘f3	♕b6
6	a3	c4
7	g3	f6

Black employs a popular method of attacking White's pawn chain.

8 exf6

In Malaniuk-Uhlmann, Tallinn 1987, White preferred to allow exchanges on e5: 8 ♗h3!? fxe5 9 ♘xe5 ♘xe5 10 dxe5 ♗c5 11 ♕h5+ g6 12 ♕e2 ♗d7 13 ♘d2 ♘e7 14 ♘f3 h6 15 0-0 0-0 16 ♖e1 ±. John Watson has suggested 8 ♘h4!? fxe5 (8...♕c7!?) 9 ♕h5+ g6 10 ♘xg6 ♘f6 11 ♕h4 ♖g8 12 ♕xf6! ♖xg6 13 ♕h4 exd4 14 ♗e2! dxc3 15 bxc3 with good play, but curiously there have been few devotees of the plan.

8 ...   ♘xf6

9 ♗g2 *(20)*

The alternatives are rare guests at tournament level:

a) 9 ♘bd2 ♗d6 10 ♗g2 0-0 11 0-0 ♗d7 12 ♕e2 ♕c7 13 ♖e1 ♔h8 14 ♘e5 ♗e8 15 f4 ♗h5 = Ratsch-Franz, Germany 1958.

b) 9 ♗h3 and now:

b1) 9....♗d6 10 ♕e2 (10 0-0 0-0 and now: 11 ♖e1?! e5! 12 ♗xc8 ♖axc8 13 dxe5 ♘g4! ∓ or 11 ♘bd2 e5 12 ♗xc8 ♖axc8 13 dxe5 ♗xe5 14 ♖e1 ♖fe8 15 ♘f1 d4 16 cxd4 ♗xd4 17 ♗e3 ♗xe3 18 ♘xe3 ♘e4 19 ♕d5+ ♔h8 20 ♘d1 ♕c5 ∓ Gillen-Harding, Dublin 1991) 10...0-0 11 ♗xe6+ ♗xe6 12 ♕xe6+ ♔h8 13 0-0 ♘a5 14 ♘bd2 ♖ae8 15 ♕h3 ♖e2 16 ♖e1 ♖xe1+ 17 ♘xe1 ♕b5 18 ♘c2 ♕e8 19 ♘e3 h6 and Black has compensation for the sacrificed pawn; S.Arkell-J.Cooper, British Ch 1990.

b2) 9...♘a5 10 ♘bd2 ♗d6 11 0-0!? (11 ♕e2 transposes to the note above) 11...0-0 12 ♘e5 (12 ♖e1 ♔h8 13 ♗xe6 ♗xe6 14 ♖xe6 ♖ae8 15 ♖xe8 ♖xe8 with an unclear position according to Botterill) 12...♗xe5 13 dxe5 ♘d7 14 ♘f3 ♘b3 15 ♗e3 ♘dc5 16 ♖b1 ♕c7 17 ♗xc5 ♘xc5 18 ♕e2 ♗d7 (18...♘d3?! 19 ♘d4 ♕xe5 20 ♕xe5 ♘xe5 21 f4 ♘d3 23 ♘xe6 ±) 19 ♘d4 ♖ae8 20 f4 ♖e7 (Botterill-Botto, Llanelli 1977) 21 ♗g2 =.

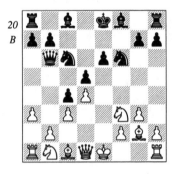

20
B

9 ...   ♗d6

10 0-0   0-0

11 ♕e2

It is necessary to prevent ...e5; Przewoznik-Uhlmann, Poland 1980, continued 11 ♘bd2?! e5! 12 dxe5 ♗xe5 13 ♘xe5 (13 ♕c2 is equal) 13...♘xe5 14 ♕e2?! (14 ♘f3!? may be better) 14...♖e8! 15 ♘f3 ♗g4 16 ♕d1 ♖ad8 17 ♗e3 ♕xb2 18 ♗d4 b6 19 h3 ♘xf3+ 20 ♗xf3 ♗xf3 21 ♕xf3 ♕e2 22 ♕f4 ♕e4 23 ♕g5 h6 24 ♕d2 ♕f5 25 ♗xf6 ♕xf6 26 ♖ad1 b5 27 ♕b2 a6 28 a4 bxa4 29 ♖a1

♕f3 30 ♖xa4 ♖e2 31 ♕c1? ♖f8 32 ♕d1 ♖xf2 0-1.

11 ...   ♔h8

This is the most popular try in contemporary practice but the alternatives merit consideration:

a) 11...♗d7 12 ♘e5 ♗e8?! (Uhlmann prefers 12...♖ae8! whereupon 13 ♘xd7 ♘xd7 14 ♗e3 keeps an edge for White) 13 ♘xc4! ♘xd4 (13...dxc4 14 ♕xe6+) 14 cxd4 dxc4 15 ♘c3 ± Alexander-Uhlmann, Munich OL (prelims) 1958.

b) 11...♘a5 12 ♘bd2 ♗d7 13 ♘e5 ♗e8 ±.

12 ♘e5   ♗xe5?!

Black instantly exchanges the powerful knight but according to Uhlmann a more restrained approach is necessary. For example: 12...♘d7! 13 f4 (or 13 ♘xc6 ♕xc6 14 ♕xe6 ♘f6 intending ...♗f5 with an unclear game) 13...♘dxe5 14 fxe5 ♖xf1+ 15 ♔xf1 ♗e7 =.

13 dxe5   ♘d7
14 ♗e3   ♕a5 *(21)*

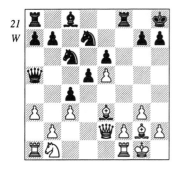

21
W

The other paths are pleasant for White:

a) 14...♘c5 15 ♘d2 ♕a5 16 f4 ♗d7 (Alexander-Uhlmann, Munich OL 1958) 17 ♘f3 ±.

b) 14...♕c7 15 f4 ♘a5 16 ♘d2 ♘c5 17 ♗xc5 ♕xc5+ 18 ♕f2 ♕xf2+ 19 ♔xf2! ♗d7 (19...g5?! 20 ♔e3 ±) 20 ♔e3 ♖ae8 (Mestel-Botterill, London 1978) 21 ♖ae1! ♗e7 22 f5!? (22...exf5 23 ♗xd5 ♖xe5+ 24 ♔d4 ♖xe1 25 ♖xe1 ±) 22...♖xf5 23 ♖xf5 exd5 24 ♔d4 ♘c6+ 25 ♔xd5 ♗e6+ 26 ♔d6 ±.

15 f4   ♘c5
16 ♘d2   ♗d7
17 ♖ad1!

White accentuates his control of the position by centralizing the queen's rook while threatening 18 ♘xc4 dxc4 19 ♕xc4 b6 20 ♗xc5 +−.

17 ...   ♗e8
18 f5!   exf5

After 18...♘xe5 19 fxe6! Black has double trouble in the form of backrank mate and a vulnerable d5 pawn.

19 ♗xd5   ♘d3!
20 ♘xc4!

White is exposed on the light squares after 20 ♗xc6?! ♗xc6 21 ♘xc4 ♕d5 22 ♖xd3 ♕xc4 intending ...♗b5 and Black is better.

20 ...   ♕xd5
21 ♕xd3   ♕xd3
22 ♖xd3   ♗h5

If Black aspires to steal the e5 pawn then White's greater activity triumphs: 22...♗f7 23 ♘d6 ♘xe5 24 ♘xf7+ ♖xf7 25 ♖d5 ♘c4 26 ♗d4! ♘xb2 27 ♖dxf5 ♖xf5 28 ♖xf5 intending 29 ♖f7 or 29 ♖b5 with advantage.

23 ♖e1?!

The problem with this move is that the pressure is taken off f5, so the previous note is now redundant. On 23 ♖d2! b5 24 ♘d6 ♘xe5 25 ♖d5 White has a clear advantage.

23 ...   ♗f7!

24 ♘d2

Not 24 ♘d6? ♘xe5 and Black wins.

24 ...   ♘xe5

25 ♖d6   ♖fe8

26 ♗d4   ♘c6

27 ♖xe8+   ♗xe8

Otherwise White will invade the seventh rank: 27...♖xe8 28 ♖d7 ♖e7 29 ♖xe7 ♘xe7 30 ♗xa7 +−.

28 ♘f3   ♔g8

29 ♔f2   b6

30 ♔e3   ♔f8

31 ♔f4   ♔e7!

32 ♖d5   g6

33 h4   h6?

It appears logical to deprive the king of the g5 square but it proves to be only a temporary measure and merely weakens g6. The best way to ensure equality is swap the roving rook: 33...♖d8 34 ♖xd8 ♘xd8. Approaching from another angle with 33...♗f7 also works, since 34 ♗f6+ ♔xf6 35 ♖d6+ ♗e6 36 ♖xc6 ♖c8 37 ♖d6 ♔e7 37 ♖d2 ♔f6 is equal.

34 ♗g7!   h5

35 ♔g5   ♖c8

36 ♖d2   ♔f7

37 ♔h6   ♖c7

The position is bleak after 37...♘e7 38 ♘e5+ ♔g8 39 ♗f6 and the g-pawn must fall.

38 ♘g5+   ♔e7 (22)

39 ♗f8+!

A stylish way to deliver the knockout blow.

39 ...   ♔f6

40 ♖d6+   ♔e5

41 ♖e6+   ♔d5

42 ♖xe8   ♘e5

43 ♗g7   1-0

Game 8
Zaitsev-Pokojowczyk
Sochi 1976

1 e4   e6

2 d4   d5

3 e5   c5

4 c3   ♘c6

5 ♘f3   ♕b6

10	exf6	gxf6
11	0-0	0-0-0
12	♖e1	

White continues in a logical fashion by pinpointing the pawn at e6.

12	...	♗g7
13	♖b1!	♔b8 (24)

13...♘ge7 can be answered strongly by 14 b3 cxb3 15 ♘xb3 ± ♗a4? 16 ♖xe6 winning.

14	b4!	cxb3
15	♘xb3	♘xb3

Black would dearly like to pin the knight but this would allow a clever riposte: 15...♗a4 16 ♖xe6 ♗xb3 17

♕f1 ♗c4 (17...♘c6 18 ♗f4+ ♔a8 19 ♘d2 +−) 18 ♗f4+ ♔a8 19 ♕e1! +−.

16 ♖xb3!

The consistent continuation. After 16 ♕xb3 ♕c6 17 ♗f4+ ♔a8 18 ♕c2 ♖e8 19 ♖ec1 the attack is less effective.

16	...	♗a4?

Krogius suggested 16...♕a6!? as an alternative.

17	♖xb6	♗xd1
18	♖bxe6	♗xf3
19	♗f4+	♔a8 (25)

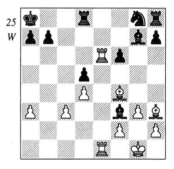

20 ♗c7!

This is the point; the sting in the tail is revealed. The danger of back-rank mate swings the game in White's favour. Nothing can be gained from 20 ♖e8 ♘h6 but after the text 20...♖c8 (20...♖f8 21 ♖e8+) 21 ♖e8 ♘e7 22 ♖8xe7 ♖cg8 23 ♗e6 wins.

20	...	♘h6
21	♗xd8	♖xd8
22	♖e8	1-0

6 a3 c4
7 ♘bd2

This flexible move-order is favoured by those who wish to incorporate g3 in their play but prefer to avoid the complications of the previous game.

7 ... ♘a5
8 g3 ♗d7
9 ♗h3

The old line 9 ♗g2 is no longer popular because in some instances g2 is useful for the manoeuvre ♘e1-g2-e3 and the bishop on h3 can stifle the option of ...f6. The game Clarke-Petrosian, Munich OL 1958 provides a good example of likely play: 9...0-0-0 10 0-0 h6!? (10...♔b8 11 ♖e1 ♘e7 12 ♘f1 ♘b3 = Alexander-O'Kelly, Hastings 1953/54) 11 ♖e1 ♘e7 12 ♘f1 (12 ♕e2 g5!? 13 ♘f1 ♘g6 14 ♘3d2 ♗e7 = Casper-Knaak, East Berlin 1982) 12...♘f5 13 ♘e3 (Clarke suggested 13 g4 ♘e7 14 ♖b1 as better) 13...♘xe3 14 ♖xe3 ♗e7 15 ♖e1 ♕b3! 16 ♕e2 ♗a4 17 ♗e3 ♔b8 (17...♕c2!) 18 ♖ad1! ♕c2 19 ♖d2 ♕f5 20 ♖f1 g5 (20...♘b3 21 ♖dd1!) 21 h3 h5 22 ♘h2 ♖dg8 23 g4 ♕g6 24 ♗f3? (24 f4!?) 24...hxg4 25 ♗xg4 ♘c6 26 f3?! ♗d8 27 ♗f2 ♘e7 28 ♖e1 ♖h6 29 ♘f1?! (29 ♗g3 ♖gh8 30 ♕g2!) 29...♖gh8 30 ♗g3 ♖xh3! 31 ♗xh3 ♖xh3 32 ♕g2 ♕h7 33 ♘e3 ♘g6 34 ♘g4 ♘f4 35 ♗xf4 gxf4 36 ♔f1 ♖g3 37 ♕f2 ♕h3+ 38 ♔e2 ♖g2 39 ♖g1 ♖xf2+ 40 ♘xf2 ♕h7 41 ♖h1 ♕g6 0-1.

9 ...

White is well [...] this typical freeing [...] a choice of alternat[...]

a) 9...h6 10 0-0 [...] now:

a1) 11...f5?! 12 [...] ♘ef3! ♘e7 14 ♖e1 [...] 16 ♕e2 ♕c7 17 b3 [...] ♘c4 19 ♘fd2 ♘b6 [...] c4! Ivanov-Suetin, [...] kiad 1978.

a2) 11...♘e7 12 [...] ♘g2 ♕c7 14 ♕f3 ♗e [...] 16 ♗g4 ♗c2 17 ♖a1 g [...] Ničevski-Vilela, Dečir [...]

a3) 11...g5 12 ♗g2 [...] h5 14 ♕e2 (14 ♗h1 [...] 14...♘h6! 15 ♘c2 ♗ [...] ♖c8 17 ♖e1 h4 18 g4 [...] Schmidt, Budapest 197[...]

b) 9...♘e7 10 0-0 h [...] 11 ♘h4 ♘c8 ± Pinter-[...] dapest 1976; 10...♘g6 1[...] 12 ♖b1 f6 13 exf6 gxf6 [...] Ilersić, corr. 1982/83) 11 [...] 12 ♘g2 and now:

b1) 12...♔b8 13 ♖b1 ♕ [...] ♘c8 15 f4 g6 16 f5 gxf5 [...] 18 ♘xg4 ♗e8 19 ♘f6 ± [...] Savon, Dubna 1976.

b2) 12...g6 13 ♘e3 h5 [...] ♗h6 15 ♗g2 ♖df8 = Plato[...] Kiev 1978.

c) 9...♕c6 10 0-0 ♕a4 [...] ♕c2 12 ♘e1 ♕g6 13 f4 [...] ♘g2 ♘f5 15 ♘e3 ± Ståhlb[...] gos, Munich OL 1958.

Game 9
Torre-Grefe
San Francisco 1991

1	e4	e6
2	d4	d5
3	e5	c5
4	c3	♘c6
5	♘f3	♛b6
6	a3	c4
7	♘bd2	♗d7
8	g3	f6?! *(26)*

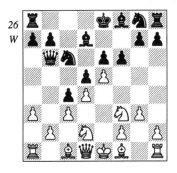

The recurring theme ...f6 is not appropriate here, as 7...♗d7 is rather slow compared to 7...♘a5 which at least uncovers the queen to support e6 and reduces the movement of the opposing queen's knight.

Kavalek-Fuchs, Havana 1966, saw yet another approach: 8...h6!? 9 ♘h4 (9 h4) 9...♘a5 10 f4 ♘e7 11 ♗h3 g6 12 ♘g2 ♘f5!? 13 g4 ♘e7 14 ♘e3 h5 15 f5 hxg4 16 fxe6 ♗xe6 17 ♗xg4 0-0-0 =.

9	exf6	♘xf6
10	♛e2	0-0-0

A brave effort to complicate matters by proposing a kingside offensive while simultaneously fending off White's attack. It is based on the misguided premise that the closed nature of the queenside allows sufficient time for a build-up of forces. After the better 10...♗d6!? 11 ♗h3 0-0 12 ♗xe6+ ♚h8 13 ♗xd7 ♘xd7 (13...♖ae8 14 ♗xe8 ♖xe8 15 ♘e5 ♘xe5 16 0-0 +−) 14 0-0 ♖ae8 15 ♛d1 Black has some compensation for the pawn.

11	♗g2	♚b8

This is too cautious and therefore slow. At least 11...h6 intending 12...g5 poses White some problems and aims to fight for the initiative.

12	0-0	♗c8
13	b3! *(27)*	

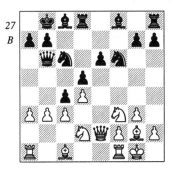

It is of considerable importance for White's attack that the b-file be opened. This is not just for the rooks to make an impression, but to facilitate c4 allowing the rest of the forces to join in the fray.

13	...	cxb3
14	♖b1	b2
15	♗xb2	♗d6
16	c4	

The opening has been a complete success for White. Black has failed to register any aggressive intent, while Torre has set in motion the decisive storming of the queenside.

16	...	♕a6
17	♖fc1	♖he8
18	♘e5	

After this move the king's bishop is uncovered to add weight to the onslaught.

18	...	♗xe5
19	dxe5	♘d7
20	♕e3	

At last the queen steps aside to avoid the pin, leaving Black with all sorts of problems.

20	...	♘b6
21	cxd5	exd5
22	♗d4	

Now both rooks are revealed to exert immense power by dominating the b- and c-files. On 22...♘a4? 23 ♗f1! ♕a5 24 ♖xc6 wins a piece.

22	...	♘c4
23	♘xc4	dxc4
24	♗a1	♖d3
25	♕c5	♘a5
26	e6!	(28)

The loss of the pawn is irrelevant when it allows the queen's bishop to deliver a devastating check.

| 26 | ... | ♗xe6 |
| 27 | ♗e5+ | 1-0 |

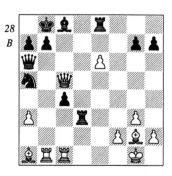

Black resigned in view of the variation 27...♔a8 28 ♕xa5! ♕xa5 29 ♗xb7#.

Game 10
Kharlamov-Shinaui
Moscow 1991

1	e4	e6
2	d4	d5
3	e5	c5
4	c3	♘c6
5	♘f3	♕b6
6	a3	a5!?

Now 7 b4 is not feasible; however, the drawback is that this move creates a weakness on b5.

7 ♗d3 *(29)*

This is considered the antidote. The idea is to reach a favourable form of the Milner-Barry Gambit where Black's inability to play ...a6 causes extra defensive problems.

The quieter 7 ♗e2 is also possible:

a) 7...cxd4 8 cxd4 ♘ge7 9 b3 (9 ♘c3!? ♘f5 10 ♘b5; Keres evaluates

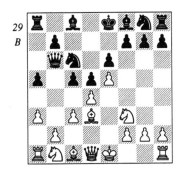

the position as better for White) 9...♘f5 10 ♗b2 ♗e7 11 0-0?! (11 g4 ♘h6 12 ♖g1 ±) 11...♗d7 12 ♔h1 h5 13 ♘c3 g5! 14 ♘a4 ♕a7 ∓ Kliavin-Klasup, USSR 1955.

b) 7...♗d7 8 b3 cxd4 9 cxd4 ♘ge7 10 0-0 ♘f5 11 ♗e3! ♗e7 12 ♘c3 0-0 13 ♗d3 ♘xe3 14 fxe3 f6 15 ♘g5!? (15 exf6 gxf6 16 ♘a4 ♕d8 17 ♖a2 with an unclear position) 15...f5 (15...fxg5 16 ♕h5 g6? 17 ♗xg6 hxg6 18 ♕xg6+ ♔h8 19 ♖f6! +−; 16...♖f5! with unclear play) 16 ♘a4 ♕d8 17 ♘h3 ♗e8 18 ♘f4 ♗f7 19 g4 g5? 20 ♘xe6 ♗xe6 21 gxf5 b5 22 fxe6 1-0 Cortlever-van Seters, Beverwijk 1958.

7 ...   ♗d7

The acceptance of the gambit is the acid test but Black has also preferred increasing the pressure on d4, e.g. 7...♘ge7 8 0-0 cxd4 9 cxd4 ♘f5 10 ♗xf5 exf5 11 ♘c3 ♗e6 12 ♘a4! ♕b5 13 ♗e3 ♗e7 14 ♘e1 0-0 15 ♘d3 ♖ac8 16 ♖c1 ♘a7 (16...♖c7 17 ♘ac5 b6? 18 a4 +−) 17 ♘ac5 b6 18 a4 ♕e8 19 ♘xe6 fxe6 20 ♕b3 ♖xc1

21 ♖xc1 ♗d8 22 h4! h6 23 ♘f4 g5 24 hxg5 hxg5 25 ♘xd5! exd5 (or 25...f4 26 ♗xf4 gxf4 27 ♘xf4 +−) 26 ♕xd5+ ♔g7 (26...♕f7 27 e6 ♕e7 28 ♗xg5 +−) 27 f4! g4 28 b3 ♖f7 29 ♕a8! +− Georgadze-Draško, Tbilisi 1985.

8 0-0

The old-fashioned 8 ♗c2!? has some followers:

a) 8...♘ge7 9 0-0 cxd4 (9...♘f5 10 dxc5! ♗xc5 11 ♘bd2 ± Tal-Sokolsky, USSR 1955) 10 cxd4 ♘f5 11 ♗xf5 exf5 12 ♘c3 ♗e6 13 ♘a4 (13 ♕a4 ♖c8 14 ♕b5 ♕xb5 15 ♘xb5 with equality, Koch-Schwertfeger, corr. 1964) 13...♕a7 14 ♗e3 ♗e7 15 ♖c1 h6 16 ♘c5 0-0 17 ♘e1 ♔h7 18 f4?! ♖g8 19 ♘ed3 ♗c8 20 ♕b3 ♖d8 21 ♘a4 b5! 22 ♕xb5 ♘xd4! ∓ Leisebein-Hunger, corr. 1985/86.

b) 8...h6 9 h4 h5 10 b3 ♘h6 11 ♗xh6?! ♖xh6 12 dxc5 ♗xc5 13 0-0 ♔f8 14 ♘bd2 f6 15 exf6 gxf6 ∓ Vatter-Korchnoi, Lugano 1986.

c) 8...♕b5 9 c4 dxc4 10 ♘c3 ♕b6 11 d5 exd5 12 ♘xd5 ♕d8 13 0-0 ♗e6 14 ♗e4 ♘d4 15 ♘f4 ♗g4 16 ♗xb7 ♖b8 17 ♗e4 ♘xf3+ 18 ♗xf3 ♕xd1 19 ♗xd1 ♗f5 20 ♘d5 ♘e7 21 ♗a4+ ♔d8 22 ♘e3 ♗d3 23 ♖d1 ♔c7 24 ♗d2 ♔b6 25 ♖ac1 ± Kiselev-Shaposhnikov, USSR 1989.

8 ...   cxd4

In answer to the push 8...a4 White should not follow the example of Dowden-Beliavsky, Lucerne OL 1982, which continued 9 dxc5?!

♗xc5 10 ♘bd2 f6 11 ♕e2 ♘ge7 ∓. A better try is 9 ♕e2 or even 9 ♔h1 to play a future f4 after the exchanges on d4.

9 cxd4   ♘xd4

In the game Maki-Hadjiyiannis, Haifa 1989, Black reacted cautiously with 9...h6?! 10 ♘c3 ♘xd4 11 ♘xd4 ♕xd4 12 ♕e2 ♘e7 13 ♔h1 ♖c8 14 f4 ♕b6 15 ♘b5 ♗xb5 16 ♗xb5+ ♘c6 17 f5 ♗e7 18 ♗xc6+ ♖xc6 19 ♕g4 exf5 20 ♕xg7 ♖f8 21 ♕g3 ♖g6 22 ♕f3 ♕e6 23 ♗f4 ♖fg8 24 ♖f2 ♗c5 25 ♖c2 b6 26 b4 ♗d4 27 ♖d1 1-0.

10 ♘xd4   ♕xd4
11 ♘c3   ♕xe5 *(30)*

As can be seen in the chapter on the Milner-Barry, at this stage Black often inserts ...a6 to stop ♘b5. As this is not possible here, other paths have been followed:

a) 11...♘h6!? 12 ♘b5 ♕xe5 13 ♖e1 ♕b8 14 ♕f3 ♗d6 15 ♘xd6+ ♕xd6 16 ♗f4 ♕e7 17 ♕g3! f6 (½-½ Zaitsev-Uhlmann, Berlin 1982) 18 ♗d6! ♕f7 19 ♖ac1 ♗c6 20 b4 axb4 21 axb4 ±.

b) 11...♕b6 and now:

b1) 12 ♔h1 ♘e7 13 f4 g6 14 ♖e1 (14 ♕e2!?) 14...♗c6 15 ♗e3 d4 16 ♗f2 ♘f5 17 ♗e4 ♗e7 18 ♕f3 0-0 19 ♗xc6 ♕xc6 20 ♘e4 ♖ac8 21 g4 ♘e3 22 ♗xe3 dxe3 23 ♖xe3 ♖fd8 24 ♖c3 ♕b5 25 ♖b3 = Rosenthal-Gerstner, Bundesliga 1991/92.

b2) 12 ♕g4?! f5 13 exf6 ♘xf6 14 ♕g3 ♗e7 15 ♕xg7 ♖g8 16 ♕h6

♕d4 17 ♖d1 ♕g4 18 ♗f1 ♖g6 19 ♕f4 ♕h5 20 ♗e2 ♕h3 21 ♕f3 e5 22 ♕xh3 ♗xh3 23 g3 ♗e6 ∓ Shteinberg-Silov, Kharkov 1967.

b3) 12 ♕e2 ♘e7 13 ♗g5 h6 14 ♗d2 g6 15 ♗e3 d4 16 ♘e4 ♘d5 17 ♗d2 ♗e7 18 h4 ♗c6 19 ♖fc1 ♕c7 20 ♘c5 ♗xc5 21 ♖xc5 ♕e7 22 ♖ac1 ♕xh4 23 ♗b5 0-0 24 ♗xc6 bxc6 25 g3 ♕h3 26 ♖1c4 ♘e7 27 ♖xd4 ♘f5 28 ♖d3 +− Schlosser-Claesen, Adelaide 1988.

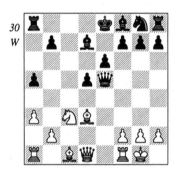

30
W

12 ♖e1   ♕d6

In normal lines of the Milner-Barry 12...♕b8 is popular, but now 13 ♘xd5 has more venom due to the threat of ♘b6.

13 ♘b5   ♕b8

13...♗xb5 leaves Black's king stranded in the centre of the board, after which a game Prié-Villeneuve, Paris 1990, continued 14 ♗xb5+ ♔d8 15 ♕h5 ♘f6 16 ♕xf7 ♕e7 17 ♕xe6 ♕xe6 18 ♖xe6 ♗c5 19 ♗g5 ♗d4 20 ♖d1 ♗xb2 21 ♖xd5+ ♔c8 22 ♖c5+ ♔d8 23 ♖c2 1-0.

14	♕f3	♗d6
15	♕xd5	♗xh2+
16	♔h1	♘e7 *(31)*

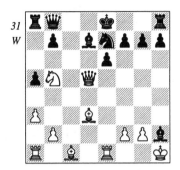

17 ♕d4

White is poised to demolish the opposition. The queen exerts considerable pressure by hitting g7, while preventing castling due to the need to defend d7.

17	...	♗c6
18	♗g5!	f6
19	♖xe6	

Now White's rooks crash through into Black's position, sealing his fate.

19	...	♗e5
20	♕c5	0-0
21	♖xe7	♗xb5
22	♕xb5	♕d8
23	♖xe5	fxg5
24	♖ae1	♕f6
25	♖f5	♕h6+
26	♔g1	♖fd8
27	♕xb7	♖ab8
28	♕f7+	♔h8
29	♖fe5	1-0

Game 11
Prié-de la Villa Garcia
León 1991

1	e4	e6
2	d4	d5
3	e5	c5
4	c3	♘c6
5	♘f3	♕b6
6	a3	♘h6 *(32)*

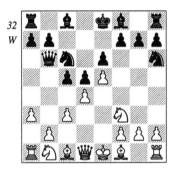

This system has experienced fluctuating bouts of popularity. The idea is to exert pressure on d4 while taking White outside normal lines.

7	b4	cxd4
8	cxd4	

The alternative 8 ♗xh6 doubles the h-pawns at the cost of opening up the g-file. Practice indicates that it deserves respect: 8...gxh6 9 cxd4 ♗d7 (9...♗g7 10 ♘c3 f6 11 ♘a4 intending ♗b5 ± ; 9...♖g8! followed by ...♖g4 is unclear according to Fedorowicz) 10 ♗e2 (not 10 ♘c3? ♘xb4 −+) 10...a5 (10...♖g8 10 0-0 ±; 10...♗g7 11 0-0 ±) 11 b5 ♘e7 12

♘c3 a4 13 0-0 ♕a5 14 ♕d2 ♘c8 (14...♖c8? 15 ♘xd5 +–) 15 ♖fc1 ♘b6 16 h3! ♖c8 17 ♘h2 ♘c4 18 ♗xc4 ♖xc4 19 ♘g4 ♗xb5 20 ♕b2! ♗c6 21 ♘xd5! ♖xc1+ (21...♕xd5? 22 ♘f6+ +–; 21...♗xd5 22 ♖xc4 ♗xc4 23 ♘f6+ ♔d8 24 ♕xb7 +–; 21...exd5 22 ♖xc4 dxc4 23 ♘f6+ ♔e7 24 d5! ♗xd5 (24...c3 25 ♕a2 +–) 25 ♕d4! ♔e6 26 ♖d1 +–) 22 ♖xc1 ♗xd5 (22...exd5 23 ♖xc6! bxc6 24 ♘f6+ +–) 23 ♘f6+ ♔e7 24 ♘xd5+! ♕xd5 25 ♕b4+ ♔e8 (Rogers-Velimirović, Vršac 1987) 26 ♖c8+! ♔d7 27 ♕c3 +–.

8   ...   ♘f5
9 ♗e3!

The question of how to defend the d-pawn is important. The text is a refinement on the old line that was based on two games at Wijk aan Zee in 1989; 9 ♗b2 ♗e7 (9...♗d7 10 g4 ♘h6 11 h3 f6 12 ♘c3 fxe5 13 dxe5 ♗e7 {13...♘f7 14 ♘a4 ♕d8 15 h4 ±} 14 ♘a4 ♕d8 15 ♖c1 0-0 16 ♘c5 ♗xc5 17 ♖xc5 ♘f7 18 ♗g2 = Sveshnikov-Lputian, Sochi 1993) and now:

a) The stem game, Fedorowicz-Dokhoian, Wijk aan Zee 1989, continued 10 ♗d3 ♗d7 (10...a5!? 11 ♗xf5 exf5 12 ♘c3 ♗e6 13 b5 a4! 14 0-0 ♘b8 15 ♗c1 ♘d7 is unclear; Campora-Dokhoian, Wijk aan Zee 1989) 11 0-0 g5 (11...0-0 12 ♘c3 ♘cxd4 13 ♘xd4 ♕xd4 14 ♗xf5 ♕xd1 15 ♖fxd1 exf5 16 ♘xd5 ±; 11...♘fxd4 12 ♘xd4 ♘xd4 13 ♕g4!

±) 12 ♗xf5 exf5 13 ♘c3 ♗e6 14 ♘a4 ♕b5 (14...♕d8 15 ♘c5 b6 16 ♘xe6 fxe6 17 ♖c1 ♖c8 18 b5 ♘a5 19 ♖xc8 ♕xc8 20 ♘xg5! ±) 15 ♘c5 g4 16 ♘e1 ♗xc5 17 dxc5 a5 and now 18 ♕d3! ♕xd3 19 ♘xd3 gives White a clear advantage.

b) 10 ♗e2 ♗d7 11 0-0 is an attempt to revive Fedorowicz's plan, which so far has proved uniformly successful:

b1) 11...0-0 12 ♕d2 a6 13 ♖d1 f6 14 ♘c3 fxe5 15 dxe5 ♖ad8 16 ♖ac1 ♕a7 17 ♗d3 ♘h4 18 ♘xh4 ♗xh4 19 ♖f1 ♘xe5 20 ♗b1 ♘g4 21 g3 ♗g5 22 ♕c2 ♖f5 23 ♖ce1 ♖df8 24 ♖e2 ♗e3 25 ♘d1 ♗b5 26 ♘xe3 ♘xe3 27 ♖xe3 ♗xf1 28 g4 d4 29 gxf5 dxe3 30 fxe6 1-0 Grosar-Jelen, Bled 1992.

b2) 11...♖c8 12 ♕d2 0-0 13 ♖d1 ♘h4 14 ♘xh4 ♗xh4 15 ♕f4 ♗e7 16 ♗d3 f6 17 ♕h4 h6 18 ♕g3 fxe5 19 dxe5 ♗g5 20 ♘c3 ♗f4 21 ♕g6 ♘xe5 22 ♕h7+ ♔f7 23 ♗e2 ♖g8 24 ♗h5+ ♔f8 25 ♘e2 ♖c4 26 ♘xf4 ♖xf4 27 ♗xe5 ♕xf2+ 28 ♔h1 1-0 Relange-Bauer, French Ch 1993.

9   ...   f6
10 ♗d3! *(33)*

This move has largely put 6...♘h6 out of business. Black sprung a surprising sacrifice to secure a draw in Romanishin-Lputian, Erevan 1988. After 10 b5 ♘xe5! 11 dxe5 ♘xe3 12 fxe3 ♕xe3+ 13 ♕e2 ♕c1+ 14 ♕d1 with perpetual check.

10   ...   ♘xe3

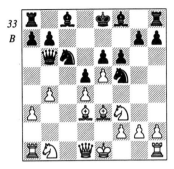

33 B

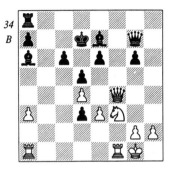

34 B

11 fxe3   fxe5?!

White also has a pleasant position after the safer 11...f5 12 0-0 ♗e7 13 ♘c3 intending 14 ♘a4 and 15 ♖c1 or ♘e2-f4 and ♕e1 with some advantage.

12 b5   e4

After 12...♘a5 13 ♘xe5 the central knight is strong and the threat of ♕h5+ is lethal.

13	**bxc6**	**exd3**
14	**♘e5**	

There is no hurry to take on d3 when the king can can be pursued instead.

14	**...**	**bxc6**
15	**♕h5+**	**g6**
16	**♘xg6**	**hxg6**
17	**♕xh8**	**♕c7**

In response to 17...♕b2, White can avoid a calamity by means of 18 0-0! +−.

18	**0-0**	**♕g7**
19	**♕h4**	**♗a6**
20	**♘d2**	**♗e7**
21	**♕f4**	**♔d7**
22	**♘f3** *(34)*	

Once again the weakness in Black's camp imposed by the lack of control over e5 is emphasized by the manoeuvres of the knight, which constitute a prelude to taking control of the seventh rank.

22	**...**	**♗d6**
23	**♘e5+**	**♔c7**
24	**♕f7+**	**♕xf7**
25	**♖xf7+**	**♔b6**
26	**♖b1+**	**♔a5**
27	**♘xc6+**	**♔a4**
28	**♔f2**	**♗xa3**
29	**♔e1**	**♗c4**
30	**♖xa7+**	**♖xa7**
31	**♘xa7**	**♗d6**
32	**♘c8**	**♗c7**
33	**♘b6+**	**♔a3**
34	**♔d2**	**♔a2**
35	**♖b4**	**1-0**

Game 12
Galdunts-Ambartsumian
Armenian Ch 1991

1	**e4**	**e6**
2	**d4**	**d5**

3	e5	c5
4	c3	♘c6
5	♘f3	♕b6
6	a3	♗d7

Black is prepared to allow White's plan of gaining space on the queenside, since he plans to seize control of the c-file.

7	b4	cxd4
8	cxd4	♖c8 (35)

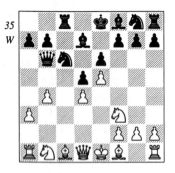

The move-order is important, as now 9 ♘c3? is ruled out by the reply 9...♘xb4.

The text is an improvement on 8...♘ge7, as played in Kamber-Michaud, Germany 1993, which saw White secure a crushing advantage: 9 ♘c3 ♘f5 10 ♘a4 ♕c7 11 ♗b2 ♗e7 (11...b6 12 ♖c1 g6 13 ♗a6 ♗h6 14 ♖c3 ♖b8 15 h4 was slightly better for White in the game Zaichik-Rozentalis, USSR 1987) 12 ♗d3 ♖c8 13 0-0 f6 14 ♖c1 ♕d8 15 ♘c5 b6 16 ♘xd7 ♕xd7 17 ♕a4 ♗d8 18 ♖xc6! ♖xc6 19 ♗b5 ♘e7 20 ♖c1 1-0.

9	♗b2

The alternatives 9 ♗e3 and 9 ♗e2 are discussed in the next illustrative game.

9	...	♘a5

A game Roos-Paulsen, Baden-Baden 1990, saw a passive approach being exploited: 9...a6 10 ♗d3 ♘a7 11 ♘c3 ♘e7 12 0-0 ♘b5 13 ♘a4 ♕a7 14 ♘c5 ♗c6 15 a4 ♘c7 16 b5 b6 17 ♘xa6 ♘xa6 18 bxa6 ♗d7 19 ♕e2 ♘c6 20 ♖fc1 ♗b4 21 ♗a3 ♗xa3 22 ♖xa3 ♘b4 23 ♖xc8+ ♗xc8 24 ♗b5+ ♔e7 25 ♕d2 ♘xa6 26 ♕g5+ 1-0.

The spectacular 9...♘xb4?! used to be acknowledged as a refutation of the variation. Angelov-Poriazov, Plovdiv 1988 continued 10 axb4 ♕xb4+ 11 ♕d2 (11 ♗c3 ♖xc3 12 ♘xc3 ♕xc3+ 13 ♘d2 ♕xd4 and Black wins) 11...♖c2 12 ♗c3 ♕b3 13 ♕e3 ♘h6 14 ♗e2 ♘f5 15 ♕d3 ♖c1+ 16 ♗d1 ♗b5 17 ♕xb5+ ♕xb5 18 ♔d2 ♖xd1+ 0-1. However, Abramović pointed out that the sacrifice is faulty: 12 ♗a3! ♕b3 13 ♕d3 ♗b4+ 14 ♘bd2 ♖c3 15 ♘xb3 ♖xd3 16 ♗xb4 with a clear advantage.

10	♘bd2

In Petronić-Paulić, Belgrade 1988, White conceded the c4 square to Black and equality arose after 10 ♗c3?! ♘c4 11 ♕b3 (after 11 ♗d3, Parma considers 11...♘h6 12 0-0 ♗e7 13 ♘bd2 ♘e3 14 fxe3 ♖xc3 15 ♕e2 0-0 unclear, whilst 11...♗e7 12 0-0 ♘h6 13 ♕e2 ♘f5 = was Klinger-Arencibia, Gausdal 1986) 11...a5 12

♗d3 a4 13 ♕d1 ♘e7 14 0-0 ♗b5 15 ♗c2 ♕c6 16 ♖e1 h6.

10 ...   ♘c4
11 ♘xc4!

This is the best way to seek an edge. After 11 ♗xc4 dxc4 12 ♖c1 (12 ♗c3?! ♘e7 13 ♘e4 ♘d5 14 0-0 ♗e7 15 ♕c2 h6 ∓ Afek-Khuzman, Berlin 1990) Black equalizes by sacrificing a pawn: 12...c3! 13 ♗xc3 ♘e7 14 0-0 ♘d5 15 ♘e4 ♗e7 16 ♗d2 0-0 17 ♘c5 ♗c6 18 ♗g5 ♕d8 19 ♕d2 ♘c7 20 ♕e3 b6 21 ♘e4 ½-½ Sax-Nogueiras, Lucerne 1989.

11 ...   dxc4
12 ♖c1   a5 *(36)*

Black counter-attacks by neglecting the defence of c4 in favour of an assault on b4. At this critical juncture, Black has investigated other possibilities:

a) 12...c3 13 ♖xc3 ♖xc3 14 ♗xc3 ♘e7 15 ♗d3 ♘d5 16 ♗d2 ♗e7 17 0-0 0-0 18 ♕c2 h6 19 ♖c1 ♖c8 20 ♕xc8+ ♗xc8 21 ♖xc8+ ♗f8 22 b5 g5 23 a4 a5 24 h4 ♔g7 25 hxg5 hxg5 26 ♗xg5 ♗e7 27 ♗e3 ♗b4 28 ♗e4 ♕a7 29 ♗xd5 exd5 30 ♗g5 ♗f8 31 ♗f6+ ♔g8 32 ♗e7 1-0 Murey-Touzane, Podolsk 1991.

b) 12...♗b5 13 ♘d2!? (13 d5 is possible) 13...c3 14 ♖xc3 ♖xc3 15 ♗xc3 ♗xf1 16 ♘xf1! ♘e7 17 ♘e3. Psakhis considers the position to be in White's favour.

c) 12...♕a6 13 d5! exd5 14 ♕xd5 ♗e6 (14...♘e7 15 ♕e4 b5 16 ♗e2 ♕g6 17 ♕e3 ♘c6 18 ♘h4 ♕e6 19

h3 h5 20 f4 with an unclear position; Motwani-Wegener, Vienna 1991) 15 ♕e4 ♘e7 16 ♗e2 ♗d5 17 ♕d4 b5 18 0-0 ♕b7 19 ♖fd1 ♗e6 (19...♗c6 20 e6! +−) 20 ♘g5 ♘f5 21 ♕f4 ♗e7 22 ♘xe6 fxe6 23 ♗f3 ♕c7 24 ♗d5! ♕b6 (24...exd5 25 ♕xf5 intending e6 +−) 25 g4 ♖f8!? 26 ♗h1 ♘h4 27 ♕g3 ♖d8 28 ♖xd8 ♕xd8 29 ♕e3 a6 30 f4 ± Afek-Psakhis, Israel 1990.

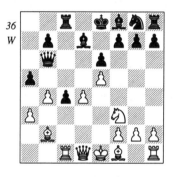

36
W

13 ♘d2   axb4
14 ♘xc4   ♕d8

In the game Sveshnikov-Nevednichy, Bled 1991, Black lost control of d6: 14...♕a7?! 15 axb4 ♗xb4+ 16 ♗c3 ♗xc3+? (16...♗e7!?) 17 ♖xc3 ♔f8 19 ♖a3 ♕b6 20 ♘d6 ♖d8 21 ♕f3 ♘h6 22 ♗d3 ±.

15 axb4   b5

The b-pawn is taboo due to the danger of ♘d6+: 15...♗xb4+ 16 ♗c3 ♗xc3+ (16...♗e7 17 ♗a5 +−) 17 ♖xc3 ±.

16 ♘d6+   ♗xd6
17 exd6   ♘f6

18 ♖c5

Sveshnikov has suggested 18 ♗d3 0-0 19 0-0 ♗c6 20 d5! ± as another course of action to be considered.

18 ...   0-0
19 ♗d3   ♘d5
20 0-0   ♘xb4?!

The act of stealing a pawn allows a violent attack to be unleashed. Black has to find recourse in the alternative. After 20...♕b6 21 ♕h5 f5 22 ♖fc1 play might proceed:

a) 22...♖a8!? 23 ♕e2 ♖a2 24 ♗b1 ♖a6 25 ♗d3 ♕xd6 26 ♗xb5 ♗xb5 27 ♖xb5 ♖a2 28 ♖a5 ♘f4! 29 ♕d2 ♖xb2 30 ♕xb2 ♘d3 31 ♕d2 ♘xc1 32 ♕xc1 ♕xb4 33 ♖e5 ♕xd4 34 ♖xe6 ♖d8 = Sveshnikov-Lputian, Moscow 1991.

b) 22...♕xd6 23 ♗xb5 is better for White according to Sveshnikov.

c) 22...♘xb4 23 ♖xc8 ♗xc8 24 ♕e2! (24 ♖xc8? ♖xc8 25 d7 ♖f8 26 ♗f1 ♘d5 27 ♕e8 ♕d6! 28 d8♕ ♕xd8 29 ♕xe6+ ♔h8 30 ♗xb5 ♘c7 31 ♕e5 ♘xb5 32 ♕xb5 ♕b8 −+) and now:

c1) 24...♘xd3? 25 ♖xc8 ♘f4 26 ♖xf8+ ♔xf8 27 ♕e5 +−.

c2) 24...♕xd6? 25 ♗a3 ♗b7!? (25...♕xd4 26 ♗xb4 ♕xb4 27 ♖xc8 +−) 26 ♕d2! ♕d5 27 ♗f1 ♘c6 (27...♘a2 28 ♖c5! ♕b3 29 ♖xb5 ♕xa3 30 ♖xb7 ♘c3 31 ♕e3! +−) 28 ♗xf8 ♔xf8 29 ♕f4 +−.

c3) 24...♗d7 25 ♗a3 ♕a5! =.

21 ♖h5   f5 (37)

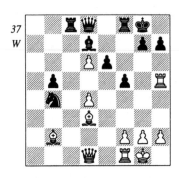

The battering of the kingside will reach a climax after 21...g6 (or 21...♘xd3 22 ♕xd3 g6 23 d5!) 22 d5! when the domination of the dark squares ensures victory: 22...♘xd5 (or 22...gxh5 23 ♗xh7+ ♔xh7 24 ♕xh5+ ♔g8 25 ♕h8#) 23 ♖xh7 ♔xh7 24 ♕h5+ ♔g8 25 ♕h8#.

22 d5!

This advance of the d-pawn is the keystone of White's attacking ambitions: it opens the long dark-squared diagonal and disrupts Black's pawn structure.

22 ...   exd5

In his notes to the game (upon which these notes are based) Galdunts demonstrates the possible complications:

a) 22...♘xd3 23 ♕xd3 ♖c4 24 ♕h3 h6 25 dxe6! ♗xe6 26 ♖xh6 gxh6 27 ♕xh6 ♖g4 (27...♕d7 28 ♕h8+ ♔f7 29 ♕h5+ ♔g8 30 ♕g6+ +−) 28 h3 ♖g5 29 ♕e6+ intending ♖c1 +−.

b) 22...♘xd5 23 ♗xf5 exf5 (or 23...♖xf5 24 ♖xf5 exf5 25 ♕xd5+

♔f8 26 ♖e1 +−) 24 ♕xd5+ ♚h8 25 ♕d2!! +−.

23	♕b3	♘xd3
24	♕xd3	♖c4

The game is brought to an abrupt finish after the alternatives: 24...♖f7 25 ♕h3 h6 26 ♖xh6 gxh6 27 ♕xh6 +− or 24...♗e6 25 ♕h3 h6 26 ♖xh6 gxh6 27 ♕xh6 +−.

25 ♕xd5+

The point of Black's defensive rook manoeuvre is revealed upon 25 ♕h3 h6 26 ♖xh6 gxh6 27 ♕xh6 d4 28 ♕g6+ ♚h8 29 ♕h6+ with a draw.

25	...	♚h8
26	♕d2!	

Now 27 ♕h6 is ominous.

26	...	♚g8
27	♗xg7	♚xg7
28	♕h6+	♚f7
29	♖e1	

The rook is brought into play to aid the king hunt.

29	...	♖e4
30	♖xe4	fxe4
31	♕xh7+	♚f6
32	♕h6+	♚f7
33	♕h7+	

It would be a fitting finish to a fine game if White (in time-trouble) had found 33 ♖g5! ♕f6 34 ♕h5+ ♚e6 35 ♖g6 +−.

33	...	♚f6
34	♕xe4	♖g8
35	♖h6+	♚f7
36	♕d5+	

36 ♖h7+ ♚f6 (36...♖g7 37 ♕d5+) 37 ♖e7 is a clean kill (Nunn).

Now victory is only achieved by Black failing to fathom the onslaught.

36	...	♚g7
37	♕h5	♗f5
38	g4	♗d3?

38...♕e8 is a sterner defence.

39	♖e6	♚f8
40	♖e7	♗g6
41	♕h6+	1-0

Game 13
Langner-Bashkov
Ostrava 1991

1	e4	e6
2	d4	d5
3	e5	c5
4	c3	♘c6
5	♘f3	♕b6
6	a3	♗d7
7	b4	

White has experimented with the flexible 7 ♗e2:

a) 7...c4 8 ♘bd2 ♘a5 transposes into Game 2, Sveshnikov-Eingorn, Palma 1989.

b) 7...♘ge7 8 dxc5 ♕c7 9 0-0 ♘g6 10 b4 ♘gxe5 11 ♘bd2 g6 12 ♖e1 ♘xf3+ 13 ♘xf3 ♗g7 14 ♘d4 a6 15 ♗g5 0-0 16 ♕d2 f6 17 ♗h6 e5 18 ♗xg7 ♚xg7 19 ♘xc6 ♗xc6 20 ♗d3 ♖ad8 21 ♖e3 ♕d7 22 ♖ae1 ♖f7 23 ♗c2 ♕c7 24 ♖h3 ♗d7 25 ♕h6+ ♚g8 26 ♗xg6 ♖g7 27 ♗xh7+ ♚f7 28 ♖f3 ♕c6 29 ♕h5+ ♚e7 30 ♖xe5+ fxe5 31 ♕xe5+ 1-0 Kettner-Schmitt, Baden-Baden 1990.

c) 7...♘h6 8 b4 cxd4 9 ♗xh6 (9 cxd4 ♘f5 10 ♗b2 ♗e7 11 0-0 f6 = Beckett-Bus, Oakham 1992) 9...d3! 10 ♗xd3 gxh6 11 0-0 ♗g7 12 ♖e1 0-0 13 ♘bd2 f6 14 exf6 ♗xf6 ∓ Sveshnikov-Razuvaev, Palma 1989.

7 ...   cxd4

8 cxd4   ♖c8

9 ♗e3 *(38)*

With this useful move White aims to develop the kingside briskly. It has grown in popularity as a viable alternative to the standard 9 ♗b2. The position offers fresh challenges as the bishop can be easily exchanged, but at least that would boost the support for d4 and open the f-file for future attacking operations. White has occasionally employed 9 ♗e2:

a) 9....♘ge7 10 0-0 ♘f5 11 ♗b2 (11 ♗e3 ♗e7 12 ♘bd2 f6 13 ♗d3 ♘xe3 14 fxe3 ♔d8!? 15 ♖c1 ♘xe5 16 ♖xc8+ ♗xc8 17 ♘xe5 fxe5 18 ♕g4 is unclear; Blatny-Teske, Leipzig 1988) 11...♗e7 12 ♕d2 0-0 13 ♖d1 f6 14 ♘c3 fxe5 15 dxe5 ♗e8 (15...♔h8?! 16 ♖ac1 ♕d8 17 ♗d3 intending ♘e2 ±) 16 ♖ac1 ♗h5! (16...♘h4? 17 b5! ♘xf3+ 18 ♗xf3 ♘xe5 19 ♘xd5 ♘xf3+ 20 gxf3 exd5 21 ♖xc8) 17 ♘a4 ♕d8 18 ♘c5 ♗xc5 19 ♖xc5 ♘h4 20 ♘xh4 ♗xe2! (20...♕xh4 23 f3 ±) 21 ♕xe2 ♕xh4 22 ♖dc1 with equality, Sveshnikov-Lputian, USSR 1990.

b) 9...♘xd4?! 10 ♘xd4 ♖xc1 11 ♕xc1 ♕xd4 12 ♕c3 ±.

c) 9...a5 10 b5 ♘xd4 11 ♘xd4 ♖xc1 12 ♕xc1 ♕xd4 13 ♕c3?! (13 ♕c7! ♕xa1 14 ♕b8+ ♔e7 15 ♕d6+ ♔e8 16 ♕b8 ±) 13...♗c5! 14 0-0 ♕xc3 15 ♘xc3 ♗d4 16 ♖ac1 ♗xe5 ∓ Striković-Čabrilo, Prokupjle 1987.

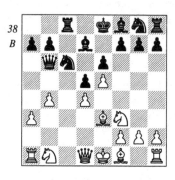

38
B

9 ...   ♘h6

There are a lot of supporters for 9...♘ge7, which is designed to occupy f5 as a way to put pressure on d4 while reserving the option of taking on e3. The problem is that it allows White to exchange on f5. After 10 ♗d3 ♘f5 play might proceed:

a) 11 ♗xf5 exf5 12 0-0 ♗e7 13 ♕d2 0-0 14 ♘c3 ♗e6 15 h4 (15 ♖fc1 a5 16 b5 ♘a7 17 ♕d3 h6 18 ♘d2 ♕d8 19 ♘a4 b6 20 ♖xc8 ♕xc8 21 ♘b1 ♕b7 22 ♘bc3 ♖c8 23 ♗d2 ♗d8 24 ♘b2 = Haba-Schmidt, Prague 1990) 15...a5 (15...♖fe8 16 ♗g5 a5 17 ♗xe7 ♖xe7 18 b5 ♘a7 19 ♖fb1 ♖c4 20 ♘d1 ♖cc7 21 a4 ± Andrienko-Danielian, Jurmala 1991) 16 b5 ♘a7 17 ♕b2 ♖c4 18 ♘d2 ♖c7 19 ♖fb1 f4 20 ♗xf4 ♕xd4 21 ♘e2 ♕xb2 22 ♖xb2 ♘c8 23 ♗e3 ♗xh4

24 b6 ♖d7 25 ♘b3 d4 26 ♘exd4
♖d5 27 ♘c5 ♗g4 28 ♘xb7 ♖xe5 29
♘c6 ♖h5 30 ♖c1 ♗f6 31 ♖bb1 ♘e7
32 ♘bxa5 1-0 Andrienko-Kiriakov,
Alma-Ata 1991.

b) 11 0-0 ♗e7 (11...♘d8!? 12
♗xf5 exf5 13 ♕d2 ♗b5 14 ♖c1
♖xc1 15 ♕xc1 ♗e7 16 ♘c3 =
Shrentzel-Pein, Haringey 1989) 12
♘bd2 0-0 13 ♘b3 ♘b8 14 ♘c5 ♗b5
15 ♗g5 ♗xd3 16 ♕xd3 h6 17 ♗xe7
♘xe7 18 ♖fc1 ♕c7 19 ♕d2 ♕b6
20 h3 ♖c7 21 a4 ♘bc6 22 ♖ab1
♖fc8 23 b5 ♘a5 24 g4 ♖e8 25 ♔g2
♖cc8 26 ♘d7 ♕d8 27 ♘f6+! gxf6
28 exf6 ♔h7 29 fxe7 ♕b6 30 ♕f4
1-0 Grosar-Ottavi, Rome 1990.

10 ♗d3   ♘g4
11 0-0   ♘xe3

In the game van der Werf-Jolles,
Groningen 1990, White had a vigorous offensive after 11...♗e7 12
♘bd2 ♘xe3 13 fxe3 0-0 14 ♘b3
f6?! 15 exf6 ♗xf6 16 ♘c5 ♖cd8 17
♘e5! ♗xe5 (17...♗c8 18 ♕h5 g6
19 ♘xg6 +−) 18 ♗xh7+! ♔xh7 19
♖xf8 ♖xf8 20 ♘xd7 ♕d8 21 ♘xf8+
♕xf8 22 ♕h5+ ♔g8 23 dxe5 ♕b8
1-0.

12 fxe3   g6

The system involving this move
has a good reputation, based on the
game Piriši-Khuzman, Balatonber-
eny 1988, which continued 13 ♔h1
(not 13 ♘g5? ♘xe5! ∓) 13...♗g7 14
♘g5?! 0-0 15 ♕g4? ♘xe5! 16 dxe5
♕xe3 17 ♖a2 ♕xd3 18 ♖af2 ♖c4 19
♕h3 ♕xh3 20 gxh3 ♗e8 21 ♘d2

♖c3 22 a4 h6 23 ♘gf3 ♗xa4 24 ♖e1
b5 25 h4 ♖fc8 26 h5 ♖c1 0-1.

However, White's play can be
dramatically improved by launching
a kingside attack using both his
knights to invade the dark squares
around the black king.

13 ♘c3 *(39)*

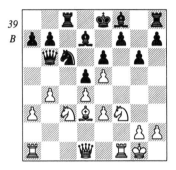

39
B

13 ...   ♗h6
14 ♕e1   0-0
15 ♘d1

This is the start of a slow but
powerful manoeuvre to harass the
bishop.

15 ...   ♗g7
16 ♘f2   ♕d8

Even at this early stage Black is
obliged to go on the defensive by
thwarting White's plan of an eventual ♕h4. On 16...f6 17 exf6 ♗xf6
18 ♘g4 ♗g7? 19 ♕h4 ♕d8 20 ♘g5
h5 21 ♗xg6 Black is destroyed.

17 ♘g4   a6
18 ♕g3   ♘b8?! *(40)*

Black chooses a faulty plan,
which he will not get the time to put

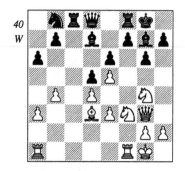

40
W

into effect. After ...♗b5 the idea is that White's attack will be stunted, while a rook invading at c3 will prove to be a distraction.

The only way to make an impression on the game is to play 18...f6

19 exf6 ♗xf6 20 ♘xf6+ ♖xf6 21 ♘g5!, but this is in White's favour nevertheless.

19	♕f4	♗b5
20	♗xb5	axb5
21	♘f6+	♗xf6

Now 21...♔h8 loses to 22 ♘xh7! ♔h7 23 ♘g5+ ♔g8 24 ♕h4.

22	exf6	♔h8
23	♘e5	♖c7
24	♖f3	

The final key to White's victory; the rook will be added to the attack on the h-file.

24	...	♖g8
25	♕h4	♕f8
26	♖h3	1-0

2 Milner-Barry Gambit

The concept of 6 ♗d3 followed by sacrificing at least the d-pawn was popularized by the Englishman Sir Stuart Milner-Barry. This cavalier approach naturally attracted Tal who revelled in the tactical possibilities. In recent times, Rozentalis and Sveshnikov, in particular, have refined the approach to the point where only one pawn is discarded in pursuit of the black king. The gambit is difficult to contend with, and will appeal to aggressive players. If Black is unprepared for them, the complications are extremely difficult to fathom over the board.

Game 14
Strauts-Kantoris
USSR 1985

1	e4	e6
2	d4	d5
3	e5	c5
4	c3	♘c6
5	♘f3	♕b6
6	♗d3	(41)

The most active posting for the bishop.

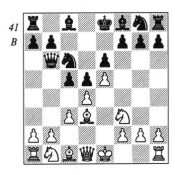

41
B

| 6 | ... | cxd4 |

It is misguided to try to transpose to other lines with 6...♘ge7?!. This occurred in Milner-Barry–Trott, England 1951: 7 dxc5 ♕c7 (7...♕xc5 8 b4 ♕b6 9 ♗e3 ±) 8 ♘a3 ♘xe5 9 ♘b5 ♘xd3+ 10 ♕xd3 ♕xc5 11 ♗e3 d4 12 ♗xd4 ♕c6 13 ♘e5 ♕xg2 14 ♘d6+ ♔d8 15 ♗b6+ 1-0.

A common error is 6...♗d7 when White can continue with 7 0-0 as in the illustrative game or take the chance to seize the initiative. After 7 dxc5! ♗xc5 (7...♕c7 8 ♗f4 ♗xc5 9 0-0 ♘ge7 10 b4 ♗b6 11 a4 ±) play might proceed:

a) 8 0-0 and now:

a1) 8...♘ge7? 9 b4 ♗xb4 10

cxb4 ♘xb4 11 ♗e3 ♕c7 12 ♘a3 ♕c3 13 ♘b5 ♕xd3 14 ♘c7+ ♔d8 15 ♕xd3 ♘xd3 16 ♘xa8 +− Molnar-Joppien, Vienna 1990.

a2) 8...f6 9 b4 ♗e7 10 ♗f4 fxe5 (10...♖c8 11 ♘bd2 ♕d8 12 a3 f5 13 c4 g5? 14 ♘xg5 1-0 Almeida-Purgimon, Andorra 1987) 11 ♘xe5 ♘xe5 12 ♗xe5 ♘f6 (12...♗f6 13 ♕h5+ g6 14 ♗xg6+ hxg6 15 ♕xg6+ +−) 13 ♘d2 0-0 14 ♘f3 ♗d6 15 ♕e2! ♖ac8 16 ♗d4 ♕c7 17 ♘e5 ♗e8 18 ♖ae1 ♗xe5 19 ♗xe5 ± Nimzowitsch-Salwe, Karlsbad 1911.

a3) 8...a5!? 9 a4 (9 ♕e2 f6 10 ♗f4 ♘ge7 11 ♘bd2 ♘g6 12 ♗g3 0-0 13 ♘b3 ♗e7 14 exf6 ♖xf6 15 ♘bd4 = Rubinetti-Ivkov, Palma de Mallorca 1970) 9...♘ge7 (9...♘ce7 10 ♘a3 ♘g6 11 ♕e2 ♘8e7 12 ♘b5 ♗xb5 13 ♗xb5+ ♘c6 14 h4 h6 15 g3 ♘ge7 16 ♔g2 ♖d8 17 ♗d2 ♕a7 18 ♖ad1 ♗b6 19 h5 0-0 20 ♗d3 with unclear play; Mellado-Bykhovsky, St. Barbara 1992) 10 ♘a3 ♘g6 11 ♕e2 0-0 12 ♘b5 ♖ad8 13 h4 f6 14 exf6 gxf6 15 ♗h6 ♖fe8 16 b4! axb4 17 a5 ♘xa5 18 cxb4 ♗xb4 19 h5 ♘c4 20 hxg6 ♗xb5 21 gxh7+ ♔f7 22 ♖ab1 ♕d6 23 ♘g5+! fxg5 24 ♗xg5 e5 25 ♕h5+ ♔g7 26 ♖xb4 e4 27 ♖xb5 ♕c6 28 ♖xb7+ Jonkman-Načinović, Holland 1993.

b) 8 ♕e2 a5 9 ♘bd2 a4 (after 9...♕c7?! 10 0-0 ♘ge7 11 ♘b3 intending ♘bd4 White has the advantage; C.Hawthorne-Evans, Bristol 1983) 10 b4 axb3 11 ♘xb3 ♗a3! 12

0-0 ♘ge7 13 ♗d2 ♘g6 14 ♘bd4! ♗e7 15 ♖fe1 0-0 16 h4! f5 17 exf6 ♗xf6 18 ♖ab1 ♕a7 19 ♗e3 ♘xd4 20 cxd4 ♗e8 21 ♘g5 ♗xg5 22 hxg5! ♘f4 23 ♗xf4 ♖xf4 24 g3 ♖f8 25 ♕xe6+ ♗f7 (Hort-Andersson, Reykjavik 1972) 26 ♕h3! g6 27 ♕g4 ±.

7 cxd4 ♗d7

It would be a grave error to grab the pawn because of 7....♘xd4?? 8 ♘xd4 ♕xd4 9 ♗b5+ picking up the queen.

8 0-0

The move-order involving 8 ♘c3 is also perfectly playable. The older lines are somewhat doubtful:

a) 8 ♗e2?! ♘ge7 9 b3 ♘f5 10 ♗b2 ♗b4+ 11 ♔f1 0-0 12 ♗d3 f6 13 ♗xf5 exf5 and Nimzowitsch felt Black was better, so he switched to 6 ♗e2 to save a tempo.

b) 8 ♗c2?! ♘b4 9 ♘c3 ♘xc2+ 10 ♕xc2 ♖c8 11 0-0 ♘e7 12 ♖d1 ♘c6 13 a4 ♘a5 ∓ Basjouni-Uhlmann, Prague 1954.

8 ... ♘xd4
9 ♘xd4

The speculative 9 ♘g5!? can be traced to the game Sørensen-Thapper, Karlskrona 1963, which continued 9...g6 10 ♗e3!? ♗c5 11 ♘c3 h6 12 ♘a4 ♗xa4 13 ♕xa4+ ♔f8 with an unclear position. It has since been heavily analysed by the Malmö chess club and has become popular in correspondence chess. It is certainly useful as a surprise weapon, although its soundness has not yet been confirmed by strenuous competitive play. For example:

a) 9...g6 10 ♗e3 and now:

a1) 10...♕xb2 11 ♘c3!? (not 11 ♗xg6? ♘e2+! –+; 11 ♘xf7 ♕xa1 12 ♘d6+ or 12 ♘xh8 ♘c6 is unclear according to Krantz) 11...♕xc3 12 ♖c1 ♕a5 13 ♗xd4 ♗h6 14 h4 ♘e7 15 ♕f3 ♗xg5? (15...0-0 16 ♗c5 ♕d8 17 ♕f6 ♗xg5 18 hxg5 is unclear) 16 hxg5 0-0 17 ♗c5 ♖fe8 18 ♕f6 ♘c6 19 ♖fe1 ♕d8 20 ♕f4 b6 21 ♗d6 ♖c8 22 ♗a6 1-0 Krantz-Tiemann, corr. 1992.

a2) 10...♗c5 11 ♘c3 and now:

a21) 11...♘f5? 12 ♗xf5 ♗xe3 (Stork-Pinarelli, Malmö 1979) 13 ♘xd5! exd5 14 ♗xd7+ ♔xd7 15 ♕xd5+ ♔c8 16 fxe3 ♘e7 17 ♖ac1+ ♔b8 18 ♕xf7 ♕xe3+ 19 ♔h1 ♕xg5 20 ♕f8+! +– Krantz.

a22) 11...♘e7 12 ♖c1 0-0 (or 12...♖c8 13 ♘a4 ♕b4 14 ♘xc5 ♖xc5 15 ♖xc5 ♕xc5 16 ♘xf7! 0-0 17 ♘h6+ ♔g7 18 ♘g4 ♖c8 19 ♘f6 ♖c7 20 ♕g4 ♘ec6 21 ♕h4 h5 22 ♘xh5+ gxh5 23 ♕f6+ ♔g8 24 ♕g6+ ♔f8 1-0 Keogh-Walsh, Dublin 1976; 12...♘b3!? Krantz) 13 ♕g4! h5 14 ♕f4 ♘ef5 15 ♗xf5 ♘xf5 16 ♗xc5 ♕xc5 17 ♘ce4 ♕e7 18 ♘f6+ ♔g7 19 ♖c7 ♖fd8 20 g4 hxg4 21 ♕xg4 b6 22 h4 a5 23 h5 +– Schipper-Luers, corr. 1989.

b) 9...h6?! 10 ♕h5 (10 ♘xf7!? ♔xf7 11 ♕h5+ ♔e7 12 ♘c3 is another idea) 10...0-0-0 11 ♘xf7 ♗e8

12 ♘c3 ♖d7 13 ♗g6 intending 14 ♗e3 ± (Krantz).

c) 9...f6? 10 ♕h5+ g6 11 ♗xg6+ ± (Krantz).

d) 9...♘e7?! 10 ♘xh7 ±.

e) 9...f5 10 exf6 ♘xf6 11 ♘xh7! 0-0-0 (11...♘xh7 12 ♕h5+ ♔d8 13 ♗xh7 ♘c2 14 ♗g5+ ♗e7 15 ♗xe7+ ♔xe7 16 ♕g5+; 14...♔c8 15 ♖c1 ♕xb2 16 ♕g6 +–) 12 ♘g5 ♗d6 13 h3 ♖h4 14 ♗e3 ♖dh8 (14...♕xb2 15 ♘c3 intending 16 ♘xf7) 15 ♘d2 ♘g4!? 16 ♗xd4 ♕xd4 17 ♘df3 ♗h2+ (Stork-Ohlsson, Sweden 1987) 18 ♘xh2 ♘xh2 19 ♔xh2 ♕e5+ 20 g3 +–.

f) 9...♗e7 and now:

f1) 10 h4 h5? 11 ♗e3! ♗c5 (or 11...♕xb2 12 ♘xf7! ♔xf7 13 ♗xd4; 11...♗xg5 12 hxg5 ♕xb2 13 g6 ♕xa1 14 gxf7+ ♔xf7 15 ♗xd4) 12 ♘c3 ♘e7 13 ♖c1 ♖c8 14 ♘a4 ♗xa4 15 ♕xa4+ ♘ec6 (Sørensen-Dehlryd, Malmö 1979) 16 ♖xc5! ♕xc5 17 ♖c1 and 18 ♗xd4 +–.

f2) 10 ♘h7?! ♘c6 11 ♕h5 0-0-0 12 ♕xf7 ♕d4 13 ♕xg7 ♘xe5 14 ♔h1 (14 ♕xh8? ♘f3+!) 14...♕xd3 15 ♖e1 ♕xh7 16 ♕xe5 ♗f6 17 ♕d6 e5 18 ♗f4 exf4 19 ♖c1+ ♗c6 0-1 Rohrich-Heyken, Dortmund 1993.

g) 9...♘c6!? 10 ♖e1 (Harding considers 10 ♗xh7 ♘h6 followed by ...♗e7 to be unclear) 10...♗c5 (10...g6 11 ♕f3 ♘h6 12 ♕f6!? =) 11 ♕f3 ♘xe5 (11...♘h6 12 h3!) 12 ♖xe5 f6 13 ♕h5+ ♔e7 14 ♕f7+ ♔d8 15 ♕xg7 ♗xf2+ 16 ♔h1 ♕d4?

17 ♘xe6+ ♗xe6 18 ♖xe6 ♕xd3 19 ♕f8+ +− (Harding).

h) 9...♗c5!? 10 ♘xh7 (10 ♘c3 g6 11 ♗e3 transposes to note 'a') 10...♘c6! 11 ♕h5 (with the idea 12 ♘f6+) 11...♘h6 (11...0-0-0 12 ♕xf7 ±) 12 ♘c3 intending 13 ♘a4 with equal chances (Harding).

9 ... ♕xd4
10 ♘c3 ♕xe5 *(42)*

The major alternative 10...a6 is examined in Game 16, Sveshnikov-Razuvaev. Black should accept the challenge as the less common ideas are just not good enough:

a) 10...♗b4?! 11 ♘b5 ♕xe5 12 ♕g4! ♗a5 13 ♗f4 ♘h6 14 ♕g3 ♕h5 15 ♗xg7 ♖g8 16 ♕xh6 ♕g4 17 ♗g3 a6 18 ♘d6+ ♔e7 19 ♕e3 ♗b4 20 ♘f5+ 1-0 Kottnauer-Palmer, England 1961.

b) 10...♕b6?! and now:

b1) 11 ♕g4 h5 12 ♕g5 g6 13 a4! ♗h6 (not 13...a6? 14 ♗xg6 fxg6 15 ♕xg6+ ♔d8 16 ♘xd5! +−; 13...♗e7 14 ♕f4 ♗b4 15 ♘b5 with compensation according to Tal) 14 ♕h4 a6 15 ♗xh6 ♘xh6 16 ♕f6 ♖f8 17 ♘xd5 ♕d8 18 ♕f4 exd5 19 ♕xh6 ♕e7 20 ♕e3 ♗c6 21 ♖ac1 ♖g8 22 f4 ♔f8 23 f5 gxf5 24 ♕h6+ ♖g7 25 ♖xf5 ♗d7 26 ♖c7 ♕e6 27 ♕h8+! ♖g8 28 ♕xh5 ♖c8 29 ♖xc8 ♗xc8 30 ♖f6 ♕e7 31 ♕h6+ ♖g7 32 ♖d6 ♕xe5 33 ♕h8+ 1-0 Tal-Ståhlberg, Stockholm 1961.

b2) 11 a4 ♘e7 (11...a5? 12 ♗e3 ♗c5 13 ♗xc5 ♕xc5 14 ♖c1 ♕b6 15 ♕g4! ± Möhring-Forintos, Halle 1958) 12 ♗e3 ♕d8 13 ♗g5! h6 14 ♘b5! ♗c6 15 ♘d6+ ♔d7 16 ♘xf7 ♕c7 17 ♘xh8 hxg5 18 ♕e2 ♘f5 19 ♗xf5 exf5 20 e6+ ♔e7 21 ♕h5 ♔xe6 22 ♖fe1+ ♔d6 23 b4 d4 24 ♕g6+ 1-0 Moles-Miyasaka, Skopje 1972.

c) 10...♘ge7?! 11 ♘b5 ♕xe5 12 ♖e1 (Keres suggests 12 f4! ♕b8 13 f5 a6 14 ♕f3 with advantage to White) 12...♕b8 13 ♕f3 ♗b5 14 ♗xb5+ ♘c6 15 ♕xd5 ♗d6 16 ♗xc6+ bxc6 17 ♕xc6+ ♔e7 18 ♗e3 ♖c8 19 ♕e4 h6 20 ♗d4 ♗xh2+ 21 ♔h1 ♕f4 22 ♕b7+ ♕c7 23 ♕b3 ♗d6 24 ♗xg7 ♕a5 25 ♕b7+ ♔e8 26 ♕f3 ♖ab8 27 ♖ad1 ♗e7 28 ♔g1 ♖b5? 29 ♕d3 ♖d5 30 ♕h7 ♗f8 31 ♗xf8 1-0 Corden-Knox, British Ch 1969.

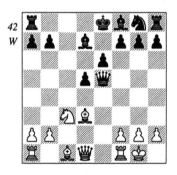

42
W

11 ♖e1 ♕d6

This old-fashioned move attempts to hang on to the d-pawn, but it is the first step on a perilous journey for Black.

The more resolute 11...♕b8 is covered in Game 16, Borg-P.Nikolić.

It is not wise to play 11...♕c7? since 12 ♘xd5 merely gives White a tempo. Play can continue:

a) 12...♕d8 13 ♗f4 ♖c8 14 ♕b3 ♗c6 15 ♗c4 ♗e7 16 ♘xe7 ♘xe7 17 ♖ad1 with a clear plus for White, Clarke-Elliott, England 1959.

b) 12...♕a5 13 ♖xe6+ fxe6 (certainly not 13...♗xe6? 14 ♗b5+ ♔d8 15 a4! ♗xd5 16 ♕xd5+ 1-0 Friedmann-Beneda, corr. 1974) 14 ♕h5+ ♔d8 (14...g6? 15 ♘f6+) 15 ♗g5+ ♘f6 16 ♘xf6 ♗e7! 17 ♘e4 and White has the better game due to Black's stranded king.

12 ♘b5 ♕b8 *(43)*

There are still those reckless enough to continue 12...♗xb5 13 ♗xb5+ ♔d8 and hope to survive the onslaught. White should be able to claim a sizeable advantage by following general attacking ideas based on sacrificial combinations at d5, penetrating on the c-file and preventing Black developing his forces. For example:

a) 14 ♗e3 ♘e7 15 ♖c1 ♘f5 16 ♗c5 ♕f4 (16...♕xc5!) 17 g3 ♕g5 18 ♕xd5+! exd5 19 ♗b6+ axb6 20 ♖e8# (1-0) Foulds-Lang, New Zealand 1956.

b) 14 ♕h5! and now:

b1) 14...g6 15 ♕f3 f6 (15...f5 16 ♗f4 ♕b6 17 ♕xd5+! +–) 16 ♗f4 e5 17 ♖xe5! fxe5 18 ♗xe5 ♕xe5 19

♕xf8+ ♔c7 20 ♖c1+ 1-0 Moyer-Kozmarek, corr. 1969.

b2) 14...♔e7 15 ♕h4+ ♘f6 16 ♗d2! a5 17 ♖ac1 intending ♗f4 with excellent chances according to Griffiths.

b3) 14...♕e7 15 ♗f4 (15 ♗g5!?) 15...♘f6 15 ♕f3 ♖ac8 16 ♖ac1 ±.

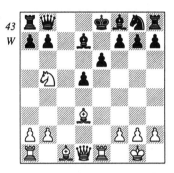

43
W

13 ♕f3 ♗d6
14 ♘xd6+

Flashy play led to success in Tal-Nei, USSR 1958, which finished in brilliant fashion after 14 ♕xd5 ♗xh2+ 15 ♔h1 ♗c6 16 ♕g5! ♘f6 17 f4 h6 18 ♕xg7 ♖g8 19 ♖xe6+! fxe6 20 ♗g6+ ♔d8 21 ♕xf6+ 1-0.

14 ... ♕xd6
15 ♗f4 ♕b6
16 ♕g3 g6

On 16...♔f8 comes 17 ♗c7! ♕c6 (17...♕xb2? 18 ♗e5!) 18 ♖ec1 ♕a4 19 b3 ♕d4 21 ♗e5 +–.

17 ♗e5 f6
18 ♗xg6+ ♔e7

There is no long-term reward in taking the offered piece: 18...hxg6

19 ♕xg6+ ♔d8 20 ♕g7 fxe5 21 ♕xh8 ♔e7 22 ♕g7+ ♔d6 23 h4! ±.

19	♗h5!	fxe5
20	♕g7+	1-0

Game 15
Borg-P.Nikolić
Kavala 1985

1	e4	e6
2	d4	d5
3	e5	c5
4	c3	♘c6
5	♘f3	♕b6
6	♗d3	cxd4
7	cxd4	♗d7
8	0-0	♘xd4 (44)

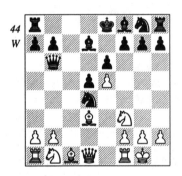

44
W

9 ♘xd4

The Czech player Jiri Nun has investigated the intriguing alternative 9 ♘bd2:

a) 9...♘e7 10 ♘xd4 ♕xd4 11 ♘f3 ♕a4 12 b3 ♕a5 13 ♗d2 ♕d8 14 ♖e1 h6 15 b4! a6 16 a4 ♘c6 17 ♖b1 ♗e7 18 b5 axb5 19 axb5 ♘a5 20 ♘d4 ♘c4 21 ♗xc4 dxc4 22 ♕g4

with a slight plus for White, Nun-Razuvaev, Sochi 1989.

b) 9...♘c6!? 10 ♘b3 ♘ge7 11 ♗e3 ♕c7 12 ♖c1 ♘g6 and White has insufficient compensation for the pawn; Nun-Schmittdiel, Prague 1990.

9	...	♕xd4
10	♘c3	♕xe5
11	♖e1	♕b8

Black's intention is to avoid his queen being harassed and to develop his kingside quickly.

12	♘xd5	♗d6
13	♕g4	

This is Milner-Barry's original idea to maintain the tension. Now the queen targets g7 and sets a trap if the h-pawn is grabbed: 13...♗xh2+? 14 ♔h1 ♗e5 15 ♗f4 ♗xf4 16 ♕xg7 ♕d8 17 ♕xh8 +−. The obvious 13 ♕h5 to protect h2 soon runs into trouble: 13...♔f8 14 ♘c3 ♘f6 15 ♕h4 ♗c6 16 ♗g5 ♗e5! (16...♘d5? 17 ♘xd5 ♗xd5 18 ♗c4! ±) 17 f4?! (after 17 ♗b5!? h6 the pin of the pawn is ineffective due to the threat of 18...♗xh2+) 17...♗d4+ 18 ♔h1 h6 19 f5 ♔g8 20 ♗e3 ♗xe3 21 ♖xe3 exf5 22 ♗xf5 g5! 23 ♕d4 ♕f4 and Black can hang on to the extra pawn; Bisguier-Westerinen, Netanya 1971.

13	...	♔f8
14	♗d2	h5

The queen is dislodged from its optimum square. Less accurate is 14...♗c6 15 ♗c3! e5 16 ♘e3 h5 17 ♕h3 ♘f6 18 ♖ad1 e4 19 ♗c2 ♗e5

20 &b4+ &g8 21 ©f5 g6 22 &d6
We8 23 ©e7+ &g7 24 &xe5 Wxe7
25 Wc3 Hhd8 26 h3 Hac8 27 Hxd8
Hxd8 28 &xe4 ± Soylu-Züger, Haifa
1989.

15 Wh3 *(45)*

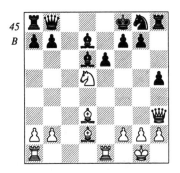

15 ... exd5?!

The start of an hallucinatory se-
quence. Black's idea is to add another pawn to the war chest and
develop his knight with gain of
tempo. However, there is still the
nigglesome problem of co-ordinat-
ing the rooks, while the black king is
liable to be threatened with back-
rank combinations.

In Pyhälä-McDonald, Gausdal
1990, Black preferred to activate his
knight immediately: 15...©h6!? 16
©e3 &g8 17 ©c4 (17 &c3! ©g4 18
©xg4 hxg4 19 Wxg4 &xh2+ 20 &f1
Wf8 21 g3 Hd8 22 He5! &c8 23 &c2
Hd5 24 Hae1 f5 25 Wg5 Hxe5 26
&xe5 &d7 27 Hd1 Wf7 28 Wd8+
&e8 29 &a4 &h7 30 &xe8 Wxe8 31
Wxe8 Hxe8 32 Hd7 f4 33 &g2 fxg3

34 fxg3 1-0 Finkel-Slutzkin, Ramat
1992; 17 g3 is unclear – Borg)
17...&c7 18 Wxh5 ©f5 19 Wg5
&xh2+ 20 &f1 is again unclear.

Another approach is possible:
15...&c6 16 ©e3 (16 ©b4 &d7 17
©d5 &c6 18 ©b4 ½-½ Motwani-
Brunner, Clichy 1991) 16...©f6 17
©c4 &c7 18 &c3 ©d5 19 ©e5
©xc3 20 ©xf7!? &h2+ (20....&xf7
21 Wxe6+ &f8 22 Wf5+ &g8 23
&c4+ &d5 24 &xd5 ©xd5 25
Wxd5+ &h7 26 Wf5+ with a drawn
position – analysis by I.Kuznekov)
21 &h1 ©e4 22 &xe4 &xf7 23
&xc6 Hh6 24 &d7 &e5 25 f4 &xf4
26 &xe6+ &f8 27 Had1 1-0 Sal-
nikov-Prudnikov, USSR 1991.

16 Wxd7 &xh2+
17 &h1 ©f6
18 Wf5

It is essential for White to maintain a grip on the situation by keeping his queen strongly centralized.
There is no joy to be gained from 18
We7+ &g8 19 g3 ©g4! when Black
is on top.

18 ... &d6
19 Hac1

The dormant rook is brought to
the scene of battle.

19 ... Wd8
20 &g5 &e7?!

A possible improvement is to seek
sanctuary in the ending: 20...Wd7 21
&xf6 Wxf5 22 &xf5 gxf6 23 Hed1
with equal chances.

21 He5! &g8 *(46)*

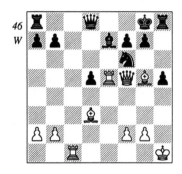

22 &xf6

White has the luxury of another line that preserves an advantage: 22 &ce1 &f8 23 &xf6 (23 &e8 &xe8 24 &xe8 &xe8 25 &xf6 gxf6 26 &xd5 ±) 23...&xf6 24 &xf6 gxf6 25 &xd5 ± (analysis by Borg).

22	...	&xf6
23	&xd5	&e8
24	&d7?!	

After this move it is clear that White has managed to establish a commanding position, although it will take time to convert to victory. However, the strongest remedy against the prospect of exchanging queens is to allow the other rook to take up residence on the seventh rank: 24 &c7! &xb2 (24...&d8 25 &xd8 &xd8 26 &d7 +—) 25 &c4 g6? 26 &xg6+! fxg6 27 &f5+ +—.

24	...	&e5
25	&xe5	&xe5
26	&xb7	

To exploit the initiative to the utmost, Black should be forced into complete passivity: 27 &c4 &f8 28

&xb7 &d4 29 f3 when a queenside pawn will romp home to promotion.

26	...	g6
27	&c4	&h7
28	&d1	&g7!

A stubborn manoeuvre which shields the king and protects the g-pawn after the bishop takes on f7.

29	&dd7	&h7
30	&xf7	&c8
31	g3	&c2
32	&g2	a5

The task is easy after 32...&xb2 33 &xa7 &c3 34 a4 +—.

33	&a7	&xb2
34	&xa5	&c3
35	&c5?	

White prepares to meet 35...&d4 by 36 &xg6+ &xg6 37 &xd4, but f2 can be attacked from another direction. The right response is 35 &a6! &h6 36 a4 &e1 37 &f6 winning.

35	...	&e1
36	&cc7	&xf2+
37	&h3	&h6
38	&c4	&xd7
39	&d7	½-½

Game 16
Sveshnikov-Razuvaev
Belgrade 1988

1	e4	e6
2	d4	d5
3	e5	c5
4	c3	&c6
5	&f3	&b6
6	&d3	cxd4

7	cxd4	♗d7
8	0-0	♘xd4
9	♘xd4	♕xd4
10	♘c3	a6

Tal introduced this move, which has the virtue of ruling out ♘b5.

11 ♕e2 *(47)*

This is an important moment for White. For some time the alternatives were the trusted continuations. However, theory has evolved to the point where the text is accepted as being the best chance for the initiative, as the rook is free to hassle the queen from d1 and the e-pawn is preserved. The other paths are:

a) 11 ♔h1 and now:

a1) 11...♘e7 12 f4 g6? (12...♘c6 13 a3! ±; 12...0-0-0 13 ♕e2 ♕b6 14 ♗e3 d4 15 ♖ac1 ♔b8 is unclear – Schwarz) 13 ♕e2 ♕b6 14 ♗e3 ♕d8 15 ♕f2 ♘c6 16 ♗b6 ♕c8 17 f5! ♘xe5 18 fxe6 ♗xe6 19 ♕f6 ♘xd3 20 ♕xh8 ♕c6 21 ♕d4 ♕c4 22 ♕e3 ♖c8 23 ♖ad1 ♘xb2 24 ♘xd5 ♘xd1 25 ♘f6+ ♔e7 26 ♕a3+ 1-0 Wade-Cafferty, British Ch 1957.

a2) 11...♕xe5 12 ♖e1 (12 f4 ♕d6 13 ♗e3 ♗e7 14 ♗d4 ♘f6 15 ♗e5 ♗xe5 16 fxe5 ♕xe5 17 ♕g4 h5 18 ♕b4 ♘e7 ∓ Wade-Menvielle, Palma de Mallorca 1966) 12...♕d6 13 ♕f3 ♗e7 14 ♗f4 ♕b6 15 ♕g3 ♘f6 16 ♗e5 ♔f8 17 ♖ac1 ♖c8 18 ♘e2 ♖xc1 19 ♖xc1 ♘e8 20 ♖c7 ♗b5 21 ♖c8 f6 22 ♗d4 ♕a5 with an equal position, Brinck-Claussen–Sørensen, Copenhagen 1989.

b) 11 ♖e1 and now:

b1) 11...♘e7 12 ♗e3 (12 ♘e2 ♕xe5 13 ♗f4 ♕f6 14 ♕b3 e5? 15 ♕xb7! ♗c6 16 ♕c7 ± Natapov-Karlsson, USSR 1972) 12...♕xe5 13 ♕f3 ♘g6 14 ♗xg6 hxg6 15 ♗f4 ♕h5 16 g4 ♕h3 17 ♕xh3 ♖xh3 18 ♘xd5 ♖c8 with unclear play; Parkanyi-Anka, Budapest 1990.

b2) 11...♗b4? 12 ♗e3 ♕xe5 13 ♗c5 ♕f4 14 ♘xd5 +-.

b3) 11...♕b6 12 ♕e2 (12 ♕g4!?) 12...♘e7 13 ♗g5 ♘c6 14 ♖ad1 ♗e7 15 ♗c1 0-0-0 16 a3 f6 17 exf6 gxf6 18 b4 ∓ McDonald-McKay, Scotland 1988.

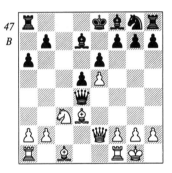

11 ... **♘e7**

The knight heads for c6 to put immediate pressure on e5 and prepare ...♘b4 to exchange on d3. The alternative treatments are not so forcing:

a) 11...♗b4?! 12 ♖d1 ♘e7 (12...♕b6 13 ♕g4 ±) 13 ♗xa6 ♕b6 14 ♗d3 0-0 15 ♗e3 ♕c7 16 ♕h5 g6 17 ♕h4 ♘c6 18 f4 ♗e7 19 ♕h6 ± Rozentalis-Neverov, Odessa 1989.

b) 11...♕h4 12 f4 ♘h6 13 ♗e3 ♖c8 14 ♖f3 ♗c5 15 ♗xc5 ♖xc5 16 ♖af1 ♕e7 17 ♖h3 ♘f5 18 ♕f2 ♗c6 19 g4 d4 20 ♘d1 ♘e3 21 ♘xe3 dxe3 22 ♕xe3 ♖a5 23 a3 g6 ½-½ Rozentalis-Epishin, USSR Ch 1990.

c) 11...♖c8 and now:

c1) 12 a3 g6 13 ♔h1 ♗g7 14 f4 ♕a7 15 ♗e3 ♕b8 16 ♕f2 ♖c6 17 ♖ae1 ♘e7 18 ♗c5 h5 19 ♗b4 ♕d8 20 ♘e2 0-0 21 ♕a7 ♖e8 22 ♘d4 ♖c8 23 ♕xb7 a5 24 ♗d6 +– Pirrot-Maiwald, Bad Wörishofen 1991.

c2) 12 ♖d1 ♗c5 13 ♗c2 (13 ♗xa6 ♕xf2+ 14 ♕xf2 ♗xf2+ 15 ♔xf2 bxa6 ∓) 13...♕h4 14 g3 ♕e7 = Cuartas-Mecking, Bogota 1977.

c3) 12 ♔h1 ♗c5 13 ♗g5 h6 14 ♗d2 ♘e7 15 ♖ac1 (perhaps 15 f4!?) 15...♕h4 16 f4 ♘f5 17 ♗xf5 exf5 18 b4 ♗a7 19 ♘xd5 0-0 = Padevsky-Darga, Siegen OL 1970.

d) 11...♕a7 12 ♔h1 ♗c5 13 f4 ± Lane-Sims, Cardiff 1981.

12 ♔h1

A necessary precaution as the e-pawn has to be supported, otherwise Black has a comfortable game. For example: 12 ♖d1 ♕h4 (12...♘c6 13 ♗xa6 ♕xe5 14 ♗xb7 ♕xe2 15 ♘xe2 ♖a7 16 ♗xc6 ♗xc6 =) 13 g3 ♕b4 14 ♗d2 ♕b6 15 b4 ♘c6 16 a3 ♕c7 17 f4 ♘d4 18 ♕f2 ♘b3 19 ♖a2 ♘xd2 20 ♕xd2 ∓ Ozanne-Bauza, Novi Sad OL 1990.

12 ...   ♘c6

White obtained an advantage in the game Formanek-Byrne, Atlanta

1967, after 12...♕h4 13 f4 ♗c6 14 b4 ♘f5 15 ♗xf5 ♗xb4 16 ♗d2 ♗xc3 17 ♗xc3 exf5 18 ♕c2 ♕g4 19 ♗b4 ±. If 12...♘g6? to hit e5 then the knight soon becomes a liability: 13 f4 ♕b6 14 f5 exf5 15 ♘xd5 ♕a5 16 ♗c4 ♗e6 17 ♖d1 ♖c8 18 ♗e3 ♗c5 19 b4! ♗xb4 20 ♗b6 ♕a4 21 ♘c7+ ♔e7 22 ♗xe6 fxe6 23 ♕c4 ♖hd8 24 ♗c5+ 1-0 C.Hawthorne-Boyne, Paignton 1983.

13 f4   ♘b4

On 13...♗c5 comes 14 a3! (14 ♗d2 ♘b4 15 ♖f3 ♘xd3 16 ♖xd3 ♕f2 17 ♕g4 0-0-0 18 b4 ♗a7 19 ♕d1 ♗c6 ∓ Zila-Borsov, Budapest 1990) 14...♗a7 15 ♗d2 g6 16 ♖f3 ♕b6 17 ♗e3 ♕c7 18 ♗xa7 ♖xa7 19 ♕f2 with reasonable chances for both sides; Luchan-McEntee, Chicago 1989.

14 ♖d1

Not 14 ♗b1?! ♕c4 15 ♕d1 d4 16 ♘e4 ♗b5! 17 ♖e1 d3 ∓ Miles-Wise, British Junior Ch 1970.

14 ...   ♘xd3

The principal argument against 14...♗c5 is line 'c', with which White secures an enduring edge in the endgame:

a) 15 ♗b5? ♕f2 16 ♗xd7+ ♔xd7 17 ♕g4 ♘d3! 18 h3 h5 19 ♕xg7 ♖ag8 20 ♕xf7+ ♔d8 –+.

b) 15 ♗xa6 ♕f2 16 ♕xf2 (16 ♗b5 ♕xe2 17 ♗xe2 =) 16...♗xf2 (Organdziev-Draško, Skopje 1992) 17 ♗e2 0-0 (17...♔e7 18 f5!) 18 ♗d2 (intending ♘e4) 18...♘c2 19

♖ab1 ♘e3 20 ♖dc1 ♖fc8 is unclear (Draško).

c) 15 ♗xh7 ♕f2 16 ♕xf2 ♗xf2 17 ♗b1 ♔e7 18 h3 ♖ac8 19 f5 exf5 20 ♖f1 ± Blasek-Kishnev, Gelsenkirchen 1991.

15 ♖xd3 ♕c4

The retreat 15...♕b6 is aimed at nullifying White's attack by shielding the queen behind the rest of Black's forces:

a) 16 ♗e3 ♗c5 17 ♗xc5 ♕xc5 18 f5 (18 ♕d2 0-0? {18...♗c6 19 ♖c1 ±} 19 ♘xd5! ♗b5 20 b4 ♕a7 21 ♘e7+ ♔h8 22 ♖h3 b6 23 f5 ♕xe7 24 f6 ♖fd8 25 ♕c2 1-0 Rogovskoi-Kolomoitsev, Volgograd 1989) 18...♗c6! (18...exf5 19 ♘xd5 ♗b5 20 ♕e3 ♕xe3 21 ♘c7+ ♔e7 22 ♘d5+ ♔f8 23 ♖xe3 g6 24 e6 =; 18...d4 19 b4! ♕c7 {19...♕xb4 20 ♘e4 is unclear} 20 ♖ad1 dxc3 21 ♖xd7 ♕xd7 22 ♖xd7 ♔xd7 =) 19 ♕g4 0-0-0 20 fxe6 fxe6 21 ♘e2 (21 ♘a4!? ♕a5 {21...♕e7 22 ♘b6+ ♔c7 23 ♕d4} 22 ♖c1 ♔b8 23 ♘c5 d4 =) 21...♔b8 22 ♘d4 ♖c8 23 h3 ♕e7 24 ♖f3 ♗d7 25 ♘b3 = Pirrot-Müller, Bundesliga 1989/90.

b) 16 a4 g6 17 f5 gxf5 18 ♖xd5 ♗c6 19 a5 ♕c7 20 ♖d3 ♖g8 21 ♖g3 ♖xg3 22 hxg3 0-0-0 ∓ Dyke-Henly, New York 1989.

16 b3 ♕c7
17 ♗b2 ♗c6

A game Wallyn-Mednis, Cannes 1992, saw another approach: 17...b5 (17...♖c8 18 f5!) 18 ♖c1 (18 ♕f2 b4

19 ♘e2? ♕c2!) 18...♕b7 19 ♕d2 (19 f5! b4 {19...♖g8 20 fxe6 fxe6 21 ♕h5+ g6 22 ♕xh7 ♖g7 23 ♕h8 ♗c6 24 ♘e2 ±; 19...♕e7 20 f6 ±; 19...♖c8 20 ♖f1 ±} 20 ♘xd5 exd5 21 e6 fxe6 22 f6 ♖c8 {22...g6 23 f7+ +−; 22...gxf6 23 ♕h5+ ♔e7 24 ♕h4 ♖g8 25 ♗xf6+ ♔e8 26 ♕xh7+−} 23 ♖f1 ♔d8 24 fxg7 ♗xg7 25 ♗xg7 ♖g8 26 ♕e5 ♖c6 27 ♖df3 ♗e8 28 ♗h6 ♕c7 29 ♕d4 ♕b6?! {29...a5 is unclear} 30 ♕h4+ ♔c8 31 ♖f8 ♖xf8 32 ♖xf8 ♔d7 33 ♗f4 ♗g6 34 ♕f6 ♖c8 35 ♕g7+ 1-0 Mololkin-Pechenkin, Volvograd 1993) 19...♖c8! 20 ♖d1 ♗e7 21 f5!? b4 22 ♘xd5 exd5 23 f6 ♗e6 24 fxe7 ♕xe7 25 ♖g3 g6 ∓. Byrne and Mednis only consider 18 f5? b4 19 ♘d1 ♗b5 winning but I believe there is significant room for improvement on White's play: 18 f5! b4 19 fxe6! fxe6 20 ♘xd5 exd5 21 e6 and now:

a) 21...♗b5 22 ♕h5+ g6 23 ♕xd5 ♗c6 24 ♖c1 ♗xd5 (24...♖c8 25 ♖xc6! ♕xc6 26 ♕d7+ +−) 25 ♖xc7 ♗e4 26 ♖dd7! ♖g8 27 e7 ♗g7 (27...♗h6 28 ♗f6! {intending ♖d8+ and e8♕+} 28...♗f7 29 e8♕+! ♔xe8 30 ♖e7+ +−) 28 ♗xg7 ♖xg7 29 ♖d8+ ♖xd8 30 exd8♕+ ♔xd8 31 ♖xg7 +−.

b) 21...♗c6 22 ♖c1 0-0-0 23 ♖f3 (23 ♖3d2!? ♔b7 24 ♖dc2 d4 25 ♖xc6 ♕xc6 26 ♖xc6 ♔xc6 27 ♕xa6+ ♔d5 28 ♕c4+ ♔e5 29 ♕c7+ ♗d6 30 ♕xg7+ ♔xe6 31 ♗xd4 ♖hf8 32 g3 =; 24...♖d6 25 ♗e5

♖xe6 26 ♗xc7 ♖xe2 27 ♖xe2 ♔xc7
28 ♖ec2 +−; 24...♖ac8 25 ♖xc6
♕xc6 26 ♖xc6 ♖xc6 27 e7 +−)
23...♖d6 (23...♔b8 24 ♖f7 ♗b5 25
♕xb5+ +−; 23...♔b7 24 ♖f7 ♗e7 25
♗e5 ♖d6 26 ♗xd6 ♕xd6 27 ♖xc6!
♔xc6 28 ♕xa6+ ♔c5 29 ♕a7+ ♔c6
30 ♖xe7 +−) 24 ♕xa6+ ♕b7 (or
24...♔b8 25 ♗e5 ♗b5 26 ♖xf8+
♖xf8 27 ♕xd6 ♖f1+ 28 ♖xf1 ♕xd6
29 ♗xd6+ +−; 24...♔d8 25 ♖f7 ♗e7
26 ♗e5 ♗b7 27 ♕xd6+ ♗xd6+ 28
♖cxc7 ♗xc7 29 ♖xc7 ♗a6 {29...♗a8
30 e7+ ♔e8 31 ♖c8+ +−} 30 ♖a7
♗c8 31 ♗xg7 ♖g8 32 ♗f6+ ♔e8
33 ♖a8 +−) 25 ♕xb7+ ♔xb7+ 26
♖f7+ ♔a8 (26...♔a6 27 ♗d4;
26...♔b8 27 ♗e5) 27 e7 ♗xe7 28
♖xe7 ± is analysis by Lane and Ady.

18 ♖c1 ♖d8

Black must be constantly on
guard against the familiar theme of
undermining d5: 18...♗e7 19 f5! ±.

19 ♕f2 ♗e7
20 ♘e2 0-0
21 ♘d4

White continues to manoeuvre
with great verve and prepares for an
attack based around the advance f5.

21 ... ♕d7
22 f5 exf5 (48)
23 ♖g3!

The final phase of the attack com-
mences; the major pieces are transferred to the kingside to storm the
monarch's citadel. Now 23...♗h4
can be rejected in view of 24 ♖xg7+
♔xg7 25 ♕xh4 (intending ♕f6+ and

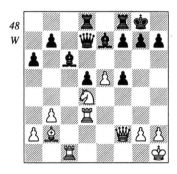

♘xf5) 25...f6 26 e6 ♕c7 27 e7 ♕xe7
28 ♘xf5+ +−.

If instead 23 ♘xf5, Black can
confuse the issue by 23...d4! 24
♖xd4 ♕e6 which activates the light-
squared bishop.

23 ... g6
24 ♕f4

Another direct move which
threatens ♕h6 and ♖h3.

24 ... ♖fe8
25 ♘xf5 ♗f8
26 ♗d4 ♖e6

The rook thwarts a future e6
which would release the bishop. On
26...f6!? comes 27 exf6 ♖e4 28
♘e7+ (28 ♕f2 ♖de8 with counterplay) 28...♔f7 29 ♕f2 with a clear
plus for White.

27 ♘h6+ ♗xh6

There is nothing to be gained
from 27...♔g7 when 28 ♖f1 seals
Black's fate.

28 ♕xh6 ♖de8
29 ♖f1 ♕c7
30 ♖h3 f5
31 exf6 ♕f7 (49)

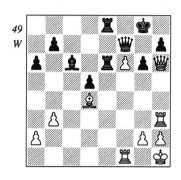

A classy finish is available after 31...♖e1 32 ♕xh7+! ♕xh7 33 f7+ ♕xf7 34 ♖h8#.

32 ♕xh7+!   1-0

3 Classical Variation

Modern practitioners of the Advance have often adopted the positional 6 ♗e2 to claim a slight advantage without undue risk. It has been incorporated into the repertoires of such players as Bronstein, Kosten and Nunn. The line has a reputation for the middlegame to drift into equality if White is not accurate.

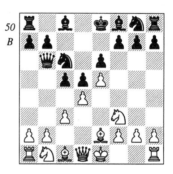

Game 17
Nunn-Schmittdiel
Dortmund 1991

1	e4	e6
2	d4	d5
3	e5	c5
4	c3	♘c6
5	♘f3	♕b6
6	♗e2 (50)	

The bishop is developed on e2 in order to keep d4 over-protected. If left undisturbed, White intends a gradual build-up of forces which would benefit from the extra space afforded by the Advance Variation

6 ...   cxd4

The double-edged alternative 6...♘h6 is examined in Game 19, Kosten-Brunner. There are a number of dubious possibilities:

a) 6...♘ge7? 7 dxc5! ♕c7 (after 7...♕xc5 8 b4 ♕b6 9 b5 Keres claimed that White is much better) 8 ♘d4 ♘xe5? (8...♕xe5 9 0-0 ±) 9 ♘b5 ♕xc5 10 ♕d4 +− Euwe-Kramer, Zaandam 1946.

b) 6...f6 7 0-0 fxe5 (7...♗d7 ♘a3) 8 dxe5! g6 (8...♘ge7 9 ♗d3!? ♘g6 10 ♖e1 ♗d7 11 ♕e2 0-0-0 ± Lane–Mitchell-Baker, London 1981) 9 ♖e1 ♘h6 10 ♘a3 ± Mackenzie-Gunsberg, Frankfurt 1887.

c) 6...♗d7 7 0-0 and now:

c1) 7...♖c8 8 dxc5 ♗xc5 9 ♘bd2 (9 b4 ♗f8 10 ♘a3 ± Antoshin-Bannik, USSR 1955) 9...♕c7 10 ♘b3 ♗b6 11 ♗f4 ♘ge7 12 ♖e1 f5 13 h4 0-0 14 h5 ♘d8 15 h6 ♘f7 16 hxg7

♔xg7 17 ♕d2 ♘g6 18 ♘bd4 ♗xd4
19 cxd4 ♕c2 20 ♗d3 ♕xd2 21
♗xd2 a6 22 a4 ♗c6 23 a5 ♖fc8 24
♖a3 ± Thipsay-Depasquale, Thessaloniki OL 1988.

c2) 7...0-0-0 8 ♘a3 cxd4 9 cxd4
♔b8 10 ♘c2 ♖c8 11 ♖b1 ♘h6 12 b4
♗e7 13 ♗xh6 gxh6 14 ♕d2 ± Zlotnik-Damsky, Moscow 1968.

7 cxd4   ♘h6

A transposition normally occurs after 7...♘ge7 8 ♘c3.

However, White has an extra option available. Play may continue 8 ♘a3!? (8...♗xa3 is no longer possible) 8...♘f5 9 ♘c2 ♗b4+ (9...h5 10 0-0 ♗d7 11 ♗g5 ♗e7 12 ♗xe7 ♔xe7 13 ♕d2 a5 14 ♗d3 ♘cxd4 15 ♘fxd4 ♘xd4 16 ♕e3 +− P.Morris-S.Morris, Dublin 1991) 10 ♔f1 ♗e7 11 h4 (11 g3 ♗d7 12 ♔g2 h5 13 h3 ± Klaman-Chistiakov, USSR 1949) 11...f6 12 g4 ♘fxd4 (12...♘h6 13 exf6 +−) 13 ♘cxd4 fxe5 14 ♘xc6 bxc6 15 ♘xe5 0-0 16 f4 ♗d6 17 ♘c4 ♕c7 18 ♘xd6 ♕xd6 19 ♔g2 1-0 Bronstein-Borges, USSR 1988.

Lesser known alternatives are:

a) 7...♗b4+ 8 ♔f1!? ♗d7 9 a3 ♗e7 10 ♘c3 f6 11 b4 ♖c8 12 ♘a4 ♕d8 13 h4 b6 14 ♖h3 ♔f8 15 ♗f4 ± Dückstein-Lombard, Austria 1974.

b) 7...♗d7 8 ♘c3 ♘h6 9 a3! ♘f5 10 ♘a4 ♕d8 11 h4 ± Hübner-Dückstein, Clare Benedict 1972.

8 ♘c3

The alternative 8 b3 is studied in the next game.

8 ...   ♘f5
9 ♘a4 *(51)*

To deflect pressure off d4. Less convincing is 9 ♔f1 when Black can play:

a) 9...♗d7!? 10 ♘a4 ♕a5 11 ♗d2 ♕d8 12 ♗f4 f6 13 ♗d3! ♘fxd4 14 ♘xd4 ♘xd4 15 ♕h5+ ♔e7 16 ♗e3 ♗xa4 17 ♗xd4 ♗e8 18 ♕h3 with unclear play; Dunhaupt-Khasin, corr. 1975-77.

b) 9...♗e7 10 h4 h5 11 g3 ♗d7 12 ♘a4 ♕d8 13 ♗f4 g6 14 ♖e1 ♖c8 = Hecht-Pietzsch, Germany 1964.

c) 9...h5 10 h4 ♗d7 11 ♘a4 ♕d8 12 g3 ♗e7 13 ♗f4 ♖c8 14 ♖c1 ♘a5 15 ♘c5 0-0 16 b4 ♗xc5 17 dxc5 ♘c4 18 ♔g2 b5 19 ♘d4 ♘xd4 20 ♕xd4 f6 21 ♖he1 fxe5 22 ♗xe5 ♘xe5 23 ♕xe5 ♖f5 24 ♕d4 ♕f6 25 ♕xf6 gxf6 26 ♖cd1 e5? 27 ♗d3 +− Lane-Dighton, London 1981.

d) 9...♘fxd4!? and now:

d1) 10 ♗e3 ♕xb2 11 ♘xd5 ♕xe2+! 12 ♕xe2 ♘xe2 13 ♘c7+ ♔d7 14 ♘xa8 ♘c3 15 ♘d4 ♗b4 16 a4 ♘xd4 17 ♗xd4 b6 18 ♗c3 ♗a6 −+ Schuermans-Claesen, Belgian Ch 1987.

d2) 10 ♘a4 ♕b4 11 ♗d2 ♕e7 12 ♗g5 f6 13 exf6 gxf6 14 ♘xd4 fxg5 15 ♗h5+ ♔d8 16 ♖c1 ♘xd4 17 ♕xd4 ♗g7 and in Boey's opinion Black is better.

9 ...   ♕a5+

9...♗b4+ 10 ♗d2 ♕a5 transposes to the text.

10 ♗d2   ♗b4

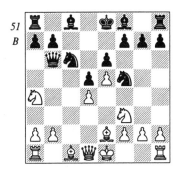

11 ♗c3   b5

Black has tried other moves here:

a) 11...♗xc3+ 12 ♘xc3 ♕b6 (12...♕b4 is met by 13 a3!) 13 ♗b5 (the line 13 ♘a4!? ♕a5+ 14 ♔f1 is unclear according to Keres) 13...0-0 (13...♗d7 14 ♗xc6 ♗xc6 15 ♕d2 ± Gurtner-Jurković, Geneva 1991) 14 ♗xc6 ♕xb2 15 ♘a4 ♕b4+ 16 ♕d2 ♕xd2+ 17 ♔xd2 bxc6 18 ♘c5! ± Nimzowitsch-Ståhlberg, 1934.

b) 11...♗d7 12 a3! ♗xc3+ 13 ♘xc3 0-0 (13...h5 14 0-0 ♖c8 15 ♕d2 with a distinct plus for White; Nimzowitsch-Spielmann, Stockholm 1920) 14 0-0 ♖ac8 15 b4 ± Mokry-Casper, Dečin 1978.

c) 11...a6!? 12 g4 ♘fe7 13 0-0 h5 14 ♗xb4 ♕xb4 15 a3 ♕a5 16 h3 hg 17 hg ♘g6 18 b4 ♕d8 19 ♕d2 ♘h4 20 ♕f4 ± Kupreichik-Seoyev, Sukhumi 1973.

12 a3   ♗xc3+
13 ♘xc3   b4
14 axb4   ♕xb4
15 ♗b5

The best chance for success.

Other continuations make fewer demands on Black's forces:

a) 15 ♕a4 ♗d7 (15...♕xa4 16 ♖xa4 ♗d7 17 g4 ♘fe7 18 0-0 0-0 19 ♖fa1 ♖ab8 ∓) 16 ♕xb4 ♘xb4 17 0-0 ♘c2! 18 ♖ad1 ♔e7 19 ♖d2 ♘b4 20 ♖a1 a5! ∓ Dushak-Voronkov, corr. 1973.

b) 15 ♖a4 ♕xb2 16 ♘b5 0-0 17 0-0 ♗d7 18 ♖a1 ♘xe5! 19 ♖b1 ♘xf3+ 20 gxf3 ♕xb1 21 ♕xb1 ♖ab8 22 ♕a1 ♗xb5 23 ♗xb5 ♖xb5 and Black is better according to Hutchings.

15 ...   ♗d7
16 ♗xc6

Also worthy of interest is 16 ♕a4!? ♕xb2 17 ♘xd5!? exd5 18 0-0 ♘fxd4 19 ♖fb1 ♘f3+ 20 gxf3 ♕c3 21 ♖c1 ♕b4 22 ♗xc6 ♕xa4 23 ♖xa4 ♗xc6 24 ♖xc6 ± Kupreichik-Ulybin, Moscow 1989.

16 ...   ♗xc6
17 ♕d2 *(52)*

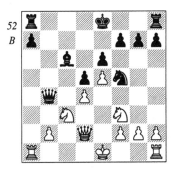

This position is critical for the future of the line. White can activate his rooks along the a- and c-files and possibly advance his kingside pawns to keep Black busy on both flanks. Black has play against b2 and a fairly solid position.

17 ...   ♗b5

A device to temporarily prevent White castling, and misguidedly encouraging White to exchange pieces to steer the game towards a draw.

Completing development with the obvious 17...0-0 is a less committal strategy:

a) 18 g4 ♘e7 19 0-0 a5 20 ♘e1 (20 h4!?) 20...f6 21 ♘c2 ♕b6 22 f4 fxe5 23 fxe5 = Zankovich-Nedochetov, Simferopol 1989.

b) 18 0-0 ♖fb8 19 ♖ab1 and now:

b1) 19...♕e7 20 ♖fc1 ♖b7 21 ♘e2 ♗b5 22 ♘g3 ♘xg3 23 hxg3 ± Dunworth-Bus, Cappelle la Grande 1991.

b2) 19...♗b5 20 ♖fd1 ♗c4 21 g4 ♘h6 22 h3 ♖b6 23 ♘g5 ♗b3 24 ♖dc1 ♖ab8 25 ♕d3 g6 26 ♕e3 ♔g7 27 ♘f3 ♕e7 28 ♕f4 ♘g8 29 ♖a1 ± Kamber-Borgstadt, Lugano 1989.

18 ♘xb5   ♕xb5
19 ♖a5   ♕b6
20 0-0   0-0
21 ♖c1

Naturally, White activates his king's rook in an attempt to control the c-file.

21 ...   ♖ab8
22 ♖c2   h6
23 ♖ac5   ♖b7
24 g4

Now that the rooks have found strong posts, the second stage of the long-term plan is instigated. The kingside pawns begin an advance to force the knight to retreat and create various attacking possibilities.

24 ...   ♘e7
25 h4   ♖fb8

Black is banking on the threat to b2 to curtail White's ambitions.

26 h5   ♕d8
27 ♕c1   ♕f8
28 g5!

Despite the quiet nature of the position, White is pursuing vigorous action on the kingside to provoke weaknesses.

28 ...   ♔h7
29 ♕f4   ♘f5
30 ♖c7   ♕d8
31 ♕c1

The rook is maintained on the seventh rank and under the stifled conditions Black is running out of useful moves.

31 ...   ♖b3
32 ♖c8   ♖xc8
33 ♖xc8   ♕a5 *(53)*
34 ♕c6!

This is the culmination of White's strategy. The c-file has proved to be of the utmost importance to infiltrate the heart of Black's camp, while the kingside pawns cover the monarch's escape squares. There is no time to take the knight: 34...♖xf3 (34...♘e7 35 ♕e8 ♘xc8 36 g6+) 35 ♖h8+! (certainly not 35 ♕e8?? ♕e1+ −+)

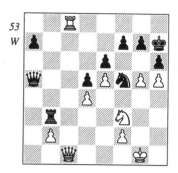

53
W

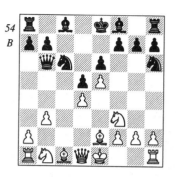

54
B

35...♔xh8 36 ♕e8+ ♔h7 37 g6+ fxg6 38 hxg6#.

34	...	♕a1+
35	♔g2	♘h4+
36	♘xh4	1-0

Game 18
Galdunts-Naroditsky
Moscow 1991

1	e4	e6
2	d4	d5
3	e5	c5
4	c3	♘c6
5	♘f3	♕b6
6	♗e2	cxd4
7	cxd4	♘h6
8	b3 (54)	

White embarks on a plan to reinforce d4 at the cost of giving up the right to castle.

It is an error to seek a positional treatment by doubling the h-pawns: 8 ♗xh6? ♕xb2 9 ♘bd2 gxh6 10 0-0 ♗g7 (or even 10...♘xd4! ∓) 11 ♘b3 ♕a3 and White has insufficient compensation for the pawn;

P.Morris-Ryan, Dublin 1991.

8	...	♘f5
9	♗b2	♗b4+

Also possible is 9...♗e7 10 0-0 ♗d7 11 g4 (11 ♔h1 0-0 12 ♗d3 ± Lputian; 11 ♗d3 g5 {11...♘fxd4 12 ♘xd4 ♘xd4 13 ♕g4 ♗c5 14 ♕xg7 0-0-0 with unclear play} 12 ♗xf5 exf5 13 ♘c3 ♗e6 14 a4 ♕d8 with an unclear game according to Hertneck) 11...♘h4 12 ♘xh4 ♗xh4 13 ♘a3 0-0 14 f4 f6 15 ♔g2! fxe5 16 dxe5 ♖f7! 17 ♕d2 ♖af8 (Kupreichik-Hertneck, Debrecen 1992) 18 g5 ♕b4 19 ♕xb4 ♘xb4 20 ♗c1 d4 21 ♗c4! ♘d5 (21...h6 22 ♗d2 ♘c6 23 g6 ♖f5 24 ♗d3 ♗e8 25 ♗xf5 ♖xf5 26 ♘b5 ♗xg6 27 ♘d6 ±; 21...♗c6+ 22 ♔h3 ♗g5 23 ♗d2! +−) 22 ♗xd5 exd5 23 ♘c2! ♗b5 24 ♖f3 ♗e2 25 ♘xd4 ♗xf3+ 26 ♘f3 ♖xf4 27 ♗f4 ♖xf4 28 ♖c1 ±.

Black chose to develop the queen's bishop in the game Yudasin-Illescas, León 1993: 9...♗d7 10 g4 ♘fe7 11 ♘c3 ♘g6 12 ♕d2 f6 (12...♗b4 13 ♖c1! intending a3 and b4 ±; 12...h5 13 g5 with the aim 0-0 and ♘a4-c5 ±; 12...♗e7 13 ♖c1 followed by ♘a4-c5 – Yudasin) 13 ♘a4 (13 ♗d3? fxe5 14 ♗xg6+ hxg6 15 dxe5 ♗e7 ∓) 13...♗b4!? (13...♕a5 14 ♕xa5! ♘xa5 15 ♘c5 ±; 13...♕c7 14 ♖c1! fxe5! 15 ♘xe5 ♘gxe5 16 dxe5 ±; 13...♕d8 14 exf6 ♕xf6 15 ♘c5 is unclear) 14 ♘xb6 ♗xd2+ 15 ♔xd2 axb6 16 exf6 gxf6 17 h4! h6! (17...♘f4 18 ♗f1 h5 ±; 17...e5 18 dxe5 ♘gxe5 19 ♘h2 intending f4 ±) 18 h5 ♘f4 19 ♗f1 ♖g8 (19...e5 20 dxe5 ♗xg4 21 ♖h4 ♗xf3 22 ♖xf4 ♗xh5 23 ♖xf6 ±) 20 ♖h4 e5 21 dxe5 ♖xg4 22 ♖h2 (22 exf6 ♖xh4 23 ♘xh4 ♔f7 ∓) 22...f5 23 ♘d4 ♘xd4 24 ♗xd4 ♘e6 25 ♗xb6?! (25 ♗b2! ♘c5 26 ♗e2! ±) 25...♖b4!=.

10 ♔f1 *(55)*

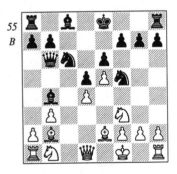

The king serenely side-steps the check to ensure the safety of d4. White can solve with the problem of activating the rook by playing h4 followed by ♖h3. Another idea is g4, to push back the knight, followed by a pawn storm when the rook is ideally placed on h1. Black often takes advantage of the situation by ...f6 and then utilizing the f-file. This can lead to a direct attack on the king or the undermining of the protection given to d4.

10 ...   0-0

This is Watson's recommendation and is potentially the most dangerous line available. Less confrontational approaches are feasible:

a) 10...♗e7 and now:

a1) 11 h4 ♗d7 (11...h5 12 ♗d3 intending ♗xf5 ±) 12 ♘c3 (12 g4 ♘h6 13 ♖g1 f6 with unclear play) 12...♘cxd4 13 ♘xd5 exd5 14 ♘xd4 ♘xd4 (14...♗c5? 15 e6! ♗xd4 {15...fxe6 16 ♘xf5 exf5 17 ♕xd5 ±} 16 exd7+ ♔xd7 17 ♖b1 ♗xb2 18 ♕xd5+ ±) 15 ♗xd4 (15 ♕xd4!?) 15...♗c5 16 ♗xc5 ♕xc5 17 ♖c1 ♕a5 18 h5!? (18 ♗g4!? ♗e6 19 ♗xe6 fxe6 {19...♕a6+ 20 ♕e2 ♕xe6 21 ♖h3 0-0 22 ♖hc3 =} 20 ♕h5+ g6 21 ♕g4 0-0 with unclear play) 18...h6 19 ♗g4 ♗e6 20 ♖h3 0-0 (20...♕xa2 21 f4!) 21 ♔g1 = Kosten-Lputian, Altensteig 1989.

a2) 11 ♘c3 ♕d8 12 g3 f6 13 ♔g2 fxe5 14 dxe5 0-0 15 ♖c1 ♗d7 (15...b6!? 16 ♘b5 ♗b7 17 ♘bd4 ±) 16 ♗d3 (16 ♘b5 and ♘bd4 ±) 16...♕e8 (16...g5?! 17 h3 ±) 17 ♘e2 ♕f7 18 ♖f1 ♖ad8 19 a3 g5 20 h3 ♗e8 (20...h5 21 b4 g4 22 hxg4 hxg4 23 ♘h2 +−) 21 b4 a6 22 ♕d2 h6 23 ♖ce1 d4 24 ♗e4 d3 25 ♘c1 ♘fd4

(Sveshnikov-Portisch, Biel IZ 1993) and now 26 ♕xd3! gives White the advantage.

b) 10...h5 and now:

b1) 11 ♘c3 ♗xc3 (11...♘xd4? 12 ♘a4 +−) 12 ♗xc3 ♗d7 13 ♕d2 a5 (Kholmov-Petrosian, USSR Ch 1949) 14 h4! =.

b2) 11 h4 ♗d7 (11...h5 12 ♖b1!? ♗d7 13 b4 ♖c8 = Lane-Bowden, London 1981) 12 a3 ♗e7 13 b4 a6 14 g3 0-0 15 ♔g2 f6!? 16 ♘c3! ♘cxd4 17 ♘xd5 exd5 18 ♘xd4 fxe5 19 ♘f3 ± Bigot-Watzl, corr. 1954-6.

11 ♘c3

It used to be assumed that the old main line was unclear after 11 g4 ♘h6 but exhaustive analysis indicates that Black has a pleasant game. For example:

a) 12 h3 ♗d7 13 a3 ♗e7 14 b4 f6! 15 exf6 ♖xf6 and now:

a1) 16 ♘c3!? ♖af8 17 ♘a4 ♕c7 18 ♖c1?! (18 ♔g2!?) 18...♖xf3! 19 ♗xf3 ♕f4 20 ♔g2 ♘xd4 21 ♗xd4 ♗xa4 22 ♕d3 ♗c6 23 ♕e3 ♕f7 24 ♖fe1 e5! 25 b5 exd4 26 ♕b3 d3 27 ♖e3 d4 28 ♕xf7+ ♔xf7 29 ♖xe7+ ♔xe7 30 bxc6 bxc6 ∓ Franke-Treffler, New York 1975.

a2) 16 ♔g2 ♖af8 17 ♘bd2 ♘f7 18 b5 (18 ♖f1!?) 18...♘a5 19 a4 ♘g5! 20 ♖f1 ♘xf3 21 ♘xf3 ♘c4 22 ♗c1 ♗d6 ∓ Bönsch-Thormann, E.Germany 1975.

b) 12 ♖g1 f6! 13 exf6 ♖xf6 14 g5 (14 ♘c3!?) 14...♖xf3! and now:

b1) 15 gxh6 ♖f7 16 ♗d3 e5 17 ♕h5 e4 18 ♗e2 ♗e6 (18...g6! ∓ Botterill) 19 ♘c3 ♗xc3 20 ♗xc3 ♘xd4 21 ♕e5 ♘f5! 22 ♗h5 ♖e7 23 ♗g4 and now Botterill-Ligterink, London 1978 was agreed drawn, but Botterill felt that 23...d4! 24 ♔e1 ♗f7 25 ♕xf5 e3! 26 f4 dxc3 27 ♕g5 ♕f6 would have left Black clearly better.

b2) 15 ♗xf3 ♘f5 16 ♖g4 ♗d7 17 ♘c3! ♘cxd4 18 ♘xd5 ♕b5+ 19 ♔g2 ♘xf3 20 ♘c7 ♕c6! 21 ♕xf3 ♕xc7 intending ...♗c6 and ...♘h4+ gives Black the edge according to J.Watson.

11 ... f6
12 ♘a4 ♕d8 *(56)*

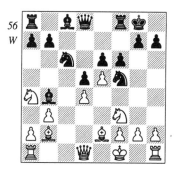

13 h4!

This is an improvement on the standard reference: 13 a3?! ♗e7 14 b4 fxe5 15 dxe5 ♗d7 ∓ Sorokin-Sokolsky, USSR 1951.

Rather than instantly trying to contain Black on the queenside, White signals aggressive intentions.

13	...	fxe5
14	dxe5	♗e7
15	♗d3	

White is combining the merits of attack and containment. Now the bishop has more scope and g4 is a real possibility.

15	...	h5
16	♖c1	♕e8
17	♔g1	♕f7

Black has doubled on the f-file but it is still difficult to conjure up counterplay. Another problem is responding to White's increasing influence on the queenside, with the bothersome ♘c5 difficult to prevent.

18	♕e2	g6
19	a3	♕e8
20	♖h3	

The long-term plan is working extremely well. White is gradually closing down the queenside with a3 intending b4, while the rook has emerged on the kingside. All this is designed to severely limit Black's opportunities by forcing cramped conditions.

20	...	♗d7
21	♘c5	♖b8
22	b4	♗d8
23	b5	♘a5
24	♘d4	

At the moment, the black knight is denying the rook access to g3 so it is logical to liquidate it.

24	...	♘xd4
25	♗xd4	♖f4
26	♖g3	1-0

Game 19
Kosten-Brunner
Altensteig 1989

1	e4	e6
2	d4	d5
3	e5	c5
4	c3	♘c6
5	♘f3	♕b6
6	♗e2	♘h6

This is a sly way to avoid the line given in Game 17, Nunn-Schmittdiel by delaying the capture on d4.

Instead of White's next move, the only other option is 7 b3 cxd4 8 cxd4 ♘f5 which is featured in Game 18, Galdunts-Naroditsky.

| 7 | ♗xh6 | |

The most testing way to treat this move-order. For the sake of doubled h-pawns, Black counts on steering the game towards relatively unfamiliar territory by castling swiftly and following up with ...f6.

| 7 | ... | gxh6 |

Black fell for a trap in the game Survila-Skoblikov, Podolsk 1978, after 7...♕xb2! 8 ♗e3! ♕xa1 9 ♕c2 cxd4 10 ♘xd4 ♘xd4 11 ♗xd4 ♗a3 12 ♗b5+ ♔d8 13 0-0 ♕b2 14 ♕a4 ♗e7 15 ♕a5+ 1-0.

| 8 | ♕d2 | ♗g7 (57) |

It is difficult for Black to get by without following the plan laid out in the text. For example:

a) 8...cxd4 9 cxd4 ♗d7 10 0-0 0-0-0 11 ♘c3 ♘a5 12 ♖fc1 ♔b8 13 ♕f4 ♗e8 14 ♗d3 ♖c8 15 ♖c2 ♕d8

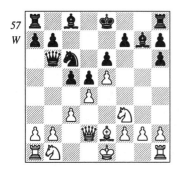

16 ♖ac1 ♘c4 17 ♘e2 ♘b6 18 ♖xc8+ ♘xc8 19 ♘g3 ♘b6 20 ♘h5 ♘d7 21 ♘f6 ♘xf6 22 exf6+ ♕d6 23 ♘e5 a6 24 g3 ♖g8 25 ♖c3 ♖h8 26 ♕c1 ♕d8 27 ♗xa6! bxa6 28 ♖b3+ ♔a8 29 ♘xf7! 1-0 Lukin-Georgadze, Spartakiad 1967.

b) 8...♗d7 9 0-0 ♗g7 10 ♘a3 0-0 11 ♘c2 cxd4 12 cxd4 f6?! 13 ♗d3 fxe5 14 ♘xe5 ♘xe5 15 dxe5 ♕xb2 16 f4 ♖ac8 17 ♖ab1 ♕c3 18 ♕e3 b6 19 ♘d4 ♕c5 20 ♗a6 ♕c3 21 ♗d3 ♕c5 22 g4 ♕e7 23 ♖f3 ♔h8 24 ♖e1 ♖ce8 25 ♖h3 ♖g8 26 ♔h1 ♗f8 27 ♖g1 ♕b4 28 g5! ♗c5 29 ♖xh6 ♖g7 30 ♕h3 ♖ee7 31 ♗xh7 ♖xh7 32 g6 1-0 Sveshnikov-Filipenko, USSR 1975.

| 9 | 0-0 | 0-0 |
| 10 | ♘a3 | cxd4 |

A natural reaction is 10...f6?! to undermine the centre, but in Kupreichik-Khuzman, Sverdlovsk 1987, it was shown to be flawed: 11 exf6 ♖xf6 12 dxc5! ♕xc5 13 b4 ♕f8 14 ♘c2 ♗d7 15 b5 ♘e7 (or 15...♘a5 16 c4 ±) 16 ♘e5 ♖d8 17 ♘d4 ♘g6 18

♘xd7 ♖xd7 19 ♗g4 ♖d6 (19...♘f4 20 ♖ae1 ♖d6 21 g3 h5 22 ♗d1 is slightly better for White) 20 ♘xe6! ♖fxe6 21 ♗xe6+ ♖xe6 22 ♕xd5 ♕f7 (22...♘f4 23 ♕xb7 ♗xc3 24 ♖ad1 ±) 23 f4! ♖e7 24 ♕f3 ±.

11	cxd4	♗d7
12	♘c2	f6
13	exf6	♖xf6
14	b4!	*(58)*

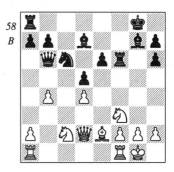

An energetic response to the situation. The aim is to dislodge the black knight from control of e5, so White can occupy the dominating square and contain the backward e-pawn. If 14...a6 15 a4 ensures b5.

14	...	♖af8
15	b5	♘e7
16	♘e5	♗e8
17	a4	

The theme of expansion on the queenside and maintaining the stronghold on e5 also featured in the game Kupreichik-Lautier, Belgrade 1988: 17 g3 h5 18 a4 ♘f5 19 a5 ♕c7 20 ♖ac1 ♘d6 21 ♘e3 ♕e7 22

♕b2 h4 23 d3 hxg3 24 hxg3 ♘e4 25 ♗xe4 dxe4 26 b6 axb6 27 ♕xb6 ♕a3 28 ♘eg4 ♖xf2 and now Bykhovsky supplies the following line to demonstrate that White can win: 29 ♘xf2! ♕xg3+ 30 ♔h1 ♖f6 (or 30...♖xf2 31 ♖xf2 ♕xf2 32 ♕e6+ ♔h8 33 ♕h3 +−) 31 ♘fg4 ♕h3+ 32 ♘h2 +−.

17   ...   ♘f5

Black has insufficient compensation for the exchange after Bykhovsky's suggestion 17...♘g6 18 ♘g4 ♖f4 19 g3 ♖xd4 20 ♘xd4 ♕xd4 21 ♕xd4 ♗xd4.

18	♖ae1	♔h8
19	f4	♕d8
20	♘e3	♘d6
21	g3	

White has managed to implement the short-term plan of securing e5 and stunting the power of the doubled rooks with f4 and g3. The next stage is to increase operations on the kingside to force the black pieces into a passive role.

21	...	♘e4
22	♕b4	♖g8
23	♘3g4	♗f8
24	♕b2	♖f5
25	♗d3	

White plays to eliminate Black's only genuinely active piece.

25	...	♗h5
26	♗xe4	dxe4
27	♘e3	♖f6
28	♖c1! *(59)*	

A high-class quiet move. The

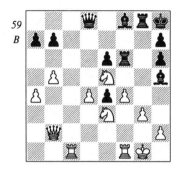

rook swings across to the c-file revealing the hidden agenda. With Black's pieces in disarray the time is right to penetrate the enemy camp.

28	...	♗g7
29	♖f2	♖ff8
30	♘g2	

There is still need for caution: 30 ♖fc2? ♖xf4 31 gxf4 ♗xe5+ 32 ♖g2 ♗xd4 −+.

30	...	♗f3
31	♖fc2	♕b6
32	♖c5	h5
33	♕d2	♕d6

Still Black continues to put up stubborn resistance. The idea is 34...♗xg2 35 ♔xg2 (the queen is now obliged to guard d4) 35...h4 to undouble the pawns.

34	♘h4	♗g4
35	♖c7	♗f6
36	♘g2	♖g7
37	♖xg7	♗xg7
38	♕e3	♗f5

The loose e-pawn requires Black to take defensive measures.

| 39 | ♘h4 | ♔g8? |

An understandable mistake, as the the rook was obliged to guard against ♘f7+.

40	♘xf5	exf5
41	♕b3+	♔h8
42	♘f7+	1-0

4 Euwe Variation

The first prominent player to recommend 5...♗d7 was Max Euwe. It is now accepted as one of Black's main lines due to the flexibility available by retaining the options of ...f6, ...♘ge7 and ...♛b6. The theory and understanding of the positions that arise have been influenced by such players as Mikhail Gurevich, Viktor Korchnoi, Nigel Short and Predrag Nikolić. White has various alternatives that can gain the initiative with the confrontation commencing in the middlegame.

Game 20
Ivanchuk-Short
Novi Sad OL 1990

1	e4	e6
2	d4	d5
3	e5	c5
4	c3	♘c6
5	♘f3	♗d7

The starting point of the variation.

6 ♗e2

This natural move has long been White's most popular choice. The main alternatives 6 dxc5 and 6 a3 are discussed later in this chapter.

6 ...   f6!?

Black takes the opportunity to attack the pawn chain now that the e-file has been blocked.

7 0-0! *(60)*

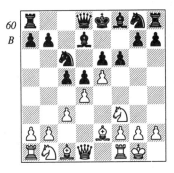

In the game Wang-Galliamova, Subotica wom IZ 1991, White managed to secure a slight pull after 7 exf6 ♘xf6 8 0-0 ♗d6 9 ♗e3 ♘g4 10 ♗g5 ♛b6 11 ♘a3 0-0 12 ♘b5 ♗b8 13 h3 ♘f6 14 dxc5 ♛xc5 15 ♗e3 ♛e7 16 c4 a6 17 ♘c3 ♛d6 18 ♖e1 ♗c7 19 ♛d2 ♖ad8 20 ♖ad1 ♗e8 21 cxd5 exd5 22 g3. However, Black's play can be improved upon and taking on f6 is considered harmless.

A poor alternative is 7 c4!? cxd4! 8 cxd5 exd5 9 exf6 ♘xf6 10 ♘xd4

♗c5 11 ♘xc6?! (11 ♘b3? ♗xf2+ 12 ♔xf2 ♘e4+ –+) 11...♗xc6 12 0-0 0-0 13 ♘d2 ♕b6 14 ♕b3 ♖ae8! 15 ♕xb6 ♗xb6 16 ♗d3 ♘g4 17 ♘f3 ♖xf3! 18 gxf3 ♘e5 19 ♗e2 d4 ∓ Kupreichik-Dolmatov, USSR 1980.

7 ... fxe5

Not 7...♕b6 8 dxc5 ♗xc5 9 b4 ♗e7 10 ♗f4 ♕c7? 11 exf6 ♕xf4 12 fxg7 ♗f6 13 g3 ♕d6 14 gxh8♕ ♗xh8 15 ♘g5 +– Andruet-Tal, Marseille 1989. An interesting try is to put pressure on e5 with 7...♕c7:

a) 8 ♗f4 ♘ge7 and now:

a1) 9 ♗d3 f5 10 ♖e1 c4 11 ♗c2 ♘g6 12 ♗g3 ♗e7 13 h4 0-0 14 b3 b5 15 ♘bd2 ♕d8 16 h5 ♘h8 17 a4 cxb3 18 ♘xb3 b4 19 ♘c5 bxc3 20 ♖a3 ♗xc5 21 dxc5 ♕a5 22 ♕d3 ♘b4 23 ♕xc3 ♖fc8 ½-½ Galdunts-Komarov, USSR 1991.

a2) 9 ♗g3 ♘f5 10 exf6 ♘xg3 11 f7+! (11 fxg3 gxf6 12 ♘h4 0-0-0! ∓ J.Watson) 11...♔xf7 12 fxg3 ♔g8 13 dxc5 ♗xc5+ 14 ♔h1 ♖f8 15 c4 d4 16 a3 ♗e7 17 ♘bd2 g6 18 b4 e5 19 c5 ♔g7 20 ♗d3 ♖e8 21 ♕e2 a6 22 h3 ♖hf8 23 g4 ♗e6 24 ♗e4 ♘b8 25 ♖ac1 ♗d8 26 ♘c4 ♗xc4 27 ♕xc4 ♖f4 28 ♖ce1 ♘d7 29 g3 ♖f7 30 ♘xd4! +– Prié-Dimitrov, France 1990.

a3) 9 ♘a3!? a6 10 ♗g3 ♘f5 11 exf6 ♘xg3 12 f7+ ♔xf7 13 fxg3 ♔e8 14 c4 cxd4 15 cxd5 exd5 16 ♗d3 ♗e7 17 ♘c2 ♔d8 ± Bastian-Lobron, Bundesliga 1990.

b) 8 ♖e1 fxe5 (8...0-0-0!? 9 ♗f4

♘ge7 10 ♕d2 ♘g6 11 ♗g3 ♕b6 =) 9 ♘xe5 ♘xe5 10 dxe5 0-0-0 with an unclear position according to J.Watson.

8 ♘xe5 ♘xe5
9 dxe5 ♗c6!? *(61)*

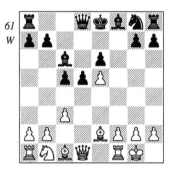

The idea is to strengthen the centre in preparation for castling queenside.

The game Glek-Yurtaev, USSR 1987 featured a different approach: 9...♘e7!? 10 ♗g5 ♕c7 11 ♗h5+ g6 12 ♗f6 ♖g8 13 ♗g4 ♗g7 (13...0-0-0 14 ♘d2 ±) 14 ♖e1 ♔f7 15 c4! d4 (15...♗xf6 16 exf6 ♔xf6 17 ♘c3 ±) 16 ♘d2 ♗c6 17 b4! b6 18 b5 ♗b7 19 ♗f3 ±.

In recent times, Black has strived to take advantage of the loose e-pawn by 9...♕c7, but with only limited success:

a) 10 c4 and now:

a1) 10...♕xe5 11 ♗h5+! g6 12 ♗f3 0-0-0 (12...d4 13 ♗xb7 ♖b8 14 ♗f3 ♗g7 ±) 13 ♖e1 ♕d6 (13...♕d4 14 ♕xd4 cxd4 15 cxd5 exd5 16 ♗f4!

±; 13...♕f5 14 ♘c3! d4 15 ♕b3 ♗c6 16 ♗xc6 bxc6 17 ♘e4 ±) 14 ♘c3! dxc4 (14...d4? 15 ♘e4 ♕b6 16 b4! wins) 15 ♕e2 ♘f6 (15...♗g7!? 16 ♕xc4! ±) 16 ♕xc4 ♗e7 17 ♗f4 ♕d4 (17...♕b6 18 b4! ♕xb4 19 ♖ab1! +−; 17...♕a6! 18 ♕xa6 bxa6 19 b4 c4 gives White an edge) 18 ♘b5!! ♗xb5 19 ♗xb7+ 1-0 Romanishin-Ivanchuk, Irkutsk 1986.

a2) 10...d4 11 ♗f4 ♘e7 12 ♘d2 ♘f5 13 ♗d3 ♗e7 14 ♘e4 0-0 15 ♕g4 ♔h8 16 ♕h3 ♕d8 17 ♗d2 ♗e8 18 g4 ♘h4 19 f4 ♗g6 20 ♗e1 h6 21 ♗xh4 ♗xh4 22 f5 ♗f7 23 fxe6 1-0 Zaitsev-Tarjan, Quito 1977.

b) 10 f4 and now:

b1) 10...♘e7 11 ♘d2 g6 12 ♘f3 ♗g7 13 ♕e1 0-0 14 ♕h4 ♘f5 15 ♕h3 ♕b6 16 g4 ♘e7 17 c4 ♖ae8 18 b3 ♘c6 19 ♗d3 ♖e7 20 ♘g5 with a small plus for White; Rozentalis-Pähtz, Germany 1991.

b2) 10...0-0-0 11 ♗e3 ♘e7 12 ♘a3?! g5 13 ♘b5 ♗xb5 14 ♗xb5 ♘f5 15 ♗d2 c4 16 ♗a4 ♗c5+ 17 ♔h1 g4 18 ♗c2 ♘g3+! 19 hxg3 ♕g7 20 f5 ♕g6! 0-1 Becker-Bruckner, Bundesliga 1985/86.

c) 10 ♗f4 ♘e7 11 ♘d2 0-0-0 12 ♘f3 h6 13 h4 g5 14 hxg5 ♘g6 15 ♗g3 ♗e7 16 ♗d3 ♖dg8 17 c4 dxc4 18 ♗xc4 hxg5 19 ♕b3 ♘f4 20 ♖fd1 ♖g6 21 ♗xf4 gxf4 22 a4 ♖hg8 23 ♔f1 ♔b8 24 a5 ♗c6 25 a6 ♖xg2 26 ♗xe6 ♗h4 27 ♖d2 ♗xf3 28 ♗xg8 ♖g1+ 0-1 Kholmov-Naumkin, USSR 1983.

10 ♗d3

Now 11 ♕h5+ is White's threat. The game Sax-Speelman, Hastings 1990/91, continued 10 c4!? ♘e7 11 ♗g4 ♕d7 12 ♘c3 dxc4 13 ♕e2 ♘f5 14 ♕xc4 ♘d4 15 a4 h5 16 ♗h3 ♕f7 17 f4 ♖d8 18 ♖f2 with equality.

10 ...   ♕d7
11 ♗g5

A necessary move if White wants to maintain the pressure by preventing queenside castling. On 11...♗e7 12 ♕h5+ g6? 13 ♗xg6+ wins.

11 ...   ♘h6
12 ♘d2   ♘f7
13 ♗h4   ♗e7

If the pawn is taken, then White exploits the open e-file: 13...♘xe5?! 14 ♕h5+ ♘f7 15 ♖fe1 ♗e7 16 ♘f3 ♗xh4 17 ♕xh4 ♕e7 18 ♕g4 0-0 19 ♖xe6 ±.

14 ♗xe7   ♕xe7
15 f4   0-0-0
16 ♕e2

White is busy centralizing his pieces to have greater influence, and preparing f5 in an attempt to secure a passed pawn.

16 ...   ♔b8
17 ♖ae1   g6
18 a3

Now White embarks on a task to disturb Black's pawn formation. The idea is b4 followed by a future a4, while ...c4 would give up control of the d4 square.

18 ...   c4
19 ♗c2   ♕c5+

20	♕f2	d4!

Black must not allow White to consolidate with ♘f3, as a knight on d4 would be strong.

21	♗e4	♘h6
22	cxd4	♕xd4
23	♘f3	♕xf2+
24	♖xf2	♖c8 *(62)*

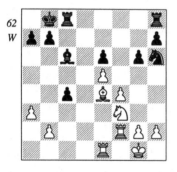

62
W

The ending offers White reasonable prospects since his forces enjoy greater harmony and he holds the initiative. Black is relying on his queenside pawn majority to pose problems.

Not 24...♗xe4?! 25 ♖xe4 ♖d1+ 26 ♖f1 ♖xf1+ 27 ♔xf1 ♖c8 28 ♘g5! when White must win a pawn.

25	♗xc6	♖xc6
26	♖d2	♘f5
27	♘g5	h5
28	♔f2	♖hc8
29	h3	b5?!

With White poised to push back the knight and take another step nearer a passed pawn, it would be better to invite complications:

29...c3! (29...h4 30 ♘e4 intending ♔f3-g4-g5) 30 bxc3 ♖xc3 31 ♘xe6 ♖xa3 and Cebalo evaluates the position as unclear.

30	g4	hxg4
31	hxg4	♘g7

If 31...♘h6 (31...♘e7 32 ♖d6 ±) 32 ♖h1! (not 32 ♔g3? c3 33 bxc3 ♖xc3+ 34 ♔h4 ♖h8 −+) 32...♘xg4+ 33 ♔f3, White wins a piece.

32	♖h1!	c3
33	bxc3	♖xc3
34	♖h7	♖3c7

The knight is trapped after 34...♖8c7 35 ♖d8+ ♔b7 36 ♖g8 +−.

35	♖h6	♖f8
36	♔e3	a5

Trying to create sufficient counterplay is a forlorn effort: 36...♖c3+ 37 ♖d3 ♖xd3+ 38 ♔xd3 ♖xf4 39 ♖xg6 +−.

37	♖xg6	♖h8
38	♘xe6	♘xe6
39	♖xe6	♖c3+

On 39...♖h3+ 40 ♔e4 ♖xa3 41 ♖b6+ ♖b7 42 ♖xb7+ ♔xb7 43 e6 White wins.

40	♔e4	♖xa3
41	♖b6+	1-0

Game 21
Anand-M.Gurevich
Manila IZ 1990

1	e4	e6
2	d4	d5
3	e5	c5
4	c3	♘c6

5 ♘f3   ♗d7
6 ♗e2   ♘ge7

If 6...♖c8, play can transpose to the note to Black's ninth move after 7 0-0 cxd4 8 cxd4 ♘ge7 9 ♘a3 (9 ♘c3!?) 9...♘f5 10 ♘c2 ♕b6 (or 10...♗e7 11 g4!? ♘h4 12 ♘xh4 ♗xh4 13 f4 ± Torre-Gausel, Manila OL 1992) 11 g4. In the game Bastian-Korchnoi, Baden-Baden 1981, an independent approach was employed: 7...♘ge7 8 dxc5! ♘g6 9 ♗e3 ♘cxe5 10 ♘xe5 ♘xe5 11 b4 ♗e7 12 f4 ♘c6 (12...♘g6 13 ♘d2 b6 14 ♘b3 ±) 13 ♘d2 ♗f6 14 ♖c1 0-0 (14...d4?! 15 cxd4 ♘xd4 16 ♘e4 ±) 15 ♘f3 ♕c7 16 ♕d2 ♖cd8 17 ♗d4 ♗e7 18 ♕e3 f6 19 ♗d3 ♖f7 20 ♖ce1 ±.

7 ♘a3

A standard idea to manoeuvre the knight to c2 where it can reinforce d4.

In the game Prié-Kindermann, Uzes 1990, White tried the adventurous 7 h4!? cxd4?! (7...♖c8 8 ♘a3 cxd4 9 cxd4 ♘f5 10 ♘c2 ♘b4 =) 8 cxd4 ♘f5 9 g4! ♘h6 10 ♗xh6 gxh6 11 g5! ♕b6 12 ♕d2 hxg5 13 hxg5 ♘a5 14 ♘c3 0-0-0 15 g6 fxg6 16 ♘g5 and achieved an advantage.

The main alternative 7 0-0 is examined later in this chapter.

7 ...   cxd4
8 cxd4   ♘f5
9 ♘c2 (63)   ♘b4

The most popular continuation, although other paths have been investigated:

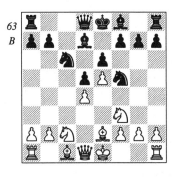

63
B

a) 9...♕a5+ 10 ♗d2 ♕b6 11 ♗c3 ♗e7 12 0-0 a5 13 a4! (13 ♘e3 g6 14 ♕d2 h5 15 g3 ♖c8 16 ♖fd1 ♘b4 17 a3 ♔f8 18 ♘xf5 exf5 19 h4 with unclear play; Lein-Dizdar, Berlin 1987) 13...0-0 14 ♘a3 f6 15 exf6 ♖xf6 16 ♘b5 ♖af8 17 ♕d2 ♘d6 18 ♖ac1 ♘e4 19 ♕e3 ♗e8 20 ♘d2 ♘xc3 21 bxc3 e5 22 ♖b1 exd4 23 ♘xd4 ♕a7 24 ♗f3 ♗f7 25 ♘b5 ♗c5 26 ♘2b3 ♖e8 27 ♘xc5 ♖xc6 28 ♕d2 ♖d8 29 ♖b1 b6 30 ♘xc5 bxc5 31 ♖b7 ♕a6 32 ♕g5 ♖cc8 33 ♖1b6 ♕d3 34 ♖xf7! ♔xf7 35 ♖b7+ ♔e6 36 ♖e7+ ♔d6 37 ♕e5+ 1-0 Rozentalis-King, Mondorf 1991.

b) 9...♕b6 10 0-0 and now:
b1) 10...a5 11 g4 ♘fe7 12 ♘h4 (12 ♘fe1 h5 13 gxh5 ♘f5 14 ♗e3 f6 15 ♗d3 0-0-0 16 ♗xf5 exf5 17 exf6 {17 ♘d3!? ♗e8 18 ♕f3 ♖xh5 19 exf6 gxf6 20 ♗f4 ±} 17...♗e8! 18 h6 18 gxf6 19 ♕d2 = Sveshnikov-Razuvaev, Moscow 1985) 12...♘g6 13 ♘g2 ♗e7 14 f4 0-0 15 ♗e3 f5 16 exf6 ♖xf6 17 h4 (17 ♗d3?! ♗d6 18 h4 ♖af8 19 g5 ♖6f7 20 ♗xg6 hxg6

21 h5 gxh5 22 ♕h5 g6! 23 ♕xg6+ ♖g7 24 ♕d3 ♘e7 25 ♕b3 ♕xb3! 26 axb3 b6 27 ♗d2 ♘f5 28 ♖f3 ♖h7 29 ♖af1?! ♗b5 30 ♖e1 ♔f7 with a clear plus for Black; Benjamin-Gulko, USA Ch 1992) 17...♗d6 18 h5 ♘ge7 19 ♗d3 ♖c8 20 ♕e2 ♖ff8 21 ♘h4 h6 (21...♘b4 22 ♘xb4 ♕xb4 23 ♖ad1 ±) 22 g5 hxg5 23 fxg5 ♘f5 24 h6!? ♘ce7 (24...♘xh4? 25 ♕h5 g6 26 ♗xg6 ♘e7 27 ♗f7+ ♔h8 28 ♕xh4 ♘f5 29 ♕h5 ±) 25 ♕h5 ♗g3? 26 g6! ♗xh4 27 hxg7 ♔xg7 28 ♕h7+ ♔f6 29 ♕xh4+ ♔g7 30 ♕h7+ ♔f6 31 ♗h6 1-0 Sveshnikov-Gulko, USSR Ch 1985.

b2) 10...♘a5 11 g4! ♘e7 (or 11...♘h6?! 12 h3 ±) 12 ♘fe1 ♗b5 13 ♘d3 h5 14 gxh5 ♘f5 15 ♗e3 ♘c4 16 a4 ♘cxe3 17 fxe3 ♗c4 18 ♘f4! ♗b3 19 ♗b5+ ♔d8 20 ♕e2 ♗xc2 21 a5 ♕c7 22 ♖fc1 ♖c8 23 a6 b6 24 ♗a4 ♕c4! (24...♕e7 25 ♗xc2 ♕g5+ 26 ♔h1 gives White an edge) 25 ♖xc2 ♕xe2 (Sveshnikov-Dolmatov, USSR 1988) 26 ♖xe2 ♗e7 27 ♖g2! ♖c4 28 ♔f2 ♗h4+ 29 ♔e2 ♖b4 30 ♔d3 ±.

b3) 10...♖c8 11 g4 ♘fe7 and now:

b31) 12 ♘fe1 h5 13 gxh5 ♘f5 14 ♗e3 ♘b4 (14...♕xb2 15 ♖b1 ♕xa2 16 ♖xb7 ±) 15 ♘xb4 ♗xb4 16 ♘d3 ♗b5 17 a4 ♗c4 (not 17...♗xd3? 18 ♗xd3 ♘xd4 19 a5 +−) 18 a5 ♕b5 19 b3 ♗xd3 20 ♗xd3 ♕d7 21 a6 b6 22 ♔h1 ♖c3 23 ♖c1 ♖xc1 24 ♗xc1 g6 25 hxg6 fxg6 26 ♖g1 ♕h7 27 ♖g2

♗e7 28 ♕g4 ♔f7 29 ♗g5 ♕h3 30 ♗xf5 exf5 31 e6+ ♔e8 32 ♕f4 ♗xg5 33 ♕xg5 ♖h6 34 ♕f6 1-0 Sveshnikov-Skalkotas, Athens 1983.

b32) 12 ♘h4!? ♘b4 13 ♘xb4 ♕xb4 14 f4 ♘c6 (or 14...♗b5 15 ♕d2 ♕a4 16 b3 ♕a6 17 ♗xb5 ♕xb5 18 f5 ♘c6 19 ♗b2 ± Sveshnikov-Gleizerov, Russia 1992) 15 ♗e3 ♗e7 16 ♘g2 f6 17 a3 ♕xb2 18 ♖b1 ♕a3 19 ♖b7 ♘d8 20 ♖d7 ♔d7 21 ♗b5 ♔c7! 22 ♕b1 ♗b4! 23 f5 ♔b6 24 ♗d7 ♖c3 (Sveshnikov-Ulybin, Russia 1992) 25 fxe6 ♖e3 26 e7 ♖b3 27 ♕h7 ♗e7 28 ♕h8 ♕b4 29 ♕xg7 ♕d4 30 ♔h1 ♕d3 31 ♖g1 ±.

10 ♘xb4

The main alternatives 10 ♘e3 and 10 0-0 are examined later in the chapter.

10 ...   ♗xb4+
11 ♗d2   ♕a5

Anand suggests the alternative 11...♕b6 12 ♗xb4 (12 a3 ♗xd2+ 13 ♕xd2 ♗b5 =) 12...♕xb4+ 13 ♕d2 ♕xd2+ with equal chances. For example: 14 ♔xd2 ♘e7 15 ♖ac1 ♘c6 16 b4 a6 17 a3 f6 ½-½ Blasek-Züger, Gelsenkirchen 1991.

12 a3!

This is an improvement on Sieiro-M.Gurevich, Havana 1986, when Black equalized after 12 ♗xb4 ♕xb4+ 13 ♕d2 ♕xd2+ 14 ♔xd2 ♘e7! 15 ♖hc1 f6! 16 ♖c5 ♔d8.

12 ...   ♗xd2+
13 ♕xd2   ♕xd2+
14 ♔xd2   f6 (64)

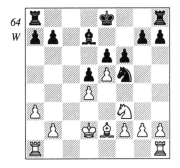

15 ♖ac1

The basis of White's game is to make the most of the extra space available to manoeuvre the pieces and force Black into a cramped position.

15 ... ♘e7
16 b4 ♔d8

If 16...♘c6 17 b5!? ♘a5 18 ♔c3 a6 19 a4 intending ♔b4 gives White excellent prospects.

17 ♗d3 ♖c8
18 ♖xc8+ ♘xc8
19 g4 h6?!

This is not the way to defend against the potential kingside pawn advance, especially when g6 is made vacant for a knight to occupy.

A more commendable solution is suggested by Anand: 19...♘b6! 20 b5 (20 exf6 gxf6 21 g5 ♘c4+ 22 ♗xc4 dxc4 23 gxf6 ♗c6 with unclear play) 20...♔e7 21 ♖c1!? when White has a small edge.

20 ♘h4 ♘e7
21 f4 a6

On 21...fxe5 22 dxe5! maintains the initiative.

22 ♖f1 ♗b5
23 f5?!

The simple 23 ♖e1 is good while 23 exf6 gxf6 24 ♖e1 ♖g8! allows Black back into the game.

23 ... h5?!

A more precise method is necessary: 23...♗xd3! 24 ♔xd3 h5 25 ♘g6 ♖h6 26 ♘f4 hxg4 27 ♘xe6+ ♔e8 27 ♘xg7+ ♔f7 when Black has at least equality.

24 ♘g6 ♘xg6
25 exf6! gxf6
26 fxg6 ♔e7 *(65)*

The line 26...♗xd3 27 ♔xd3 ♔e7 (27...hxg4 28 ♖xf6 ♔e7 29 g7 ♖g8 30 ♖g6) 28 g5 fxg5 29 ♖f7+ leaves White with a clear advantage.

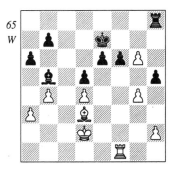

27 g5 f5
28 ♗xb5 axb5
29 ♖c1 ♔d6
30 ♔e3

The passed g-pawns provide the necessary distraction to allow the white king to advance.

30 ... ♖g8

31	♔f4	b6
32	♖c3	♖xg6
33	♖h3	♖g8
34	♖xh5	♖c8
35	g6	♖c4
36	♖g5!	♖xd4+
37	♔e3	♖e4+
38	♔f2	1-0

Game 22
Sax-Brenninkmeijer
Wijk aan Zee 1992

1	e4	e6
2	d4	d5
3	e5	c5
4	c3	♘c6
5	♘f3	♗d7
6	♗e2	♘ge7
7	♘a3	♘f5

The unusual 7...♘g6, which Larsen originally suggested, is occasionally tested:

a) 8 ♘c2 ♗e7 9 0-0 0-0 10 ♖e1 ♕c7 11 ♗d3!? c4 12 ♗xg6 hxg6 13 ♗g5 h6 14 ♗xe7 ♘xe7 15 ♘e3 = Zude-Kishnev, Munich 1992.

b) 8 h4!? ♗e7 9 g3 (9 h5!?) 9...cxd4 10 cxd4 0-0 11 h5 ♘h8 12 ♘c2 f6! 13 exf6 ♗xf6 14 b3 ♘f7 15 ♗b2 ♕a5+ (de la Villa Garcia-Korchnoi, Pamplona 1990) 16 ♔f1 with unclear play.

8	♘c2	cxd4
9	cxd4	♘b4
10	♘e3 *(66)*	

The idea is to challenge the knight, while the prospect of doubled

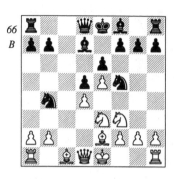

pawns is agreeable as it bolsters the d-pawn and opens up the f-file.

| 10 | ... | ♘xe3 |
| 11 | fxe3 | |

Stean states that 11 ♗xe3 ♖c8 12 0-0 ♘c2 offers a level game.

| 11 | ... | ♗e7 |
| 12 | 0-0 | |

A new idea which has revived interest in the set-up. This differs from the game Spassky-Korchnoi, Belgrade C (18) 1978 which catapulted the line into prominence: 12 a3 ♘c6 13 b4 a6 14 ♖b1 ♘a7 15 a4 ♘c6 16 ♗d2 a5 17 b5 ♘b4 18 0-0 0-0 19 ♕e1 ♔h8 20 ♕g3 f6 21 ♖bc1 f5 22 h4 ♖c8 23 h5 ♖xc1 24 ♖xc1 ♘a2 25 ♖a1 ♘b4 26 ♕h3 =.

| 12 | ... | 0-0 |
| 13 | ♗d2 | ♕b6?! |

The queen makes little impression here because the usual pressure on b2, which restrains the development of the c1 bishop, is absent.

Brenninkmeijer has put forward 13...a5!? as an alternative, with unclear play.

14	a3	♘c6
15	b4!	

White has gained space by employing a typical pawn structure while pushing back the knight.

| 15 | ... | f5 |

Another approach is 15...a6, intending ...♘a7 followed by ...♗b5 in order to exchange the light-squared bishop.

16	exf6	♗xf6
17	♗d3	♘e7
18	♕b1!	h6?!

It is a better idea to play 18...g6 in an effort to blunt the effectiveness of the b1-h7 diagonal.

| 19 | a4 | ♘f5 |
| 20 | b5 | a5 (67) |

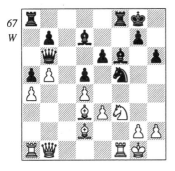

67
W

21 ♗c1!

A neat way to introduce the queen's rook into play via a2-f2 while adding the option of ♗a3.

21	...	♖fc8
22	♖a2	♕d8
23	♖af2	♕e7
24	g4	♖xc1

The only way to avoid instant calamity: 24...♘h4 (24...♘d6 25 ♗a3 and ♘e5 +−) 25 ♘xh4 ♗xh4 26 ♗h7+ ♔h8 27 ♖f7 +−.

25	♕xc1	♘d6
26	♘e5	♖c8
27	♕b1	♗e8

Now the game could have been finished off in style after 28 h4! intending 29 g5 hxg5 30 hxg5 ♗xg5 31 ♖f8+ ♕xf8 32 ♗h7+ ♔h8 33 ♖xf8#.

| 28 | g5 | hxg5 |
| 29 | ♗h7+ | |

White is beginning to lose his way as 29 ♘g4 would quickly secure the win.

29	...	♔h8
30	♖f3	g4
31	♘xg4	♗h5
32	♖g3	

Less clear cut is the ending that can be forced: 32 ♘xf6 gxf6 33 ♖h3 ♕xh7 34 ♕xh7+ ♔xh7 35 ♖xh5+ ♔g6.

32	...	♗h4
33	♖g2	♗g5
34	♗g6	♗xg4
35	♖xg4	♗xe3+
36	♔g2	e5
37	♕e1	♘c4
38	♖f7	♕e6 (68)
39	♕g3?	

In time-trouble White misses a superb opportunity to demolish his opponent by 39 ♕h4+ ♗h6 40 ♕xh6+! gxh6 41 ♖h7+ ♔g8 42 ♗f5+ +−.

| 39 | ... | ♗h6 |

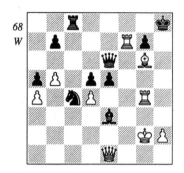

68
W

1	e4	e6
2	d4	d5
3	e5	c5
4	c3	♘c6
5	♘f3	♗d7
6	♗e2	♘ge7
7	♘a3	cxd4
8	cxd4	♘f5
9	♘c2	♘b4
10	0-0 *(69)*	

40	♖h4	♘e3+
41	♔f2	♔g8
42	♖f3?!	

Brenninkmeijer shows how White can still make progress: 42 ♖xh6! ♘g4+ 43 ♔g2 ♘xh6 (the other capture is no better: 43...gxh6 44 ♗f5! ♖c2+ 45 ♔h3 ♕xf7 46 ♕g4+ ♔f8 47 ♗xc2 ♕f1+ 48 ♕g2 +−) 44 ♖xg7+ ♔f8 45 ♖xb7 ♕g4 46 ♕xg4 ♘xg4 47 ♖f7+ ♔g8 48 b6 +−.

42	...	e4
43	♖ff4?!	♖c2+
44	♔xe3	♕e7?!

Black would actually have the better chances upon 44...♖c3+ 45 ♔f2 ♖xg3 46 ♗f7+ ♕xf7 47 ♖xf7 ♗e3+ 48 ♔xg3 ♔xf7 ∓.

45	♗f7+	♕xf7
46	♖xh6	♖c3+
47	♔f2	♖xg3
48	♖xf7	♔xf7
49	♖d6	½-½

Game 23
Sveshnikov-Dreev
St. Petersburg 1993

69
B

Sveshnikov has pioneered this course of action. The idea is that the defence of d4 can still be adequately maintained despite allowing Black to fulfil the plan of exchanging on c2.

| 10 | ... | ♘xc2 |
| 11 | ♕xc2 | h5!? |

Black is concerned about the prospect of a future g4 while even harbouring ambitions of a minor pawn storm with ...g5. The policy of direct action against d4 by 11...♕b6 is more logical although it can be easily contained. On 12 ♕d3 play might continue:

a) 12...a6 13 ♗d2 h5 14 a4 a5 15 ♖fd1 ♗e7 16 h3 ♖c8 17 ♗c3! h4 18 ♕d2 ♖a8 19 ♖db1 ♗b4 20 ♗b5 ♗xb5 21 ♗xb4 ♗d7 22 ♗c5 ♕d8 23 b4 b6 24 ♗d6 f6 25 ♖c1 ♖a7 26 b5 ♘xd6 27 exd6 g5 28 ♖a3 0-0 29 ♖ac3 ♗e8 30 ♖c7 ♖f7 31 ♖c8 ♕d7 32 ♖1c6 ♖f8 33 ♕c2 ♗h5 34 ♖8c7 ♖xc7 35 ♖xc7 1-0 Sveshnikov-Zlotnik, Moscow 1991.

b) 12...♗e7 13 a4 0-0 14 a5 ♕c7 15 ♗d2 a6 16 ♖fc1 ♗c6 17 ♕b3 ± Sveshnikov-Nikolaev, Šibenik 1990.

c) 12...♖c8 13 ♗d2 ♗b4! (or 13...♗e7 14 g4! with a clear plus for White) 14 ♗f4?! (14 ♗xb4 ♕xb4 15 a3 ♕b6 ±) 14...a6 15 a4 ♘e7 16 h4 ♗a5 17 ♖fc1 ♖xc1 18 ♗xc1 h6 (½-½ Sveshnikov-Dreev, Rostov-on-Don 1993) 19 b3 0-0 20 ♗b2 =.

12 ♗d2   ♗e7

13 ♗d3

On 13 ♕b3?!, 13...g5! poses some problems due to the threat of ...g4.

13 ...   ♕b6

The situation has changed to the extent where the standard attack on d4 is no longer feasible. Sveshnikov suggests that 13...g5 14 ♗xf5 exf5 15 ♕b3 is unclear, although the kingside pawn rush should fail without significant support from the major pieces.

14 ♗xf5   exf5 *(70)*

An enterprising idea is 14...♖c8 which seeks counter-play on the basis of the bishop exploiting the light

squares: 15 ♕b3 exf5 16 ♕xd5 ♗e6 17 ♕a5 ♕xa5 18 ♗xa5 b6 19 ♗d2 ♗d5 20 ♖fc1 ♔d7 21 ♘e1 a5! 22 ♘c2 g5 23 ♘e3 ♔e6 24 a3 f4?! (24...h4 is unclear) 25 ♘xd5 ♔xd5 26 h4 g4 27 ♗xf4 ♖xh4 28 a4 with an edge for White; Yagupov-Dreev, Rostov-on-Don 1993.

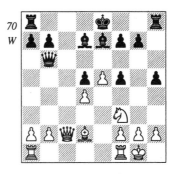

15 ♗g5!

This is the point of White's play. Black cannot castle without allowing a strong knight to be posted on g5, while grabbing the d-pawn invites the white rooks to seize the central files.

15 ...   ♗xg5

16 ♘xg5   ♕xd4

The quieter 16...0-0 17 ♕d2 leaves White in a commanding position.

17 ♖fd1   ♕h4

It would appear that 17...♕c4 defending d5 and offering the exchange of queens is Black's salvation but it fails to 18 ♕xc4 dxc4 19 ♘xf7! ♔xf7 20 ♖xd7+ ♔e6 21

罝ad1 ±. If 17...♕b6 18 罝xd5 ♗e6
19 罝d6 ±.

18	♕d2!	♕c4
19	罝ac1	♕b5
20	a4	

White spends some time molest-
ing the queen in order to take on d5
without permitting an exchange of
queens.

20	...	♕b3
21	罝c3	♕b6
22	♕xd5	0-0
23	a5	

Not 23 ♕xd7? 罝ad8 −+.

| 23 | ... | ♕xb2 (71) |

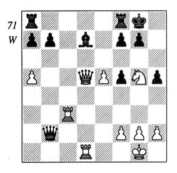

| 24 | ♕f3! | g6 |

Now the bishop leaves the board,
but there is no escape after 24...罝fd8
25 ♕xh5 ♕xc3 26 ♕xf7+ ♔h8 27
♕h5+ ♔g8 28 ♕h7+ ♔f8 29 ♕h8+
♔e7 30 ♕xg7+ ♔e8 31 ♕f7#.

25	罝xd7	罝ac8
26	罝xc8	罝xc8
27	罝d1	罝c1
28	♕d5	罝xd1+
29	♕xd1	♕xe5
30	♕d8+	♔g7
31	♕h8+!	

An unpleasant surprise for Black
which brings the game to an abrupt
finish.

31	...	♔xh8
32	♘xf7+	♔g7
33	♘xe5	♔f6
34	f4	g5
35	♔f2	gxf4
36	♘d3	b5
37	♘xf4	h4
38	♔e3	♔e5
39	♘g6+	1-0

Game 24
Hort-Tukmakov
Bern 1992

1	e4	e6
2	d4	d5
3	e5	c5
4	c3	♘c6
5	♘f3	♗d7
6	♗e2	♘ge7
7	0-0	

A standard procedure which is the
latest fashion. The intention is to relieve the pressure on d4 by undermining the knight when it occupies
f5.

| 7 | ... | cxd4 |

This relieves the tension, allowing
the b1 knight to develop quickly on
c3. In the game Thipsay-Speelman,
London 1992, the queen's rook
played a greater role after 7...罝c8 8
罝e1!? (or 8 ♘a3, transposing to

notes in Game 21, Anand-M.Gure-
vich) 8...cxd4 9 cxd4 ♘f5 10 ♘c3 a6
(10...♗e7?! 11 ♗d3! is a suggestion
by Larsen) 11 ♔h1 ♗e7 (11...♕b6?
12 ♘a4 ♕c7 13 g4! ±) 12 g4 ♘h4 13
♘xh4 ♗xh4 14 ♗e3 0-0 15 ♖g1 f6!
16 exf6 ♗xf6 and now 17 ♕d2 g6
would have been unclear.

Psakhis prefers the more patient
alternatives 7...♘f5 and 7...♘g6
which are examined later in this
chapter.

8 cxd4   ♘f5
9 ♘c3   ♗e7

See the next game for 9...♖c8.

10 g4 *(72)*

10 a3 would bring about Kamsky-
Kasparov, New York (exhibition
game) 1989, where White's passive
play was punished: 10...♖c8 11
♗f4?! g5! 12 ♗e3 g4 13 ♘e1 h5 14
♘c2 f6 15 exf6 ♗xf6 16 ♗d3 ♘ce7
17 ♕d2 0-0 18 ♗g5 ♘g6 19 ♗xf6
♕xf6 20 ♖ae1 ♘fh4 with advantage
to Black.

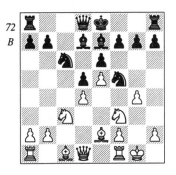

10 ...   ♘h4

There is little to recommend the
meek 10...♘h6?! after 11 h3 0-0 12
♗e3 f6 13 exf6 ♖xf6 14 ♘e5 ♖f8 15
f4 ♗b4 16 ♗f3 ♗xc3 17 bxc3 ±
Sveshnikov-Lalić, Sochi 1987.

11 ♘xh4   ♗xh4
12 ♗e3   0-0
13 f4   ♗e7

This retreat is an attempt to improve on the critical encounter Nunn-
Anand, Munich 1991. That game
proceeded: 13...f6 14 exf6 ♗xf6 15
♖c1 (Nunn considers 15 g5 ♗e7 16
♗d3 g6 intending ...♗d6 and ...♘e7
unclear) 15...g6 16 ♕d2 ♗g7 17
♗f3?! (17 ♘a4! ±) 17...♕a5! 18
♗g2 ♔h8 19 ♔h1 ♖ac8 20 h3 ♕b4
21 ♖fd1 b6 22 ♗f1 ♘a5 23 b3
♗c6?! (23...♕e7 =) 24 ♘e4! ♕e7
(24...♕xd2 25 ♘xd2 intending ♘f3
±) and now 25 ♘f2 followed by ♔g1
and ♘d3 offers White the better
chances.

14 ♗d3   f6
15 ♕c2

A clear indication of White's aggressive intentions, this forces a
weakening of the pawn structure because 15...g6? fails to 16 ♗xg6!
hxg6 17 ♕xg6+ ♔h8 18 ♖f3 winning.

15 ...   h6
16 ♕g2! *(73)*   **♗e8**

The light-squared bishop is added
to the defence to meet White's ♗b1
and ♕c2 by either ...g6, blocking the
diagonal, or by ...♔h8 followed by
...♗f7-g8.

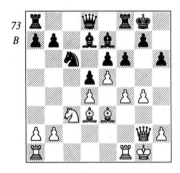

Not so good is 16...fxe5 17 fxe5 ♕b6? 18 ♘xd5! +–.

17	♖ad1	fxe5
18	fxe5	♗f7
19	♖f3	

White conducts the attack with commendable energy. Now that Black has had to waste time coping with the threats along the b1-h7 diagonal, White can successfully switch plans and prepare to double on the f-file.

| 19 | ... | ♗g5 |
| 20 | ♗f2! | |

The bishop is conserved in order to protect d4 and contemplate h4.

20	...	♔h8
21	♖f1	♗g8
22	♖xf8	♕xf8
23	h4	

Bringing the kingside pawns into the offensive has the effect of restricting Black's mobility.

23	...	♗d8
24	♗e3	♕e7
25	g5	♗b6
26	♕f2!	

Continuing the onslaught while snuffing out Black's counterplay by defending d4.

26	...	♗h7
27	g6	♗g8
28	♘b5	

Hort acknowledges that 28 ♘e2 to over-protect d4 is a winning strategy as it releases the queen and bishop for the attack.

28	...	♖d8
29	♗g5	♕d7
30	♗e3	♕e7
31	♗g5	♕d7 (74)

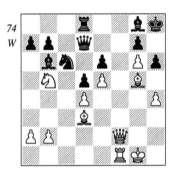

32 ♕f4!

In a moment of mutual time-trouble White finds the winning combination by preparing 33 ♗f6 with the threat 34 ♕xh6+.

32	...	a6
33	♗f6	gxf6
34	exf6	♗h7
35	g7+	

White is in the enviable position of having a choice of wins; 35 ♕xh6 and 35 f7 were also effective.

35	...	♔g8
36	♕xh6?!	

A quicker solution is 36 f7+ ♔xg7 37 f8♕+ ♖xf8 38 ♕xf8#.

36	...	♗f5
37	♕h8+	♔f7
38	♕h5+??	

The pressures of time-trouble take their toll as 38 ♖xf5! exf5 39 ♗xf5 ♕xf5 40 ♘d6+ wins.

38	...	♔xf6
39	♕h6+	♔f7
40	♗xf5	exf5
41	♘d6+	♕xd6
42	♖xf5+	♔e7
43	♕g5+	♔d7
44	♖xd5	♗xd4+
45	♔f1	♖g8!
46	♕f5+	½-½

Game 25
Blatny-Ghinda
Stara Zagora Z 1990

1	e4	e6
2	d4	d5
3	e5	c5
4	c3	♘c6
5	♘f3	♗d7
6	♗e2	♘ge7
7	0-0	cxd4
8	cxd4	♘f5
9	♘c3	♖c8

This move represents the major diversion in the line. The rook is brought into play as a waiting tactic to deter b3 before deciding where to develop the rest of the pieces.

10	♗e3 *(75)*	

White continues in traditional fashion by supporting d4.

In Petkovski-Efimov, Corfu 1991, White tried to make progress on the queenside: 10 a3 ♗e7 11 g4 (11 ♗d3 g6 12 ♘e2 ♕b6 13 ♔h1 ♘a5 14 b4 ♘c4 15 g4 ♘g7 16 ♘f4 a5 17 bxa5 ♕xa5 18 ♕e2 ± Antonio-Nolte, Manila 1991) 11...♘h4 12 ♘xh4 ♗xh4 13 ♗e3 ♗e7 14 ♖c1 ♘a5 15 ♘a4 ♘c4 16 ♗xc4 dxc4 17 ♘c5 ♗c6 18 f3 h5 19 gxh5 b5 20 ♘e4 ♖xh5 21 ♕d2 f5 22 ♕g2 ♔f7 23 ♘g3 ♖h4 24 ♘e2 g5 25 ♗f2 ♖h7 26 ♗e3 g4 27 ♘f4 ♗g5 28 d5 ♗xf4 29 dxe6+ ♔xe6 0-1.

10 ♔h1!? a6 11 g4 ♘fe7 12 ♗d3! ♘a5?! (Vatter-Kindermann, Baden-Baden 1993: 12...h5 13 gxh5 ♖xh5 14 ♘g5 g6 15 ♕f3 ♘f5 16 ♗xf5 ♘d4 17 ♗xe6 ♗xe6!; 15 ♗e3 ±) and now 13 ♘g5! h6 14 ♘h7 gives White the better chances.

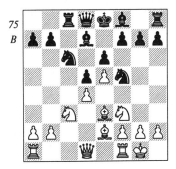

75
B

10	...	♗e7
11	♗d3	g6

If 11...♘xe3 12 fxe3 0-0 13 ♕e2 White has a good plan in doubling rooks by ♖f2 and ♖af1, with a small advantage.

12   ♖c1   0-0?!

Black hopes that in return for allowing the king to be exposed, he can take possession of the g-file with his rook.

Blatny suggests 12...♘xe3 is a superior alternative but after 13 fxe3 0-0 14 ♗b1 intending ♖c2-f2 White has good prospects.

13   ♗xf5   gxf5
14   ♗h6   ♖e8
15   h4!

A clever attacking device that prepares the deadly ♘g5 and ♕h5.

15   ...   ♗xh4 *(76)*

In his analysis of the game, Blatny reveals the depth of the offensive: 15...f6 16 ♕d2 (16 ♘b5? fxe5 17 dxe5 a6! 18 ♘d6 ♗xd6 19 exd6 ♕f6 20 ♕d2 d4! followed by 21...e5 ∓) 16...♔f7 (16...fxe5 17 dxe5 ♔f7 18 ♘g5+ ♔g6 19 h5+ ♔xh5 20 ♘f7 ♕c7 21 ♗f8!! +−; 16...♗f8 17 exf6 ♕xf6 18 ♗xf8 ♖xf8 19 ♖fe1 ±) 17 exf6 ♗xf6 18 ♘b5 ♕e7 19 ♗f4! e5 20 dxe5 ♘xe5 21 ♕d5+ +−.

16   ♕d2!   ♗e7
17   ♕f4

Black is unable to deal with the mounting pressure adequately. Now the immediate ♕g3+ is threatened, while ♘g5 and ♕h4 is dangerous.

17   ...   ♔h8
18   ♘g5   ♖f8

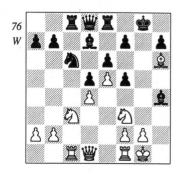

On 17...♔g8 18 ♘xe6! allows ♕g3+ +−.

19   ♕h4   ♗xg5

There is no way out of the calamity: 19...♔g8 20 ♕g3 f4 21 ♕g4 ♔h8 22 ♘xe6 +−.

20   ♗xg5   f6
21   ♗xf6+   ♖xf6
22   exf6   ♕g8
23   ♘b5   ♕g4 *(77)*

The f-pawn proves its worth on 23...♕g6 24 f7 ♖f8 25 ♘d6 e5 26 ♖xc6 ♗xc6 27 ♕e7 +−.

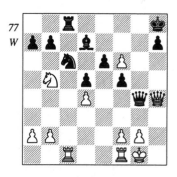

24   ♕h2!   f4
25   ♘d6   ♖f8

26	♕h6	♔g8
27	f7+	♖xf7
28	♘xf7	♔xf7
29	♕xh7+	♔e8
30	♖c3	♔d8
31	♖e1	a5
32	♖f3	♔c7
33	♕h2	e5
34	dxe5	♘d4
35	♖xf4	♘e2+
36	♖xe2	♕xe2
37	♕g3	♕xb2
38	e6	♗xe6
39	♖b4+	1-0

Game 26
Kupreichik-Levitt
Badenweiler 1990

1	e4	e6
2	d4	d5
3	e5	c5
4	c3	♘c6
5	♘f3	♗d7
6	♗e2	♘ge7
7	0-0	♘f5

This waiting move allows White to cast aside traditional methods and reposition his bishop to adapt to the changing situation.

8 ♗d3 *(78)*

The regular move, although Rozentalis-Züger, Chiasso 1991, saw White try to transpose to a previous main line in this chapter, but Black replied with an independent continuation: 8 ♘a3 cxd4 9 cxd4 ♗xa3 10 bxa3 ♕b6 11 ♗e3 0-0 12 ♗d3 ♖ac8

13 g4 ♘xe3 14 fxe3 ♕d8 15 ♕e1 f5 16 gxf5 exf5 17 ♖b1 b6 18 ♕g3 ♘e7 19 ♘g5 ♖c3 20 ♖b3 ♖c6 21 ♔h1 ♖g6 22 ♕h4 ♖h6 23 ♕f2 ♕c7 24 ♖g1 ♖g6 25 ♖bb1 h6 26 ♘h3 ♖xg1+ 27 ♖xg1 ♕c6 28 ♕h4 ♖f7 29 ♘f4 ♔f8 30 ♕h5 ♗e8 31 ♕h3 ♗d7 32 ♕g3 ♗e6 33 ♗b5 ♕c8 34 ♕h4 1-0.

8 dxc5 is an unusual line with similarities to Game 29, Sveshnikov-Popović, discussed later in this chapter. After 8...♗xc5 9 b4 play might continue:

a) 9...♗e7 10 ♗d3 g6 11 ♖e1 ♕c7 12 ♗f4 a6 13 ♘bd2 ♘a7 14 ♖c1 ♗c6 15 ♘b3 with an unclear position; Braga-Micalizzi, Rome 1990.

b) 9...♗b6 10 b5 ♘a5 11 ♗d3 a6 12 a4 ♕c7 13 ♗f4 0-0 14 ♕c2 h6 15 ♘bd2 with equality; Carlier-Barsov, Holland 1993.

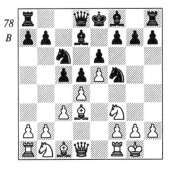

8 ... **♘h4**

The decision to exchange the kingside knights can be linked to continued pressure on d4.

The alternative 8...cxd4 has been explored. For example, after 9 ♗xf5 exf5 10 ♘xd4 ♗e7 play might continue:

a) 11 ♕b3 and now:

a1) 11...♘xd4 12 cxd4 ♕b6 13 ♕xb6 (13 ♕xd5? ♗c6 14 ♕b3 ♕xd4 15 e6 fxe6 16 ♕xe6 ♕d5 ∓; 13 ♘c3 ♗e6 14 ♕a4+ ♗d7 =) 13...axb6 14 ♘c3 ♗e6 15 ♗d2 ♔d7 16 a3 (16 ♘b5 ♖hc8 17 a4 ♖c4 {17...♖c2 18 ♗c3 f4 19 ♖fe1 and ♘a3 =} 18 b3 ♖c2 ∓) 16...♖hc8 17 ♘a2 ♖c4 (17...♖c2 18 ♗c3 f4 19 ♖fe1 intending ♘b4 =) 18 ♗c3 f4 19 ♖fd1 ♗f5 (Romero Holmes-Ulybin, Las Palmas 1992) 20 ♗b4! ♗c2 21 ♖dc1 (not 21 ♖d2? ♗xb4 −+) 21...♗b3 (21...♗g5?! 22 ♘c3 ♗b3 23 ♘b5! ♖ac8 24 ♖e1! with the idea ♘d6 ±) 22 ♖xc4 ♗xc4 23 ♗xe7 ♗xa2 = (Ulybin and Lysenko).

a2) 11...♗c8 12 f4 0-0 13 ♗e3 f6 14 exf6 (14 ♘d2 fxe5 15 ♘xc6 bxc6 16 fxe5 is unclear) 14...♗xf6 15 ♘d2 ♖e8 16 ♖ae1 ♖xe3?! (16...♔h8 ±) 17 ♘xc6 ♕e8 18 ♘e5 ♖xe1 (18...♗xe5 19 ♖xe3 ♗d4 20 cxd4 +−) 19 ♖xe1 ♗e6 20 ♕xb7 ♖b8 21 ♕xa7 ♖xb2 22 ♘df3 ♕c8! 23 ♕a3 ♖c2 24 ♖e3 d4 25 ♘xd4 ♖xa2 26 ♕d6 ♖a6 27 ♕b4 ♗d5 28 ♘xf5 h6 29 ♕b5 ♕a8? 30 ♘g4! ♖a1+ 31 ♔f2 ♖a2+ 32 ♔g3 ♖xg2+ 33 ♔h3 1-0 Kupreichik-Kosten, Torcy 1989.

b) 11 ♘f3 ♗e6 12 ♗e3 g5!? 13 ♘a3! f4 14 ♗d4 ♖g8 15 ♘e1 ♘xd4?! (15...♕a5 16 ♘ac2 ♗f5 with unclear

play) 16 ♕xd4 ♕a5 17 ♘ec2! h5 18 ♕d3 0-0-0 19 ♘d4 g4 20 ♘ab5 a6 21 ♘xe6 fxe6 22 ♘d4 ♕b6 23 b4 ♖g5 24 ♖ae1 ♔d7 (Romanishin-Hort, Biel 1987) 25 c4! dxc4 26 ♕xc4 ♖c8 27 ♕b3 and ♖d1 +−.

c) 11 ♖e1 ♘xd4 12 ♕xd4 ♗e6 13 ♕a4+ ♕d7 14 ♕xd7+ ♔xd7 15 ♗e3 g5 16 ♘d2 f4 17 ♗d4 b5 18 a4 ½-½ Gallagher-Züger, Switzerland 1992.

9 ♘g5

White is prepared to take risks by offering the d-pawn and thereby inviting complications.

A steadier response, 9 ♘xh4, is the standard continuation. Upon 9...♕xh4 play might proceed:

a) 10 ♘d2 cxd4 11 ♘f3 ♕d8 12 cxd4 ♕b6 13 ♗e3 ♘b4 14 ♗b1 ♗e7 15 a3 ♘c6 16 b3 a5 17 h4 h6 18 h5 0-0-0 19 b4 axb4 20 axb4 ♗xb4 21 ♗d3 ♔c7 22 ♖c1 ♕a5 23 ♖a1 ♕b6 24 ♖b1 ♕a5 25 ♖a1 ½-½ Prié-Murey, France 1991.

b) 10 ♗e3 and now:

b1) 10...♕d8 11 ♘d2 ♕b6! 12 ♘f3 c4 13 ♗c2 ♕xb2 14 ♕d2 ♕b6 15 ♘g5 h6 16 ♘h3 0-0-0 17 ♘f4 ♗e7 18 ♘h5 ♖dg8 19 ♖fb1 ♕d8 20 a4 ♘a5 21 ♕d1 g6 22 ♘f4 h5 23 ♗c1 ♔b8 24 ♗a3 and White has some compensation for the pawn; Vasiukov-Levitt, Græsted 1990.

b2) 10...cxd4 11 cxd4 ♕d8 (or 11...♗b4 12 a3 ♗a5 13 g3 ♕e7 14 ♘c3 f5 15 b4 ♗b6 16 ♗c2 0-0 17 ♕d2 with an edge for White, as in the game Kupreichik-Levitt, Copenhagen 1988, but not 11...♘xd4? 12 g3 +−) 12 ♘c3 ♗e7 13 f4 g6 14 g4 ♕b6 15 a3 0-0-0 (15...♘xd4? 16 ♔h1! a5 17 ♘e2 ♗c5 18 b4! axb4 19 axb4 ♖xa1 20 ♕xa1 +−) 16 b4 ♖df8 17 ♕d2 ♔b8 18 ♖ab1 ♕d8 19 b5 ♘a5 20 ♘a4 b6 21 ♖fc1 ♗c8 22 ♕c3 ♗b7 23 ♘c5! ± Blatny-Ruxton, Oakham 1990.

9	...	cxd4
10	cxd4	♘xd4
11	♕h5	♘g6
12	♘c3 (79)	

White needs to exercise caution, for example 12 ♘xf7? (12 ♘xh7? ♘f5 −+) 12...♔xf7 13 ♗xg6+ hxg6 14 ♕xh8 ♘c2 −+.

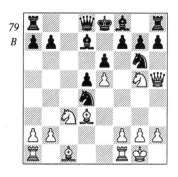

12	...	♘xe5
13	♘xe6	

The only way forward, as 13 ♖e1 g6 14 ♕h4 ♘ec6 is good for Black.

13	...	♘ef3+!
14	gxf3	♗xe6
15	♔g2	♗e7
16	♖e1	♕d7

Any attempt to castle must first deal with the threat to h7: 16...g6 17 ♕h6 (17 ♕e5 ♗f6 18 ♕xd5 0-0 with unclear play) 17...♗f8 (17...a6!?) 18 ♕f4 ♗g7 19 ♘b5! ♘xb5 20 ♗xb5+ ♔e7 21 ♕b4+ ♕d6 22 ♗g5+ f6 23 ♖xe6+ +−.

17 ♗f4

Now the rooks are connected. The immediate 17 ♘b5 fails to make an impression on the position: after 17...♘xb5 18 ♗xb5 ♕xb5 19 ♖xe6 ♕d7 Black has a material advantage.

17 ... h6

Kupreichik suggests Black should bring the knight back as a defensive measure: 17...♘c6!? 18 ♘b5 (18 ♖xe6 ♕xe6 19 ♘xd5 ♗d8 is unclear) 18...♖c8 19 ♖xe6 ♕xe6 20 ♗f5 ♕e2! 21 ♘c3 ♕xb2 also with unclear play after either 22 ♗xc8!? ♕xa1 23 ♘xd5 or 22 ♖b1 ♕xc3 23 ♗xc8 0-0 24 ♗xb7.

18	♘b5!	♘xb5
19	♗xb5	♕xb5
20	♖xe6	♔f8

If 20...♕d7 21 ♖ae1 wins.

21 ♕f5

White also has fine prospects after 21 ♖xe7 ♔xe7 22 ♖e1+ ♔f8 23 ♗d6+ ♔g8 24 ♖e7 ♖f8 25 ♖c7.

21 ... ♕d7? (80)

Black is under the misapprehension that White must head for the ending with 22 ♖e5; instead there was an amusing (for White) finish.

The game could have continued 21...♗g5! 22 ♖ae1 ♔g8 23 ♖d6!?

(23 ♗xg5 hxg5 24 ♖e7 ♖f8 25 ♖1e5
♕xb2 26 ♖xf7 ♖xh2+! =) 23...♕b2
(23...♗xf4? 24 ♖e7 ♖f8 25 ♖d8 +−)
24 ♖d7 ♖f8 25 ♖e8! (25 ♗e5 ♕d2
26 ♗d6 g6 27 ♕e5 is unclear)
25...♕f6 26 ♖xf8+ ♔xf8 27 ♕xd5!
± (Kupreichik).

22   ♖xh6!   ♕xf5
23   ♖xh8# (1-0)

Game 27
Hjartarson-Korchnoi
Amsterdam 1991

1	e4	e6
2	d4	d5
3	e5	c5
4	c3	♘c6
5	♘f3	♗d7
6	♗e2	♘ge7
7	0-0	

Black faced the unusual 7 dxc5 in
the game Velimirović-Züger, Lucerne 1989: 7...♘g6 8 ♗e3 ♘gxe5 9
♘xe5 ♘xe5 10 f4 ♘c6 11 ♘d2 b6
12 ♘b3 bxc5 13 ♘xc5 ♕b6 14
♘xd7 ♕xe3 15 ♘xf8 ♔xf8 16 ♕d2

♕xd2 17 ♔xd2 ♔e7 18 b4 ♖ac8 19
♖hc1 ♖hd8 20 ♖ab1 f6 21 ♗d3 g6
22 ♖e1 ♔d6 23 ♖f1 ♗e7 24 ♖f3 e5
25 ♖h3 ♖h8 26 b5 ♘a5 27 fxe5 fxe5
28 ♖b4 e4 20 ♖a4 1-0.

7 ...   ♘g6 (81)

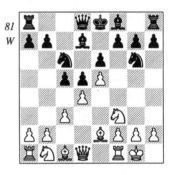

Korchnoi acknowledges that
Werner Hug first suggested this set-
up. On g6 the knight is less active
than on f5, but at least it avoids the
threat of ♗e2-d3xf5.

8 g3
In the game Mephisto Lyon-Psak-
his, Berlin 1991, the computer used a
new approach: 8 ♗g5 f6!? (8...♕b6
9 ♕d2 h6 10 ♗e3 ±) 9 exf6 gxf6 10
♗e3 cxd4 11 cxd4 ♗d6 12 ♘c3 ♘f4
13 ♘b5 ♗b8 14 ♕d2 (14 ♖e1!?)
14...♘xe2+ 15 ♕xe2 ♕e7 16 ♗h6
♕f7 and now White can improve
with 17 ♕d2! ♕h5 18 ♗f4 ±.

The major alternative is 8 ♗e3:
a) 8...cxd4?! 9 cxd4 ♗e7 (9...f6!?
10 ♘c3 ♗e7 11 ♗d3 0-0 12 exf6
♖xf6 13 ♖e1 ♕c7 14 g3 ♗e8 =
Thipsay-Gulko, Manila IZ 1990) 10

♘c3 0-0 11 ♗d3 ♗e8 12 ♖c1 f6 13 exf6 ♗xf6 14 ♕d2 ♔h8 15 ♗b1 ♖c8 16 ♖fe1 ♖c7 17 ♖cd1 ♖d7 18 ♔h1 ♗e7 19 ♘g5 ♖f6 20 f4 ± Sax-Korchnoi, Wijk aan Zee C (2) 1991.

b) 8...♗e7 and now:

b1) 9 dxc5 ♘gxe5 (or 9...♕c7!? 10 ♘a3 ♘cxe5 11 ♘xe5 ♘xe5 {11...♕xe5?! 12 ♗d4 ♕g5 13 g3! ±} 12 ♘b5 ♗xb5 13 ♗xb5+ ♘c6 14 c4 ♖d8 {14...a6 15 ♗xc6+! bxc6 16 cxd5 exd5 17 ♗d4 ±} 15 cxd5 exd5?! {15...♖xd5!?} 16 ♗xc6+ ♕xc6 17 ♗d4 0-0 18 b4 ♗f6 19 a4 ± Kharlov-Sakaev, Podolsk 1992) 10 ♘xe5 ♘xe5 11 f4 ♘c6 12 ♘d2 0-0 13 ♗d3 g6 14 ♕f3! ♗f6 (14...b6 15 cxb6 axb6 16 ♕f2 ±) 15 ♕f2 ♗g7 16 ♘f3 ♘e7 17 h4! f6 (17...♘f5 18 ♗d4! ±) 18 h5 e5 19 h6 ♗h8 20 fxe5 fxe5 21 ♗g5 ♕e8 (21...e4 22 ♕h4 ♖f7 23 ♖ae1 ♕f8 24 ♗xe7 ♕xe7 25 ♕xe7 ♖xe7 26 ♘g5 is slightly better for White) 22 ♖ae1 ♘c6 (22...e4? 23 ♖xe4! dxe4 24 ♗c4+ and Whie wins) 23 c4 ± Kharlov-Sakaev, São Paulo 1991.

b2) 9 ♗d3 ♕b6 10 ♕d2 cxd4 11 cxd4 ♘b4 12 ♗e2 ♗b5 13 ♘c3 ♗xe2 14 ♕xe2 ♘c6 15 g3 0-0 16 h4 ♖fc8 17 ♖ad1 ♘a5 18 ♘e1 ♘c4 19 ♘d3 ♘f8 20 ♘a4 ♕d8 21 b3 ♘a3 22 h5 ♘c2 23 ♘dc5 b6 24 ♘b7 ♕d7 25 ♘d6 ½-½ Sax-Nikolić, Manila OL 1992.

b3) 9 g3 cxd4 10 cxd4 f6 11 exf6 ♗xf6 12 ♘c3 0-0 13 ♕d2 (13 ♗d3!? ♗e8 14 ♕d2 e5 =) 13...♘ge7 14

♗d3 h6 (Romanishin-Nikolić, Leningrad 1987) 15 ♖fe1 =.

b4) 9 ♘e1 0-0 10 f4 ♕b6 11 ♕d2 cxd4 12 cxd4 f6 13 ♘f3 fxe5 14 fxe5 ♖ac8 15 ♘c3 ♘a5 16 ♖f2 ♘c4 17 ♗xc4 ♖xc4 18 ♖af1 ♖cc8 19 g3 ♖f5 20 h4 = Kupreichik-Nikolić, Ljubljana 1989.

| 8 | ... | ♗e7 |
| 9 | h4 | |

This advance forces the knight to retreat. Black relies on eventually breaking out of the cramped conditions whereupon White's kingside pawns might become a liability.

9	...	cxd4
10	cxd4	0-0
11	h5	

On 11 ♘a3 comes 11...f6 12 exf6 ♗xf6 13 ♘c2 ♘ge7 with equal chances.

| 11 | ... | ♘h8 |
| 12 | h6 | |

To combat Black's plan of breaking out with ...f6 it might be advisable to consider 12 ♗d3!?, e.g. 12...f6?! 13 ♕c2 with excellent prospects. Thus, 12...♘b4 13 h6 g6 14 ♘c3 ♘xd3 15 ♕xd3 is likely, when White has relinquished the useful light-squared bishop in return for greater control of e5.

| 12 | ... | g6 |
| 13 | ♘bd2 | |

The queen's knight will support d4 although Korchnoi suggests that 13 ♘c3 should be considered, to contest the central light squares. The reason for the exchange 9...cxd4 becomes apparent because otherwise White could now play 12 dxc5 (12 c4!?) 12...♗xc5 13 c4 with advantage.

13	...	f6
14	exf6	♗xf6
15	♘b3	♘f7
16	♘h2!	*(82)*

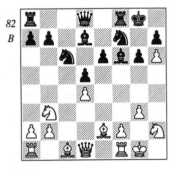

82
B

White intends either ♘g4 to restrain ...e5, or ♗g4 to target e6.

Not 16 ♗f4? g5 and ...♘xh6, nor 16 ♗e3 ♘d6 ∓.

16	...	♘d6

Now 17 ♘g4 ♘f5 is satisfactory.

After 16...e5 17 dxe5 ♘cxe5 18 ♕xd5 ♗c6! 19 ♕xd8 ♖fxd8 Black has insufficient compensation for the pawn.

17	♗g4!	♖c8
18	♘f3	♘e4

18...b6 19 ♖e1 ♘f5 20 ♗xf5 exf5 21 ♗f4 is better for White.

19	♗e3	♖f7?!

Black is slow to sense that the queen's knight should immediately

aim for f5 to hinder White's progress. On 19...e5? 20 ♘xe5! ♗xe5 21 dxe5 ♗xg4 22 ♕xg4 ♘xe5 23 ♕e6+ White has a big plus.

20	♖c1	b6
21	a3	♘e7
22	♖xc8	♕xc8
23	♘bd2	♘f5
24	♗f4?!	

Korchnoi prefers 24 ♘xe4 dxe4 25 ♘e5 ♗xe5 26 dxe5 ♘xe3 27 fxe3 ♖xf1+ 28 ♔xf1 ♗b5+ 29 ♔g2 ♗d3 30 ♕d2 intending 30 ♕f2 with a clear advantage.

24	...	♕f8?!

Black would have equal chances after the superior 24...♘xd4! 25 ♘xd4 e5.

25	♖e1	♘xh6
26	♗xh6	♕xh6
27	♘xe4	dxe4
28	♖xe4	♔g7 *(83)*

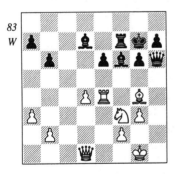

83
W

29   ♗xe6?

Just one more preliminary move would have ensured White a decisive advantage: 29 ♕c2! ♖f8 (29...♖e7

30 d5! e5 31 ♗xd7 ♖xd7 32 ♘xe5)
30 ♕c7 ♖f7 31 ♕c4.

Now Black can activate his queen
to cause a few problems.

29	...	♗xe6
30	♖xe6	♕h5
31	♕b3	♖d7

A sterner test is 31...♕f5 (intending 32...♗xd4) when Black has
counterplay after either 32 d5 g5 or
32 ♖e2 h5.

32	♖e8	♕d5
33	♕b4	♕d6
34	♕c4	♕d5
35	♕b4	♕d6
36	♕xd6	♖xd6
37	♖e4	h5
38	♔f1?!	

The best practical try is 38 ♘e5
followed by f4.

38	...	♖d5
39	♖e3	g5
40	♖c3	g4
41	♖c7+	♔h6
42	♖c6	♔g7
43	♖c7+	♔h6
44	♖c6	½-½

Game 28
Illescas-Speelman
Linares 1992

1	e4	e6
2	d4	d5
3	e5	c5
4	c3	♘c6
5	♘f3	♗d7
6	a3	

This continuation is a popular
idea, which often results in play very
similar to lines arising from 5...♕b6
6 a3. The difference is that Black is
not obliged to transpose into such
lines, but can delay moving the
queen; this offers increased flexibility.

6 ... ♘ge7 (84)

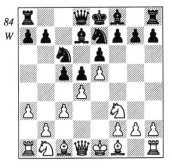

There are valid alternative treatments:

a) 6...f6 7 ♗d3 (7 b4?! fxe5 8
dxc5 e4 9 ♘d4 ♘f6 10 ♗f4 ♗e7 11
♗b5 0-0 ∓ Popchev-Dolmatov, Po-
lanica Zdroj 1987) 7...♕c7 8 0-0 c4
9 ♗c2 ♘ge7 10 ♖e1 ♘g6 11 ♘h4!
♘xh4 12 ♕h5+ g6 13 ♕xh4 f5 14
♗g5 ♕b6 15 ♖a2 h6 16 ♗f6 ♖g8
17 ♘d2 ♘d8 18 a4 a5 19 ♔h1 ♘f7
20 ♖b1 ♕c7 21 g4 ♘g5 22 gxf5
exf5 23 ♕g3 ♗e6 24 b3 ♘e4 25
♘xe4 dxe4 26 bxc4 ♗xc4 27 ♖ab2
b5 28 ♖xb5 ♗xb5 29 ♖xb5 g5 30
♗b3 ♖g6 31 ♕h3 ♕d7 32 ♕h5 ♕h7
33 ♖b7 1-0 Donguines-R.Rodriguez,
Cebu 1992.

b) 6...♖c8 7 ♗d3 (7 b4 cxd4 8 cxd4 ♕b6 9 ♗b2 transposes to Game 12, Galdunts-Ambartsumian) 7...cxd4 8 cxd4 ♕b6 9 ♗c2 g5 10 h3 ♘xd4 11 ♘xd4 ♗c5 12 ♘e2 ♗xf2+ 13 ♔f1 f6 14 ♘bc3 a5 15 ♗a4 ♘e7 16 ♗xd7+ ♔xd7 17 exf6 with an unclear position; Afek-Welin, Biel 1989.

c) 6...c4 and now:

c1) 7 g3 and now:

c11) 7...♕c7 8 h4 f5 9 ♗g2 ♘ge7 10 0-0 h6 11 ♘bd2 ♘a5 12 a4 0-0-0 13 b3 cxb3 14 ♘xb3 ♘xb3 15 ♕xb3 ♘c6 16 ♕a2 ♘a5 17 ♗e3 ♔b8 18 ♘d2 ♖c8 19 ♖fc1 ♗e7 20 h5 ♘c4 21 ♘xc4 ♕xc4 22 ♕b2 ♖hd8 23 ♗f1 ♕c7 24 c4 ♗c6 25 ♖ab1 dxc4 26 ♗xc4 ♕d7 27 ♕a2 ♗d5 ½-½ Adams-Levitt, British Ch 1989.

c12) 7...♘a5 8 ♘bd2 ♘e7 9 ♗g2 ♘c8 10 0-0 ♘b6 11 ♘e1 ♕c7 12 ♖b1 0-0-0 13 ♘df3 h6 14 h4 ♗e7 15 ♕e2 ♕c6 16 ♗h3 ♕a4 17 ♘g2 ♕b3 18 ♗e3 ♗a4 19 ♘d2 ♕c2 20 f4 ♗d7 21 ♗f2 ♘b3 22 ♗e1 ♘xd2 23 ♗xd2 g6 24 ♘e3 ♕b3 25 h5 ♖dg8 26 ♔h2 ♔b8 27 ♖fc1 ♗c8 28 ♗e1 a5 29 ♗f2 ♘a8 30 ♖g1 ♘c7 31 g4 a4 32 ♗g3 ♕b5 33 ♖bf1 ♕e8 34 ♕f3 with a slight plus for White; Anand-Garma, Calcutta 1992.

c2) 7 ♘e2 ♘a5 8 ♘bd2 f5!? 9 0-0 ♘e7 10 a4!? ♕b6 11 b4 cxb3 12 ♗a3 ♘g6 (12...♗xa4? 13 ♗b4 +−) 13 ♗xf8 ♖xf8 14 c4 dxc4 15 ♘xc4 ♘xc4 16 ♗xc4 b2 17 ♖b1 ♖c8 18

♗a2 ♖c3 19 d5 ♖a3 20 ♗c4 ♗xa4 21 ♕d2 ♕c5 22 ♕xb2 ♖xf3 23 ♕c1! ♗d7? (23...b6! 24 gxf3 ♘xe5 25 ♗b5+ ♗xb5 26 ♕xc5 ♘xf3+ 27 ♔h1 bxc5 28 ♖xb5 exd5 29 ♖xc5 ♖f7 ±) 24 ♖xb7 ♕c8 25 ♖xa7 ♘xe5 26 dxe6 ♗xe6 27 ♗b5+ ♔d8 28 ♕g5+ ♖f6 29 ♕xg7 1-0 Nikolić-Schulz, Lugano 1986.

c3) 7 ♗f4!? ♕b6 (7...♘ge7 8 h4 ♘c8 9 ♘bd2 h6 10 g3 ♘b6 11 ♗h3 ♗e7 12 h5 ♘a5 13 ♗e3 ♗a4 = Khalifman-Yusupov, Minsk 1987) 8 ♕c1 ♘ge7 9 ♘bd2 f6 10 exf6 gxf6 11 ♖b1 ♘g6 12 ♗e3 ♘a5 13 h4?! ♗d6 14 h5 ♘e7 15 ♘h4 0-0-0 16 g3 ♘f5! 17 ♘xf5 exf5 18 ♗g2 ♖he8 19 0-0 ♗xg3! 20 b4 cxb3 21 fxg3 ♖xe3 22 ♘xb3 ♖xg3 23 ♘xa5 ♕xa5 24 ♕f4 ♖dg8 25 ♖f2 ♕xa3! 26 ♖e1 ♖3g4 27 ♕d2 f4 28 ♕d3 ♖g3 29 ♕f1 ♗h3 0-1 J.Littlewood-Adams, Sheffield 1991.

c4) 7 h4 ♘ge7 8 h5 h6 9 g3 ♘a5 10 ♘bd2 ♘c8 11 ♘h4! ♘b6 12 ♘g2 ♕c7 (12...♗a4 13 ♕e2 ♗c2? 14 ♘xc4! ♘b3 15 ♘xb6 axb6 16 ♕xc2 ♘xa1 17 ♗b5+ ♔e7 18 ♕d1 ♖a5 19 b4 ♖xb5 20 ♗b2 +−) 13 ♘e3 0-0-0 (13...f6!? 14 f4 fxe5 15 fxe5 ♗e7 16 ♕g4 0-0 with an unclear position) 14 f4 ♗e7 15 ♗h3 ♔b8 16 ♕e2 ♖df8 17 0-0 a6 18 ♔h2 ♔a7 19 ♖b1 ♖hg8 20 ♘g2! ♘a4 21 ♘f3 ♗xa3 22 f5! exf5 23 ♗f4 ♕b6 24 bxa3 ♘xc3 25 ♖xb6 ♘xe2 26 ♖b2 ♘xf4 27 ♘xf4 ♗e6 28 ♘h4 ♘c6 29 ♘xf5 ♗xf5 30 ♗xf5 ♘xd4 31 ♘xd5 and White wins; Malaniuk-Bareev, USSR 1987.

d) 6...cxd4 7 cxd4 ♘ge7 8 ♗d3 ♘f5 9 ♗e3 ♕b6 10 ♘c3 ♘xe3 11 fxe3 ♗e7 12 b4 ♖c8 13 ♖c1 ♘d8 14 0-0 0-0 15 ♕b3 f5 16 exf6 ♗xf6 17 ♕c2 ♔h8 18 ♘e5 ♗e8 19 ♕f2 ♘f7 20 ♘xd5! +− Masserey-Summermatter, Silvaplana 1993.

e) 6...♘h6 7 b4 cxd4 8 cxd4 ♘f5 transposes to the text.

**7 b4   cxd4
8 cxd4   ♘f5
9 ♘c3?!** *(85)*

Illescas and Zlotnik prepared this idea based on the premise that 9...♕b6 is ineffective after 10 ♘a4.

The usual move is 9 ♗b2:

a) 9...♗e7 and now:

a1) 10 ♗d3 0-0 11 0-0 f6 12 ♗xf5! exf5 13 ♘c3 ♗e8 14 ♕d3 f4 15 e6! ♗h5 16 ♖fe1 a6 17 ♕f5! ♗xf3 18 gxf3 ♘xd4 19 ♕d3 ♘c6 20 ♘xd5 ♕e8 21 ♖ad1 ♖d8 22 ♕e4 ♕h5 23 ♘xf4 ♕g5+ 24 ♔h1 ♖xd1 25 ♖xd1 ♖d8 26 ♖g1 ♕b5 27 ♘g6! ♖e8 (27...hxg6 28 ♕xg6 ♗f8 29 ♕f7+ ♔h8 30 ♗xf6 +−) 28 ♘xe7+ ♘xe7 29 ♗xf6 +− Nikolić-Christiansen, Ljubljana/Portorož 1985.

b) 9...♕b6 10 ♗e2 and now:

b1) 10...♖c8 11 0-0 h5 (11...a6 12 ♔h1 ♗e7 13 g4 ♘h4 14 ♘c3 ♘xf3 15 ♘a4 ♕a7 16 ♗xf3 0-0 17 ♘c5 b6 18 ♘xd7 ♕xd7 19 ♗e2 b5 20 f4 f6 21 ♕d2 = Kontić-Miljanić, Nikšić 1991) 12 ♔h1 ♗e7 13 ♘c3 ♕d8 14 ♗d3 g6 15 ♖c1 a5 16 b5

♘a7 17 a4 ♖a8 18 ♘d2 ♘c8 19 ♘b3 ♘b6 20 ♘c5 ♗c8 21 ♘e2 h4 22 ♘f4 ♘c4 23 ♖xc4! dxc4 24 ♗xc4 b6 25 ♘e4 ♗b7 26 d5 h3 27 g4 ♘h4 28 f3 ♘g2 29 ♘d6+ ♗xd6 30 exd6 ♘xf4 31 dxe6 fxe6 32 ♗xh8 ± Galdunts-Orlov, Belgrade 1989.

b2) 10...♗e7 11 0-0 transposes to the notes in Game 11, Prié-de la Villa Garcia.

c) 9...b5 10 ♘c3 a6 (10...a5!? 11 ♘xb5 axb4 12 a4 ♘a5 13 ♖c1 ♘c4 14 ♗xc4 dxc4 15 ♖xc4 ♗xb5 16 axb5 ♕d5 ±) 11 ♗d3 g6 12 0-0 h5 13 ♘e2 ♗e7 14 ♗c3 ♕b6 15 ♘f4 ♘g7 16 h4 a5 17 ♕e2! axb4 18 axb4 ♖b8 19 ♖fb1 0-0 20 ♗c2 ♕d8 21 g3 ♖c8 22 ♖a3 ♘a5! 23 ♘d3 ♘c4 24 ♖a7 ♖c7 25 ♖ba1 ♕b8 26 ♘c5 ♗c6 27 ♖xc7 ♕xc7 28 ♗d2 ♖a8 29 ♕d1 ♕b8 30 ♗c3 ♖xa1 31 ♕xa1 ♕a8 ½-½ Grosar-L.B.Hansen, Bled/Rogaška Slatina 1991.

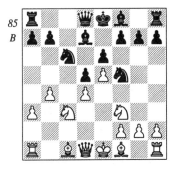

85
B

9 ...   ♖c8

9...♗e7 10 ♗d3! (10 ♗e2?! ♖c8 11 ♗b2 0-0 12 0-0 f6 13 ♖c1 ♕e8 14

♖e1 fxe5 15 dxe5 ♗d8! with an edge for Black; Miljanović-Draško, Belgrade 1987) 10...♘fxd4 11 ♘xd4 ♘xd4 12 ♕g4 gives White an advantage.

10 ♗b2　♘h4!

Black has implemented a novel procedure in order to make the defence of d4 difficult. The idea of exchanging the king's knight is not feared in the 9 ♗b2 lines because the knight can be supported by ♘1d2 or the bishop is on e7.

11 ♘xh4

In Kimpinsky-Zysk, Bundesliga 1992, White tried the surprising resource 11 ♘g1 which proved dependable: 11...♗e7 12 g3 ♘f5 13 ♘ge2 f6 14 ♗h3 fxe5 15 ♗xf5 exf5 16 ♘xd5 e4 17 ♕b3 ♗d6 18 0-0 ♘e7 19 ♘ec3 ♘xd5 20 ♕xd5 ♕e7 21 ♘b5 ♗xb5 22 ♕xb5+ ♕d7 23 ♕d5 ♗b8 24 ♕b3 ♕f7 25 ♕a4+ ♕d7 26 ♕b3 ♕f7 ½-½.

11 ...　♕xh4
12 ♘a2

The only move in view of 12 b5? (12 ♘e2? ♘xb4 —+) 12...♘xd4! 13 g3 ♖xc3! 14 gxh4 ♘f3+ 15 ♔e2 ♗xb5+ —+.

12 ...　♕e4+

12...♗e7 13 ♗d3 leaves the queen in a vulnerable state.

13 ♕e2　♕g6
14 ♖c1

It is necessary to thwart the possibility of 14...♘xb4 followed by ...♖c2. However, Illescas indicates

that the best chance is 14 ♕d3!? a6 15 ♕xg6 hxg6 intending ...♘a7, ...♗b5 and ...♖h4, which gives Black the better chances.

14 ...　♗e7
15 ♕f3　0-0
16 ♗d3　♕h6
17 0-0　f6

With White having to disrupt the harmony of his pieces to defend d4, Black is in the ascendancy. Now the plan is to introduce the light-squared bishop into the game via e8-h5.

18 ♕e2　fxe5
19 dxe5　♗g5
20 ♖ce1

Speelman suggests 20 ♖c2 as an improvement, based on the line 20...♗e8 21 b5 ♗h5 22 g4 with equal chances. Illescas points out a refinement to tip the scales in Black's favour after 21...♗f4! 22 g3 ♗h5 23 f3 ♗e3+.

20 ...　♗e8
21 g3　♗h5
22 f3　♗d2
23 ♖d1　♗e3+
24 ♔g2 (86)　♗xf3+?

This impetuous move appears to be lethal but the course of the game proves it to be faulty. Black can retain the advantage upon 24...d4.

25 ♖xf3　♖xf3
26 ♕xf3　♖f8
27 ♗xh7+!

The refutation of the sacrifice is revealed. Black is overloaded and is obliged to relinquish material.

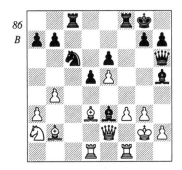

27	...	♕xh7
28	♕xe3	♕c2+
29	♕d2	♕e4+
30	♔g1	d4
31	♖e1	

Black is still posing a number of problems thanks to White's difficulty in activating his forces. A better try is 31 ♗xd4 ♖d8 32 ♘c3 ♕xd4 33 ♕xd4 ♖xd4 (33...♘xd4 34 ♔g2 ♖c8 35 ♖xd4 ♖xc3 36 a4 +−) 34 ♖xd4 ♘xd4 35 ♔f2 ♘c6 36 ♘b5 a6 37 ♘d6 b5 38 ♔e3! ♘xe5 39 ♔d4 which is a favourable ending for White.

31	...	♕d5
32	♘c1	♘xe5
33	♖xe5	♕xe5
34	♗xd4	♕e4
35	♗b2	♖f3!

On 35...♖c8, White could reply 36 ♘d3! ♖d8 37 ♕g5 ♖d7 38 ♘f2 when the knight acts as a shield to the king, ensuring an edge.

Now 36 ♘e2 is the winning try.

36 ♕d8+? ♖f8?

In time-trouble Speelman passes

up the chance of a probable draw with 36...♔h7 37 ♕h4+ ♕xh4 38 gxh4 ♖h3.

37	♕d2	♖f3
38	♘e2!	e5
39	♘c3	♕d4+
40	♕xd4	exd4
41	♘b5	d3

If 41...♖d3 42 ♔f1 ♖d2 43 ♗xd4 a6 44 ♔e1! ensures White's advantage.

| 42 | ♗c1 | a6 |
| 43 | ♘c3 | ♖f6 |

No better is 43...♔f7 44 ♗f4 intending 45 ♔g2.

44 h4

White's victory is sealed. The rook has no opportunity to enter White's camp due to the minor pieces blocking the files, while the d3 pawn will soon leave the board. White efficiently concludes the game: 44...♔f7 45 ♗f4 ♖c6 46 ♗d2 ♔e6 47 ♔f2 ♔e5 48 ♔e3 ♖g6 49 ♗e1 ♔f5 50 ♔xd3 ♖d6 51 ♔e3 ♔g4 52 ♘e2! ♖e6+ 53 ♔d3 ♖e8 54 ♗c3 ♔f3 55 ♘d4+ ♔xg3 56 ♘f5+ ♔g4 57 ♘xg7 ♖d8+ 58 ♔c2 ♖c8 59 h5 ♔g5 60 ♔d3 ♔h6 61 ♗e5 b5 62 ♗c3 ♖c6 63 ♗e5 ♖c4 64 ♘e6 a5 1-0.

Game 29
Sveshnikov-Popović
Palma de Mallorca 1989

| 1 | e4 | e6 |
| 2 | d4 | d5 |

3	**e5**	**c5**
4	**c3**	**♘c6**
5	**♘f3**	**♗d7**
6	**dxc5** *(87)*	

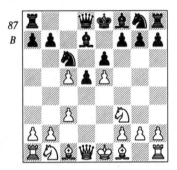

This move has its attractions as a way to avoid the heavily analysed lines. The decision to abandon the centre looks odd but it can be quite effective. Black is plunged into relatively unknown positions with White's advanced pawns staking out a spatial plus and providing attacking chances. The primary problem with the scheme is that the pawns can become a target and are particularly weak in endings. After 6 ♗d3 the game usually transposes into usual lines; in the game Kindermann-Bischoff, Munich 1989, Black continued 6...♘ge7 7 0-0 cxd4 8 cxd4 ♘c8 9 ♘c3 ♗e7 10 ♘a4 ♘b6 11 ♘c5 ♘xd4 12 ♘xb7 ♘xf3+ 13 ♕xf3 ♕b8 14 ♘d6+ ♗xd6 15 exd6 ♕xd6 16 ♗f4 ♕e7 17 ♕g3 with unclear play.

| **6** | **...** | **♗xc5** |

An almost automatic response, although Nikolenko-Shur, USSR 1991 continued 6...♕c7 7 ♘a3! (7 ♗f4 ♗xc5 8 ♗d3 h6 9 h4 ♘ge7 10 b4 ♗b6 11 a4 is unclear; Mamedov-Shur, USSR 1990) 7...♘xe5 8 ♘b5 ♘xf3+ 9 ♕xf3 ♕e5+ 10 ♔d1 ♖c8 11 ♗f4 ♕f6 12 ♕g3 ♕g6 13 ♘xa7 ♕xg3 14 hxg3 ♖xc5 15 ♗e3 ♖a5 16 ♗b6 ♖a4 17 f3 ♗d6 18 b3 ♖a3 19 ♘b5 ♗xb5 20 ♗xb5+ ♔e7 21 g4 ♖a8 22 ♗d4 e5 23 ♖e1 f6 24 f4 ♔e6 25 ♔c2 ♘e7 26 a4 ♘c6 27 ♗f2 ♖ac8 28 ♖ad1 ♘e7 29 f5+ ♔f7 30 ♗d7 ♖c7 31 ♗e6+ +−.

7   b4

This is the modern treatment of the position. The main alternative is 7 ♗d3, whereupon play might proceed:

a) 7...f5 8 ♘bd2 ♘ge7 9 ♘b3 ♗b6 10 0-0 ♘g6 11 ♖e1 0-0 12 ♘bd4 ♘xd4 13 cxd4 ♘h4 14 ♗e2 ♘xf3+ 15 ♗xf3 ½-½ Mascariñas-Meier, Switzerland 1991.

b) 7...f6 8 b4 (8 ♗f4 fxe5 9 ♘xe5 ♘xe5 10 ♗xe5 ♘f6 =; 8 exf6 ♘xf6 9 0-0 0-0 10 ♗g5 ♕e8 11 ♕e2 e5 ∓ Potick-Fiorito, Konex 1991) 8...♗e7 9 b5 ♘xe5 10 ♘xe5 fxe5 11 ♕h5+ ♔f8 12 ♕xe5 ♗f6 (Sveshnikov-Savon, Lvov 1978) 13 ♕g3! e5 14 0-0 ♘e7 15 ♗g5 ±.

c) 7...♘ge7 and now:

c1) 8 0-0 ♘g6 9 ♖e1 ♕c7 10 ♕e2 (10 ♗xg6 fxg6! 11 ♗f4 0-0 12 ♗g3 ♘e7 ∓ Sveshnikov-Balashov, USSR Ch 1976) 10...f6 11 exf6 gxf6

12 c4! d4 13 a3 0-0-0 14 b4 ♗d6 15
c5 ♗f4 16 g3 ♗xc1 17 ♖xc1 ± Pach-
man-Voiculescu, Bucharest 1954.

c2) 8 ♗f4 ♘g6 9 ♗g3 0-0 10
♘bd2 f5 11 exf6 gxf6 12 ♘b3 ♗b6
13 0-0 ♘ce5 14 ♘xe5 ♘xe5 15 ♗c2
♖f7 16 ♘d4 ♕f8 17 ♕h5 ♕g7 18
♖fe1 ♗xd4 19 cxd4 ♘c6 20 ♗f4 f5
21 ♖e3 ♕xd4 22 ♗h6 f4 23 ♗xf4
♖xf4 24 ♕xh7+ ♔f8 25 ♕xd7 ♖d8
26 ♕xe6 ♖f6 27 ♕h3 ♕xb2 28
♕h8+ ♔f7 29 ♕h7+ ♔f8 30 ♖f1 d4
31 ♖g3 ♖f7 32 ♕h6+ ♔e8 33 ♗b3
♖e7 34 ♕h3 1-0 Bastian-Geveke,
Bundesliga 1991/92.

c3) 8 b4 ♗b6 9 b5 ♘a5 10 0-0
♘g6 11 a4 ♖c8 12 ♖a2 ♘c4 13 ♖e2
a6 14 bxa6 bxa6 15 ♘a3 ♘xa3 16
♗xa3 ♗c5 17 ♗xc5 ♖xc5 18 ♗xa6
♕a5 19 ♗b5 ♗xb5 20 axb5 ♕xb5
21 ♘d4 ♕d7 22 f4 0-0 23 f5! exf5 24
e6 ♕a7 25 exf7+ ♖xf7 26 ♖e8+ ♖f8
27 ♖xf8+ ♘xf8 28 ♘xf5 ♘g6 29
♔h1 ♕d7 30 ♕g4 ♔h8 31 h4 ♖c4
32 ♕g5 ♖c8 33 h5 ♘f8 34 ♘e7
♖e8 35 ♖f7 ♘e6 36 h6 ♖g8 37
hxg7+ ♘xg7 38 ♕xg7+! 1-0 Bron-
stein-M.Gurevich, Brussels Rapid-
play 1993.

d) 7...♕c7 8 ♕e2 ♘ge7 9 ♗f4 (9
b4) 9...a6 10 0-0 f5 11 ♘bd2 0-0 12
♘b3 ♗a7 13 ♘bd4 ♘g6 14 ♗g3 f4
15 ♘g5 ♕xe5 16 ♕h5 h6 17 ♘df3
♕f6 18 ♘h7 ♔xh7 19 ♗h4 ♕f5 20
♗xf5 ♖xf5 21 ♘g5+ ♖xg5 22 ♗xg5
♖f8 with an unclear game; Fishbein-
Foisor, Saint John 1988.

e) 7...♕b6?! transposes to the line

5...♕b6 6 ♗d3 ♗d7 7 dxc5 which is
examined in the chapter on the Milner-Barry Gambit – see the note to
Black's sixth move in Game 14.

7	...	♗b6
8	b5	♘a5
9	♗d3	♕c7 (88)

In the game Kharlov-Dreev,
USSR 1991, Black chose to bring
the queen's knight back into play:
9...♘c4 10 a4 ♕c7 11 ♕e2 a6 12
bxa6 ♖xa6 13 0-0 ♘e7 (13...♖xa4
14 ♖xa4 ♗xa4 15 ♘a3 with unclear
play) 14 ♘a3 ♖xa4 15 ♘xc4 dxc4
(15...♖xa1? 16 ♘d6+ ♔f8 17 ♘g5
+−) ♖xa4 ♗xa4 17 ♗xc4 0-0 18
♗d3 ♘g6! ½-½ and now Dreev analysed 19 h4 ♗c6 20 h5 ♗xf3 21 gxf3
♕xe5! (21...♘e5? 22 ♗f4 f6 23 ♕e4
+−) 22 hxg6 ♕g3+ 23 ♔h1 ♕h3+
with a draw.

The immediate 9...♘ge7 is the
usual alternative. The game might
continue: 10 0-0 ♖c8 (10...♕c7 transposes to the text) 11 a4 ♘g6 and
now:

a) 12 ♗a3 ♗c5 13 ♗xc5 ♖xc5
14 g3 ♕c7 15 ♖e1 ♘c4 16 ♕e2 0-0
17 h4 f6 18 ♗xg6 hxg6 19 exf6
♖xf6 20 ♘d4 ♘d6 21 ♘b3 ♖c4 22
♘1d2 ♖xc3 23 ♖ac1 ♖f8 24 ♕e5
♖xc1 25 ♖xc1 ♕b6 26 ♘c5 ½-½
Sveshnikov-Balashov, Lvov 1978.

b) 12 ♖e1 f6 13 ♖a2 0-0 14
♗xg6 hxg6 15 ♕d3 ♔f7 16 ♗e3
♖h8 17 ♖ae2 ♘c4 18 ♗d4 ♖h6 19
h4 a6 20 bxa6 bxa6 21 ♘bd2 ♗xd4
22 cxd4 ♖h8 23 ♘b3 fxe5 24 dxe5

♗xa4 25 ♘bd4 ♗d7 26 g3 ♕e8 27 ♖b1 ♖f8 28 ♖b7 ♔g8 29 ♘g5 ♖d8 30 f4 a5 31 h5 a4 32 ♖h2 +– Sveshnikov-Naumkin, Moscow 1989.

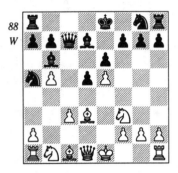

10   0-0

Now the king's rook is available to protect e5.

A refinement, 10 ♕e2!?, was tested in the game Kharlov-Kramnik, USSR 1991, which continued 10...♘e7 11 h4 h6 12 0-0 ♖c8 13 ♗f4 ♘c4 14 a4 f5 15 h5 0-0 16 ♖a2 ♗e8 17 ♘h4 d4 18 cxd4 ♘d5 19 g3 ♘a5 20 ♖c2 ♕d8 21 ♖xc8 ♕xc8 22 ♘g2 ♘b3 23 ♗e3 ♘xd4 24 ♗xd4 ♗xd4 25 ♗c4 ♗xh5 26 ♕d3 ♕c5 27 ♗xd5 ♕xd5 28 ♘f4 ♕d8 29 ♔g2 ♗f7 30 ♖d1 ♗b6 31 ♕xd8 ♖xd8 32 ♖xd8+ ♗xd8 33 ♘a3 a6 34 ♘c4 with equality.

10 ...	♘e7
11 a4	♘g6
12 ♖e1	♗c5

Black is careful not to allow White to incorporate ♗a3 into his plans.

13 ♖a2

Sveshnikov suggests another possibility: 13 h4!? f6 14 ♗xg6+ hxg6 15 ♗f4 with unclear play.

13 ...	0-0-0
14 ♗e3	♗xe3
15 ♖xe3	f6
16 ♖ae2	

The e5 strongpoint is reinforced. Now 16...fxe5 (16...♘xe5 17 ♘xe5 fxe5 18 ♖xe5 ±) 17 ♗xg6 hxg6 18 ♘xe5 is favourable for White so Black chooses to delay the capture.

16 ...	♔b8
17 h3	♗c8?!

This move gives the queen greater freedom, but the plan has a flaw. The emphasis on e5 is a sufficient rôle for the queen at the moment and there is little point in fianchettoing when e6 is under attack. A better way forward is 17...♖c8! when further pressure is applied to c3, the weak link in White's camp.

18 ♕c2!	f5

The line 18...♘f4 19 ♖e1 ♘xd3 20 ♕xd3 ♘c4 21 ♖3e2 intending ♘bd2 is assessed by Sveshnikov to be good for White.

19 ♖e1	b6
20 ♘d4	♖he8
21 g4!?	

A brave gesture to gain the initiative. As Black's forces are relatively constrained, it is deemed feasible to open the kingside.

21 ...	fxg6
22 ♗xg6	hxg6
23 ♕xg6	gxh3 *(89)*

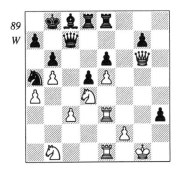

24 Rg3?!

The simple 24 Rxh3 provides excellent chances, e.g. 24...Rh8?! 25 Nxe6 Qe7 26 Nd8! (26 Rxh8? Rxh8 27 Nd4 Qh4 28 Qg2 Rh5 29 Re3 Bh3 −+) 26...Rxh3 27 Qd6+ Qxd6 28 exd6 Rh6 29 Nf7 Rf6 30 Re7 ±.

24 ... Rf8
25 f3

There is still time for 25 Rxh3 without the need to expose the king further.

25 ... Bd7
26 Rxh3 Nc4
27 Qg5 Rh8
28 Rxh8 Rxh8

29 Kg2

If 29 Re2 Qd8! 30 Rg2 (but not 30 Qxg7?? Rg8 −+) 30...Qxg5 31 Rxg5 with equality.

29 ... Nb2
30 Rh1 Rxh1
31 Kxh1 Nxa4
32 Qxg7 Kb7!?

Black can also enter the queen ending: 32...Nxc3 33 Nxc3 Qxc3 34 Qxd7 Qxd4 35 Qxe6 Qh4+ 36 Kg2 Qg5+ 37 Kh3 Qh5+ 38 Kg3 Qg5+ 39 Qg4 Qxe5+ 40 Qf4 Qc7!.

33 Kg2 Bc8
34 Qxc7+ Kxc7
35 f4?!

Now the game meanders to a draw. The last chance to keep slim winning chances is 35 Kg3 intending Kf4-g5-f6.

35 ... Kd7
36 Kf3 a6!
37 Kg4 axb5
38 Nxb5 Ba6
39 N1a3 Ke7
40 Kg5 Bxb5
41 Nxb5 Nc5
42 Nd6 ½-½

5 Systems with ...♘ge7

The introduction of the early knight sortie 5...♘ge7 is designed to put pressure on d4 without the need for ...♗d7. It has been championed by such players as Korchnoi and Portisch, who have added much to the understanding of the line. The attraction of 4...♘e7 intending 5...♘ec6 lies in its unusual knight formation which can confuse an unsuspecting opponent. It has been employed occasionally by Botvinnik and Keene. The strength of Black's positional play can be somewhat muted by accurate play and White should emerge with at least a slight advantage.

Game 30
Sveshnikov-Farago
Hastings 1984/85

1	e4	e6
2	d4	d5
3	e5	c5
4	c3	♘c6
5	♘f3	♘ge7 (90)

Black declares an intention to attack d4 via f5.

6 ♘a3

White exploits the temporarily

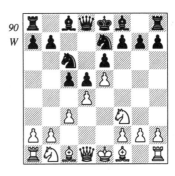

blocked diagonal to manoeuvre the knight to c2 whence it reinforces d4.

6	...	cxd4
7	cxd4	♘f5
8	♘c2	♗e7

White obtained a slight advantage in the game Psakhis-Chernin, USSR Ch 1985, after 8...♘b4 9 ♘xb4 ♗xb4+ 10 ♗d2 ♗xd2+ 11 ♕xd2 ♕b6 12 ♗d3 ♗d7 13 ♗xf5 exf5 14 0-0 0-0.

Also possible is a straightforward attempt to put pressure on d4: 8...♕b6 9 ♗d3 ♗b4+ 10 ♔f1 ♗e7 11 h4! (11 g3 ♗d7 12 ♔g2 ♖c8! 13 ♗xf5 exf5 14 b3 0-0 ∓ Short-Vaganian, Montpellier C 1985) 11...h5 (11...♗d7?! 12 g4 ♘h6 13 ♖g1 ♘g8 14 ♖b1 a5 15 ♕e2 ♘b4 16 ♘xb4 axb4 17 a3 ± Rohde-Spraggett, New York 1986) 12 g3 a5 13 ♔g2 ♗d7 14 ♗xf5 exf5 15 ♗g5 ♗xg5 16 ♘xg5 f4 17 ♕f3! ± Malaniuk-Lputian, USSR Ch 1986.

9   ♗d3   0-0?! *(91)*

At this juncture, Black has various possibilities:

a) 9...♗d7 10 0-0 ♕b6 11 ♖b1 a6 12 ♗xf5 exf5 13 ♗g5! 0-0 14 ♕d2 ♖ac8 15 ♖fc1 ♖c7 16 ♘e3 ♗e6 17 ♗xe7 ♘xe7 18 ♖xc7 ♕xc7 19 ♖c1 ♕d7 20 ♘e1 b6 21 h3 h6 22 ♘d3 ♖c8 23 ♖xc8+ ♘xc8 24 ♘f4 ♘e7 25 ♕b4! ♕c7? 26 ♕d6! ♕xd6 27 exd6 ♘c8 28 ♘xe6 1-0 Haba-Meyer, Hassloch 1991.

b) 9...♕b6 and now:

b1) 10 g4!? ♘h4 11 ♘xh4 ♗xh4 12 0-0 ♗e7 (12...f6 13 g5! ±) 13 ♗e3 ♗d7 = Plaskett-Mestel, Hastings 1986/87.

b2) 10 0-0 ♗d7 11 ♖b1 a5 (not 11...♘fxd4 12 ♘fxd4 ♘xd4 13 ♗e3 ♗c5 14 b4 +−) 12 ♗xf5 exf5 (Carlier-Rasidović, Lugano 1987) 13 ♗g5! ∓.

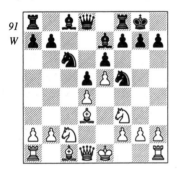

91
W

10 g4!

A survey of older sources reveals that the position is assumed to be equal, on the basis of the continuation 10 0-0. This assessment stems from the game Sax-F.Portisch, Hungary 1978, which continued 10...f6 11 ♗xf5 exf5 12 ♖e1 fxe5 13 dxe5 f4! 14 h3 ♗c5 15 a3 a5 16 ♖b1 ♔h8 (16...d4? 17 b4 d3 18 bxc5 dxc2 19 ♕xc2 ♗f5 20 ♕b3+ ±) 17 b4 axb4 18 axb4 ♕b6 19 ♖e2 ♗f5 20 ♖b2 ♗e7! 21 ♕xd5 ♖ad8 22 ♕b3 ♖d1+ 23 ♖e1 ♗xc2 24 ♕xc2 ♖xe1+ 25 ♘xe1 ♘xe5 =.

The text, which launches a dangerous attack, is a strong antidote to Black's system.

10   ...   ♘h4

If the knight retreats, then the pawn barrier can be shattered: 10...♘h6 11 ♗xh6 gxh6 12 g5!? hxg5 13 ♘xg5 ♗xg5 14 ♕h5 h6 15 h4 with good play (Kuijf).

11 ♘xh4   ♗xh4
12 g5!

This rapid sharpening of the position is the reasoning behind 10 g4. The pawn traps the bishop, so Black is obliged to take it. This opens up the g-file for the benefit of the rooks.

12   ...   ♗xg5
13 ♕h5

It would be premature to lash out with another sacrifice: 13 ♗xh7+? ♔xh7 14 ♕h5+ ♗h6 15 ♖g1 (intending ♖xg7+) 15...♖g8 16 ♔e2 ♕f8! −+.

13 ...   **h6**
14 ♖g1   **♗xc1**

White's plan is easy to follow with the natural moves ♕h5 and ♖g1 posing all sorts of problems. The ominous threat of 15 ♖xg5 dictates Black's response.

Not so good is 14...f5? (14...f6? 15 f4! wins) 15 exf6 ♕xf6 16 ♖xg5! ♕xf2+ 17 ♔d1 which is again winning for White.

15 ♖xc1   **f5**

Even at this early stage, Black is on the brink of collapse. For example: 15...♔h8 16 ♔e2 (intending ♖xg7) 16...♖g8 17 ♕xf7 ♕e8 18 ♖xg7! +−.

16 ♕xh6   **♖f7**
17 ♔e2   **♕b6**
18 ♕h4

The opening has been a great success for White. Material equality has been re-established while the onslaught continues in earnest.

18 ...   **♗d7**
19 ♖g5!   **♕xb2**
20 ♔d2 *(92)*

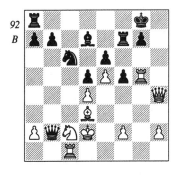

White is understandably anxious to rule out any hint of counterplay and has time to take precautions. However, Sveshnikov points out that a direct approach would reap instant dividends: 20 ♖h5 ♘xd4+ 21 ♔d1! ♖ff8 22 ♕xd4 ♕xd4 (22...♕xa2 23 ♖a1 +−) 23 ♘xd4 +−.

20 ...   **♘e7**

Other paths also offer little resistance:

a) 20...♘xe5 21 dxe5 ♕xe5 22 ♖h5 g6 23 ♖g1 ♕f6 24 ♖xg6+ ♕xg6 25 ♖h8+ ♔g7 26 ♖xa8 +−.

b) 20...♖c8 21 ♖h5 ♖ff8 22 ♖g1 +−.

21 ♖h5   **♘g6**

No better is 21...♔f8 22 ♖h8+ ♘g8 23 ♕h7 +−.

22 ♕g3!   **♘f8**
23 ♕h3

Now the other rook will be added to the attack with decisive consequences.

23 ...   **♖e7**

The resource 23...♘g6 can be rebuffed by 24 ♖g1! winning.

24 ♖h8+   **♔f7**
25 ♖g1   **♗a4**
26 ♕h5+   **g6**
27 ♖xg6!   **1-0**

Game 31
Fedorowicz-Jackelen
Porz 1988

1 e4   **e6**
2 d4   **d5**

3	e5	c5
4	c3	♘c6
5	♘f3	♘ge7
6	♘a3	

White also has other possibilities to fight for the advantage:

a) 6 ♗e3?! ♘f5 7 ♗d3 (7 ♕d2 ♘xe3 8 fxe3 ♗e7 9 ♗d3 0-0 Tolush-Botvinnik, USSR 1938) 7...♘xe3 8 fxe3 ♗e7! 9 0-0 0-0 0-0 10 ♕c2 (10 ♕e2 ♗d7 11 ♘b2 ♕b6 ∓) 10...h6 11 ♘bd2 ♗d7 12 ♖ae1 ♖c8 13 ♕b1 b5! 14 dxc5 ♗xc5 15 ♘b3 ♗e7 16 ♘bd4 b4 17 cxb4 ♗xb4 18 ♖e2 ♕b6 ∓ Heidenfeld-Donner, Lugano 1968.

b) 6 a3 cxd4 7 cxd4 ♘f5 8 ♘c3 ♗e7 and now:

b1) 9 ♗b5 ♗d7 10 ♗a4 ♕b6 11 ♘e2 f6 12 g4 ♘h6 13 exf6 ♗f8 14 ♗xh6 gxh6 15 ♕d2 0-0-0 16 ♗xc6 ♗xc6 17 ♘e5 ♗e8 18 0-0 ± Romanishin-Razuvaev, Moscow 1985.

b2) 9 ♗d3!? ♘fxd4 10 ♘xd4 ♘xd4 11 ♕g4 ♘f5 12 ♗xf5 exf5 13 ♕xg7 ♖f8 14 0-0 ♗e6 15 ♗h6 ♔d7 16 ♖fd1 ♖g8 17 ♕xh7 ♔c7 18 ♖ac1 ♔b8 19 ♘xd5 ♗xd5 20 ♖xd5 ♖xg2+ 21 ♔xg2 ♕xd5+ 22 ♔g1 b6 23 ♕xf5 +− Pyhälä-Kanko, Helsinki 1989.

c) 6 ♗e2 ♘f5 (6...cxd4 7 cxd4 ♘f5 transposes to Game 18, Galdunts-Naroditsky) 7 dxc5 (7 g4!? ♘h4 8 ♘xh4 ♕xh4 9 ♗e3 ♗d7 10 0-0 {10 ♘d2 cxd4 11 ♘f3 ♕xg4! ∓} 10...f6 11 f4 fxe5 12 dxe5 g5! with the better game for Black – Psakhis)

7...♗xc5 8 b4 ♗e7 9 b5 ♘a5 10 0-0 0-0 11 ♗d3 ♕c7 12 g4! ♘h4 13 ♘xh4 ♗xh4 14 g5 h6 15 f4 f6 16 gxf6 gxf6 17 ♕h5 fxe5 18 ♕xh4 e4 19 ♗e2 ♔h7 20 ♗e3 1-0 Ekström-Schauwecker, Switzerland 1993.

d) 6 ♗d3 is examined in the next illustrative game.

6	...	cxd4
7	cxd4	♘f5
8	♘c2	♕a5+ *(93)*

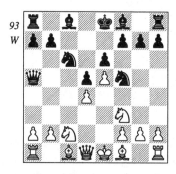

A popular way of handling the position as it lures White's queen's bishop out. This is a debatable achievement as it will over-protect d4 whilst Black argues that it will lack scope on c3.

Also feasible is 8...♘b4 9 ♘e3 ♗e7 10 ♘xf5 exf5 11 a3 ♘c6 12 ♗d3 ♗e6 13 0-0 a6 14 ♗e3 ♖c8 15 b4 when White has the slightly better chances; Vučinić-Dizdar, Pula 1990.

9	♗d2	♕b6
10	♗c3	♗e7

In the game Marjanović-Popović, Yugoslavia 1986, Black adopted an alternative plan of development: 10...♗d7 11 ♗d3 ♗e7 12 ♕d2?! (12 0-0!? ±) 12...a5! 13 a3 h5 and now 14 ♗xf5 exf5 15 h4 offered equal chances.

11 ♗d3   a5
12 a3

White is keen to nullify Black's counterplay by ruling out the chance of a piece occupying b4.

It is also possible to proceed in more robust fashion as shown by Sveshnikov-Ortega, Sochi 1987: 12 ♘e3 g6 13 0-0 ♗d7 14 ♗c2 h5 (14...0-0 15 ♘g4 intending ♘f6+ ±) 15 ♕d2 ♔f8 16 g3 ♘b4 17 ♗xf5! gxf5 (17...exf5? 18 a3 +−) 18 h4 ♗b5 19 ♖fd1 ♕a6 20 ♘g5 ♖c8 21 a3 ♘c6 22 ♘g2 ♔g7 23 ♖e1 ♗c4 24 ♘f4 ♗b3 25 ♕e3 ♕b5 (25...♗xg5? 26 ♘xe6+! fxe6 27 ♕xg5+ ♔f7 28 ♕f6+ and White wins) 26 ♖ac1 ♗c4 27 ♔g2 ♖cg8 28 ♕f3 ♔f8? 29 ♘fxe6+ 1-0.

12 ...   0-0
13 g4

This is a familiar theme, particularly when Black castles before White. One way to counter the problem is 12...h5!? but this has the drawback of weakening the kingside.

13 ...   ♘h4
14 ♖g1 (94)

A novel way to conduct the attack. The immediate threat is illusory: 15 ♘xh4 ♗xh4 16 g5 ♘xe5! 17 ♖g4 ♘xg4 18 ♕xg4 e5 19 ♕xh4

f5 and Black has very good chances. However, White can follow up with 15 ♕e2, so Black is obliged to be wary.

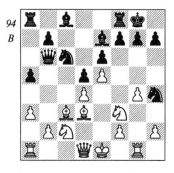

94
B

14 ...   f5
15 gxf5   ♘xf5
16 ♘e3

This removes a vital defender, and so increases the pressure on Black's kingside. Black's problems are compounded by the prospect of 17 ♗xf5 exf5 18 ♘xd5, thus forcing the issue.

16 ...   ♘xe3
17 fxe3   ♗d7
18 ♕e2

White's forces are perfectly poised to start an avalanche on the flank by doubling on the g-file or targeting h7. Black is unable to adjust swiftly enough to the changed circumstances when the queen is a remote figure and the rest of the pieces lack harmony.

18 ...   ♖f7
19 ♕g2   ♘b8

The start of a cumbersome manoeuvre to transfer the knight to f8.

20 ♕h3   g6 *(95)*

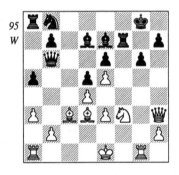

21 ♗xg6!

A stylish way to terminate the game.

21	...	hxg6
22	♖xg6+	♖g7
23	♖xg7+	♔xg7
24	0-0-0	♗f8
25	᧒g5	1-0

Game 32

Blatny-Moldovan

Stara Zagora Z 1990

1	e4	e6
2	d4	d5
3	e5	c5
4	c3	᧒c6
5	᧒f3	᧒ge7
6	♗d3	*(96)*

The most energetic reply, which has Psakhis' stamp of approval.

6 ...   cxd4

Black wisely prefers to exchange

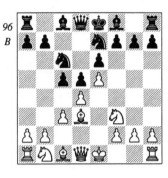

on d4 without further ado, since delaying this decision would give White more options. In Kupreichik-Lëgky, Lvov 1984, White was permitted to recapture on d4 with the knight, and gained an advantage after 6...᧒f5 7 0-0 (7 dxc5!? ♗xc5 8 0-0 b6 9 b4 ♗e7 10 b5 ᧒a5 11 ᧒d4 was unclear in Lazić-Velimirović, Yugoslavia 1991) 7...cxd4 8 ♗xf5 exf5 9 ᧒xd4! ♗e6 10 ♗e3 ♗e7 11 f4.

7	cxd4	᧒f5
8	♗xf5	

A direct course of action to relieve the pressure against d4. A survey of the alternatives reveals:

a) 8 ♗e3!? and now:

a1) 8...♗e7 9 0-0 0-0 10 ᧒c3 ᧒xe3 11 fxe3 f5 12 exf6 ♗xf6 13 ♕c2 h6 14 ᧒e2 ♗d7 15 ᧒f4 ᧒e7 (Bellon-Moles, Groningen 1968/69) 16 ᧒h5 with a distinct advantage for White.

a2) 8...♗b4+ 9 ᧒c3 0-0 10 0-0 ᧒xe3 11 fxe3 f6 12 exf6 ♕xf6 13 ♔h1 ♕h6 14 e4 ♗d6 15 e5 ♗e7 16 a3 ♗d7 17 b4 ♖ac8 18 ♘e2 ♗e8 19 ♕c1! ♕xc1 20 ♖axc1 and White has the better ending due to his territorial advantage; C.Hawthorne-Corfield, Bournemouth 1981.

b) 8 0-0?! ♘fxd4 9 ♘xd4 ♘xd4 10 ♘c3 ♘c6! 11 ♗f4 ♗e7 12 ♖e1 (or 12 ♕g4 g5!) 12...♗g5! 13 ♗g3 0-0 14 ♕h5 (Haag-Portisch, Hungary 1959) 14...g6 15 ♕e2 f5 16 exf6 ♗xf6; White has insufficient compensation for the pawn.

8 ... exf5

9 0-0 *(97)*

At this point, there is a major junction. One particular value of the little-known text is that it explodes the myth that it is necessary to prevent ...g5 in order to install a knight on f4.

After 9 ♘c3 ♗e6 play might continue:

a) 10 0-0 ♗e7 (10...h6 11 ♘e1 ♗e7 12 f4 g5 13 ♘c2 ♕b6 14 ♕d3 ± Zaitsev-Volke, Podolsk 1991) 11 ♘e1! (11 ♘e2 g5! 12 ♘e1 f4 13 f3 ♕b6 14 ♔h1 ♗f5 is even slightly better for Black; Teschner-Portisch, Monte Carlo 1969) 11...♕b6 (11...♖c8 12 ♘c2 0-0 13 ♕d3 ♕d7 14 f4 a6 15 ♗d2 ± Zaitsev-Moskalenko, Moscow 1992) 12 ♘e2 0-0 13 ♔h1! ♔h8 (13...a5 14 f4 ± Blatny-Machulsky, Alma-Ata 1989) 14 ♘d3 ♖ac8 15 ♗e3 ♘b4 16 ♘c5 ♘a6 17 ♘a4 ♕d8 18 ♘ac3 ♕d7 19 ♕d2 ♖fe8 20 f3 b5 21 ♘g3 was unclear; Thipsay-Gdanski, Manila OL 1992.

b) 10 ♗g5 ♕b6 11 0-0 h6 12 ♗c1 ♗e7 13 ♘e2 g5 14 b3 ♖c8 15 ♗b2 0-0 16 ♔h1 f4 = Markland-Moles, Birmingham 1968.

c) 10 ♘e2 and now:

c1) 10...♕b6!? 11 ♘f4 h6 12 h4 g6 13 ♔f1 (13 0-0 ♗e7 14 g3 a5 15 ♔g2 a4 16 ♖b1 ± Sax) 13...♗e7 14 g3 0-0-0 15 ♔g2 ♕b8 (15...g5 16 ♘xe6 fxe6 17 hxg5 hxg5 18 ♖xh8 ♖xh8 19 ♗g5 ♗g5 20 ♘g5 ♘d4 21 ♕d2 ± Sax) 16 ♖b1 ♗c8 (16...g5 17 hxg5 hxg5 18 ♖xh8 ♖h8 19 ♘xe6 fxe6 20 ♗xg5 ♗xg5 21 ♘xg5 ♘xd4 22 ♕d2 ♖g8 23 b4 ± Sax) 17 e6 ♗xe6 18 ♘xe6 fxe6 19 ♖e1 e5! (19...♘a5 20 ♘e5 ±) 20 ♘xe5 ♘xe5 21 ♗f4 ♗f6 22 dxe5 ½-½ Sax-M.Gurevich, Munich 1993.

c2) 10...♗e7 11 h4 ♖c8 12 ♔f1 (12 ♘f4 h6 13 ♖h3 ♔d7 14 h5 ♖e8 15 ♖g3 ♗f8 16 ♔f1 ♔c7 17 a3 ♔b8 18 b4 ± Nun-Langner, Ostrava 1991) 12...♕b6 13 ♘f4 ♘b4 14 ♗d2 ♔d7 15 ♗c3 ♕a6+ 16 ♔g1 ♖hd8 17 g3 b5 18 a4 ♘c6 19 ♕e2 ♖b8 20 ♘g5 h6 21 ♘xf7! ♖f8 22 ♘d6 ♗xd6 23 exd6 ♖fe8 24 ♘d3 ♔xd6 25 ♗d2 ♔e7 26 ♕xe6+ 1-0 Orr-Poulton, British Ch 1988.

c21) 11...h6 12 ♘f4 ♕b6 13 a3 (13 ♖h3!? g6 14 ♔f1 0-0-0 15 ♔g1 ♖dg8 16 ♖b1 g5 17 hxg5 hxg5 18 ♖xh8 ♖xh8 19 ♘xe6 fxe6 20 ♗xg5 ♗xg5 21 ♘xg5 ♕xd4 22 ♕xd4 ♘xd4 23 g3 = Sveshnikov-Temirbaev, Kuibyshev 1987) 13...0-0 14 ♕d3 ♖c8 15 ♖b1 ♘a5 16 b4 ♘c4 17 g4! g6 18 h5 fxg4 19 hxg6 gxf3 20 ♖xh6 f5 21 g7 ♖f7 22 ♘xe6 ♕b5 23 ♖h8# (1-0) C.Hawthorne-Shaw, Devon 1981.

c22) 11...♕a5+?! 12 ♔f1 h6 13 ♘f4 ♖c8 14 ♔g1! ♕b6 15 h5 ♘b4 (15...0-0!?) 16 ♗d2 ♘c2? 17 ♘xe6! fxe6 18 ♖c1 ♕xb2 19 ♘e1 ♕xd4 20 ♖xc2 0-0 21 ♖h3! ♖xc2 22 ♘xc2 ♕a4 23 ♖c3 ♕xa2 24 ♘d4 ♕a6 25 ♖g3 +− Sveshnikov-Psakhis, Sochi 1987.

d) 10 h4 ♗b4 (10...♗e7 11 ♘e2 transposes to the notes above) 11 ♗d2 ♗xc3 12 bxc3 h6 13 ♘g1!? 0-0 14 ♘e2 f6 15 ♘f4 ♗f7 16 exf6 ♕xf6 17 h5 ♖fe8+ 18 ♔f1 b5 19 a3 a5 20 g3 b4 21 ♔g2 bxc3 22 ♗xc3 a4 23 ♖b1 was equal in Vasiukov-Popović, Vršac 1989.

e) 10 a3 ♗e7 11 h4 h6 12 ♗f4 ♘a5 13 ♔f1 ♕d7 14 ♘d2 with equality; Benjamin-Vaganian, Wijk aan Zee 1989.

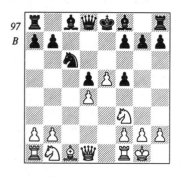

97
B

9 ... ♗e7
10 ♘c3

The rare alternatives are not convincing:

a) 10 ♘bd2 ♗e6 11 ♘b3 0-0 12 ♗e3 a5 13 ♖c1 a4 14 ♘c5 a3 15 bxa3 ♗xc5 16 ♖xc5 ½-½ Piancatelli-Marino, Rome 1990.

b) 10 a3 a6 11 b4 b5 12 ♗e3 0-0 13 ♘c3 ♗e6 14 ♕d2 ♕b6 15 ♘e2 a5 16 ♗g5 h6 17 ♗xe7 ♘xe7 18 ♖ac1 axb4 19 axb4 ♖fc8 20 ♖c5 with a slight plus for White; Salai-Hirsch, Brno/Morava 1991.

10 ... **g5!?**

For some time this prophylactic move, which rules out the usual idea ♘e2-f4, was considered the antidote to White's plan.

If 10...♗e6 11 ♘e1 transposes to note 'a' after White's ninth move.

11 ♘e1 **f4**
12 h4

The weakening of White's defensive barrier is a calculated risk to undermine Black's pawns before he can support them with his pieces.

12 ... **h6**
13 ♕h5! **gxh4**

It is more critical to steal the d-pawn: 13...♘xd4!? 14 hxg5 ♗xg5 15 ♕d1! ♘c6 16 ♕xd5 ♗f5 (or 16...♗e6 17 ♕e4) 17 ♘f3 when the complications favour White.

14 ♗xf4 **♗e6**
15 ♗e3 **♕d7**
16 ♘d3 **♗g4** (98)
17 e6!

At a stroke an escape route is exposed. If 17...♗xh5 (17...♕xe6 18

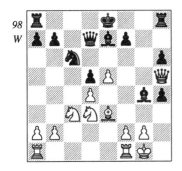

98
W

♕xd5 ♖d8 19 ♕b5 +–) 18 exd7+ ♔xd7 19 ♘f4 +–.

17	...	♗xe6
18	♗f4	0-0-0

Since 10...g5, Black's simplistic plan has been to castle long and storm the kingside. However, the way White has contrived to shatter the pawns and open up the position reveals what a risky task that can be.

19	♘b5	a6
20	♘e5!	

The game is brought to an abrupt finish. The knight cannot be captured due to 20...♘xe5 21 ♕xe5 with mate next move. Black's problems are compounded by the threat of 21 ♘xc6 and ♕e5 +–.

20	...	♕e8
21	♘xc6	♕xc6
	1-0	

Game 33
Kupreichik-Kovačević
Ljubljana/Rogaška Slatina 1989

1	e4	e6

2	d4	d5
3	e5	c5
4	c3	♘e7

This is usually a prelude to 5...♘bc6 which would return to the lines already considered.

5	♘f3	♘ec6 (99)

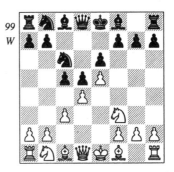

99
W

Now Black has revealed his true intentions. The idea is to keep pressure on d4 while exchanging the light-squared bishop after ...b6 and ...♗a6 or, as in the game, continue with queenside development. Other tries have not emerged with much credit:

a) 5...♘f5 6 dxc5 ♗xc5 7 ♗d3 ♘c6 and now:

a1) 8 0-0 ♘h4!? 9 ♖e1 (9 ♘bd2!) 9...♗d7 10 b4?! ♗b6 11 b5 ♘xf3+ 12 ♕xf3 ♘e7 13 ♗a3 ♖c8 14 ♕g3 ♘g6 ∓ Barden-Botvinnik, Hastings 1961/62.

a2) 8 ♗xf5! exf5 9 0-0 ♗e7 10 ♘bd2 0-0 11 ♘b3 ♗e6 12 ♕e2 ♕c7 13 ♗f4 ♖c8 14 ♖fe1 a6 15 ♗g5! ♗xg5 16 ♘xg5 h6 17 ♘f3 ♘e7 18

♘bd4 ± Basman-Keene, British Ch 1968.

b) 5...♘d7 6 a3! ♕b6 7 b4 cxd4 8 cxd4 ♘c6 9 ♗b2 intending 10 ♗d3 is considered by Szily to give White an advantage.

6 ♗e3

White can choose other paths:

a) 6 ♗d3 and now:

a1) 6...b6 7 ♗g5 ♕d7 8 0-0 ♗a6 9 dxc5 bxc5 10 ♗xa6 ♘xa6 11 c4 h6 12 ♗h4 ♘c7 13 ♘c3 ♗e7 14 ♗xe7 ♘xe7 15 ♖c1 ♖c8 16 ♕e2 0-0 17 ♖fd1 ♕c6 18 b3 ± Sveshnikov-Lputian, Moscow 1989.

a2) 6...♘d7 7 0-0 cxd4 8 cxd4 ♗e7 9 ♘c3 ♘b6 10 a3 a5 11 ♗c2 ♗d7 12 g3 ♘a7 13 h4 h6 14 ♘h2 ♕c7 15 ♗d3 ♘c4 16 a4 ♗b4 17 ♕g4 ± Maciejewski-Spreŏić, Tuzla 1989.

b) 6 ♗e2 b6 7 0-0 ♗a6 8 ♗xa6!? ♘xa6 9 ♕a4 ♘ab8 10 ♗e3 ♕d7 11 ♕c2 ♗e7 12 ♘bd2 0-0 13 g3 c4 14 ♘g5 ♗xg5 15 ♗xg5 ♘a6 16 f4 ♘c7 17 ♖f3 ♘e8 18 f5 exf5 19 ♖xf5 ♘c7 20 ♖af1 ♘e7 21 ♗xe7 ♕xe7 22 ♕d1 ♘e6 23 ♕f3 ♖ad8 24 ♕e3 b5 25 ♖1f2 h6 26 h4 ♔h7 27 ♘f1 g6 28 ♖f6 ♘g7 29 ♕f3 ♖d7 30 ♘e3 ♘h5 31 ♘xd5 ♕d8 32 g4 1-0 Soos-Havaŏi, Hungary 1991.

c) 6 a3!? a5 7 ♗d3 b6 8 ♗g5 ♕d7 9 dxc5 bxc5 10 ♘bd2 c4 11 ♗c2 ♘a6 12 b4 cxb3 13 ♘xb3 a4 14 ♘bd4 ♘c5 15 0-0 h6 16 ♗f4 ♗a6 17 ♖e1 ♗c4 18 ♘xc6 ♕xc6 19 ♘d4 ♕a6 20 ♖e3 with an equal

position; Dekić-F.Portisch, Budapest 1992.

d) 6 h4!? ♘d7 7 g3 (7 h5? f6! 8 exf6 ♘xf6 9 h6 g6 ∓ Sveshnikov-Kovaŏević, Belgrade 1988) 7...♗e7 8 ♗h3 b5 9 a3 a5 10 ♘g5 ♗xg5 11 ♗xg5 f6 12 exf6 ♘xf6 13 dxc5 0-0 14 ♘d2 ♕e7 15 ♗xf6 ♖xf6 16 b4 ♖g6 17 ♘f3 ♕f6 18 ♘d4 ♕e5+ 19 ♔f1 ♗d7 20 ♔g2 ♖f8 21 ♕e2 ♕f6 22 ♖ad1 ♔h8 23 h5 ♖h6 24 f4 ♕f7 25 ♘xb5 +− Espinoza-Paneque, Cali 1990.

6 ...   ♘d7

Also worth consideration is 6...b6 which prepares ...♗a6 and bolsters c5. Fishbein-Friedman, New York 1990 continued 7 ♗d3 ♗a6 8 ♗xa6 ♘xa6 9 ♕a4 ♘ab8 10 0-0 ♕d7 11 ♕c2 ♗e7 12 h4 ♕d8 13 ♖d1 ♘d7 14 h5 0-0 15 ♕e2 f6 16 exf6 ♗xf6 17 h6 g6 18 c4 cxd4 19 cxd5 exd5 20 ♘xd4 ♘xd4 21 ♗xd4 ♗xd4 22 ♖xd4 ♘f6 23 ♘c3 ♕d6 24 ♕d2 with advantage to White.

7 ♗d3   a5
8 ♘bd2

Kupreichik's suggestion 8 ♘g5!? merits attention, for example 8...cxd4 9 cxd4 ♗e7 (9...h6?! 10 ♕h5 hxg5 11 ♕xh8 ♘b4 12 ♕h7 g6 13 ♗xg6 +−) 10 h4 (10 ♕h5? ♗xg5! 11 ♗xg5 ♕b6 ∓) 10...♕b6 (10...h6 11 ♕h5!) 11 ♘c3 and White has an edge.

8 ...   cxd4
9 cxd4   a4?!
10 a3?!

Though White is gradually improving his position, a more adventurous course of action was called for to highlight the inadequacies of neglecting development. Rather than pushing the a-pawn, 10 ♘g5! ♗e7 10 h4 ♕b6 11 ♕g4 ♕xb2 12 0-0 was called for, when the attack continues in earnest.

| 10 | ... | ♗e7 |
| 11 | h4 | h6 *(100)* |

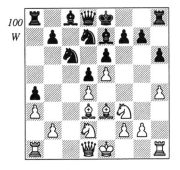

12 h5

A standard device to hem in the kingside pawns. The pawn effectively puts a block on a future ...g6, so White can continue to concentrate his resources on direct action towards snaring the king.

12	...	♘b6
13	♘h2	♘a5
14	♕g4	♗f8

An unpleasant move to make, but after 14...♔f8 15 ♖c1 White can continue in robust fashion with 0-0 and f4-f5.

| 15 | ♖c1 | ♗d7 |

16 0-0 ♘bc4!

If given no opposition, the pawn-roller f4-f5 would pose a serious problem. This inspires Black to start counterplay on the other flank.

| 17 | ♘xc4 | ♘xc4 |
| 18 | ♕e2 | |

There is nothing to be gained from trading pieces: 18 ♗xc4 dxc4 19 d5 exd5 20 ♕d4 ♗f5! 21 g4 ♗d3 and it is Black who has the better game thanks to the extra pawn.

18	...	b5
19	f4	♗e7
20	f5!?	

It is also tempting to seek complications, which emerge after 20 ♗xc4 dxc4 (20...bxc4 21 g4!) 21 f5!? (21 d5 exd5 22 f5 d4! 23 ♗xd4 ♗xf5 leaves Black with the better chances) 21...exf5 22 d5. Kupreichik considers this position to be unclear.

| 20 | ... | exf5 |

Black is positionally bankrupt after 20...♗g5? 21 ♗xc4 bxc4 (21...dxc4 22 d5! ±) 22 ♗xg5 ♕xg5 23 f6 ±.

21	♗xf5	♘xe3
22	♕xe3	♗g5
23	♕g3	♗xf5
24	♖xf5 *(101)*	♖c8?

A perilous journey appears to await Black if the rook is snatched, but Kupreichik's analysis demonstrates it is the only way to seek salvation (at least). Play might continue 24...♗xc1! 25 ♕xg7 ♖f8 and now:

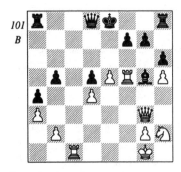

101
B

a) 26 ♘g4 ♖a6 (26...♗g5! 27 e6 ♕e7! ∓ Nunn) 27 ♘f6+ ♖xf6 (or 27...♔e7 28 ♘g8+ ♔d7 29 ♖f7+ ♖xf7 30 ♕xf7+ ♔c8 31 e6 ♗e3+ 32 ♔f1, with an unclear position) 28 exf6 ♕d6 29 ♖e5+ ♔d8 30 ♖e7 ♖e8 31 ♖xe8+ ♔xe8 32 ♕g8+ ♕f8 33 ♕g3! ♔d7 34 ♕h3+ ♔d8 35 ♕g3 =.

b) 26 e6!? ♕d6 (26...♕e7 27 exf7+ {27 ♘g4 ♗g5} ♖xf7 28 ♕g8+ ♕f8 29 ♖e5+ ♔d7 ∓ Nunn) 27 exf7!? (27 ♖xf7 0-0-0 28 e7 ♖xf7 29 ♕xf7 ♗xb2! 30 e8♕ ♗xd4+ 31

♔h1 ♖xe8 32 ♕xe8+ ♔c7 ∓) 27...♔d7 28 ♘f3 ♔c7 29 ♖f6 ♕e7 30 ♕g6 with an unclear game.

25	♖cf1	0-0
26	e6!	

With the oppressed king finally seeking shelter by castling, White administers a crushing blow by a successful breakthrough.

26	...	♕c7

If 26...f6 27 ♕f3 wins the d5 pawn.

27	♕e1!	♕e7

If Black plays 27...♗f6 to block the f-file, White can instigate a thunderous attack: 28 ♖xf6 gxf6 29 ♘g4 fxe6 30 ♕xe6+ ♔g7 31 ♖xf6 with a clear advantage.

28	♖xf7	♖xf7
29	♖xf7	♖c1

On 29...♕d6 30 ♖d7 ♕b6 31 ♕e5 ♗f6 32 ♕xd5 wins.

30	♕xc1	♕xe6
31	♖f4	1-0

6 5...♘h6

The idea is to reach positions similar to those which arise from 5...♘ge7, while thwarting ♘a3 because of ...cxd4 and ...♗xa3. The attraction of the line for Black is that it avoids main-line theory. Sveshnikov's remedy 6 dxc5 is the critical continuation, with White generally emerging on top.

Game 34
Sveshnikov-Bareev
Match: Poliot-T.Petrosian 1991

1	**e4**	**e6**
2	**d4**	**d5**
3	**e5**	**c5**
4	**c3**	**♘c6**
5	**♘f3**	**♘h6!?**

The start of the variation.

6 dxc5

Sveshnikov pounces on the chance to exploit the unusual move-order. The idea is that the exchange on c5 lures the bishop out, presenting White with the options of ♗xh6 followed by ♕d2, or b4-b5, which oblige the bishop to retreat. After 6 ♗d3 the game could transpose into Game 32, Blatny-Moldovan, or Black

might adopt an independent line: 6...f6!? 7 ♗xh6 gxh6 8 0-0 cxd4 9 cxd4 ♗g7 10 ♖e1 0-0 11 ♘bd2 ♕b6 12 exf6 ♖xf6 13 ♘b3 ♗d7 14 ♘c5 ♖d8 15 ♖c1 ♗c8 16 ♗b1 ♖df8 17 ♕d3 ♖f5 18 ♘xe6 ♗xe6 19 ♖xe6 ♕xb2 20 ♖f1 ♘xd4 21 ♘h4 ♘xe6 22 ♘xf5 ♖d8 23 ♘xh6+ and now White has a clear plus; Hendriks-Crouch, Dieren 1992.

The immediate 6 ♗xh6 normally transposes to the note to Black's sixth move, although the game Gofshtein-Soffer, Tel Aviv followed a different direction: 6...gxh6 7 dxc5 ♗g7 8 ♗b5 0-0 9 ♗xc6 bxc6 10 0-0 f6 11 ♕e2 ♗d7 12 ♖e1 ♖b8 13 b4 ♗e8 14 ♘bd2 ♗h5 15 ♕e3 ♕c7 16 ♖ac1 ♗xf3 17 ♘xf3 fxe5 18 ♘xe5 ♖f5 19 ♘g4 ±.

6 ... ♘g4?! *(102)*

Black assumes that taking away the natural defender of e5 allows the knight to enter the fray. After 6...♗xc5 play might continue:

a) 7 b4 and now:

a1) 7...♗e7 8 ♗d3 ♘g4 9 ♗f4 f6! 10 b5 ♘cxe5 11 ♘xe5 ♘xe5 12 ♗xe5 fxe5 13 ♕h5+ ♔f8 = Rozentalis-Kuporosov, Budapest 1990.

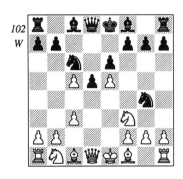

102
W

a2) 7...♗f8 8 b5 (8 ♗d3!? is worth consideration) 8...♘a5 9 ♗d3 f6 10 ♗xh6 gxh6 11 ♘d4 ♕c7 12 exf6 ♕e5+ 13 ♗e2 ♗d6 14 f7+ ♔xf7 15 g3 ♔g7 16 0-0 ♖f8 17 ♘d2 ♗d7 18 ♗g4 ♖ae8 19 ♗h3 ♖e7 20 ♕a4 ♕h5 21 ♗g2 b6 22 c4 e5 23 ♘c6 ♗xc6 24 dxc6 ♕e2 25 ♖ad1 ♗c5 26 cxd5 ♖xf2 27 ♖xf2 ♕xf2+ 28 ♔h1 ♖f7 29 ♕g4+ ♔f8 30 c7 1-0 Sveshnikov-Jolles, Torcy 1991.

a3) 7...♗b6 8 ♗xh6 (8 b5 ♘e7 9 ♗d3 ♘g6 10 0-0 0-0 11 ♗xh6 gxh6 12 a4!? f6 13 ♗xg6!? hxg6 14 ♕d3 ♔g7 15 ♘bd2 ♗d7 16 c4 fxe5 17 cxd5 {17 ♘xe5 ♗e8 18 ♖ad1 ♖c8 is unclear} 17...exd5 18 ♕xd5 ♗f5 19 ♕xe5+ ♕f6 with unclear play; Sveshnikov-Moskalenko, Rostov-on-Don 1993) 8...gxh6 9 b5 ♘e7 10 ♗d3 ♘g6 11 0-0 ♕c7 (not 11...f6? 12 ♗xg6 hxg6 13 ♕d3 ♔f7 14 exf6 ♕xf6 15 ♘bd2 ♖d8 16 ♖ae1 a6 17 ♘e5+ ♔g7 18 ♘df3 ♗d7 19 ♘d4 ♗xd4 20 ♕xd4 axb5 {20...♗xb5 21 ♖e3 ♗xf1 22 ♖f3 wins} 21 ♖e3 ♖a4 22 ♕b6 ♖f4 23 ♕c7 g5 24 ♘xd7 ♕e7 25 ♘c5 1-0 Sveshnikov-Dukhov, Moscow 1992; or 11...0-0 12 ♖e1!?; 12 a4!? unclear – Glek) 12 ♖e1 0-0 13 a4 ♗d7 14 ♖a2!? f6 (14...a6!?) 15 ♗xg6 hxg6 16 ♕d3 f5 17 ♘bd2 ♖fc8 18 ♖c2 a6 19 ♖ec1 axb5 20 axb5 ♖a3 21 ♕e2 ♕c5 22 ♘d4 ♖ca8 23 g4 f4 24 g5 h5 25 ♘2f3 ♔g7 26 ♕d2 ♖f8 27 ♖a2 ♗a5 28 ♖xa3 ♕xa3 29 ♕c2 ♕e7 30 c4 dxc4 31 ♕e4! ± Sveshnikov-Nikolaev, Moscow 1992.

b) 7 ♗xh6 gxh6 and now:

b1) 8 b4 ♗f8 9 b5 ♘e7 10 ♗d3 ♗g7 11 0-0 ♘g6 (Sveshnikov-Glek, Moscow 1991) 12 ♕e2 0-0 (12...♕c7 13 ♗xg6 hxg6 14 c4 is also unclear) 13 c4 with an unclear game according to Sveshnikov.

b2) 8 ♗d3 f6! 9 b4 ♗f8 10 b5 ♘xe5 11 ♘xe5 fxe5 12 ♕h5+ ♔d7 13 ♕xe5 ♖g8 ∓ Khalifman-Kaidanov, Moscow 1987.

In the game Mukhametov-Lempert, Moscow 1992, Black wrongly tried to delay the capture: 6...♕c7?! 7 b4! ♘g4 (7...♘xe5 8 ♗f4 ♘xf3+ {8...f6 9 ♗b5+!; 8...♘d3+ 9 ♗xd3 ♕xf4 10 ♗b5+ ±} 9 ♕xf3 ♕d8 10 ♗b5+ ♗d7 11 ♗xd7+ ♕xd7 12 0-0 ♘f5 13 ♘d2 ♗e7 14 c4 ±) 8 ♗f4 f6 (8...♘gxe5 9 ♘xe5 ♘xe5 10 ♗b5+ ±) and now 9 ♗b5! gives White an advantage.

7 ♕a4!

The point. At a stroke the queen's knight is pinned while the king's knight comes under attack. If now

7...♘h6, White maintains a clear extra pawn with 8 b4 or 8 ♗e3.

7	...	h5
8	h3	♘h6
9	♗e3	♘f5
10	♗d4	

Even though the bishop acts like a pawn, it has an important role. It protects c5 and e5, which allows White to bring out the rest of the forces with impunity.

| 10 | ... | ♗d7 |
| 11 | ♗b5 | g5?! |

An ambitious measure to induce complications by preparing g4. On 11...a6 comes 12 ♗xc6 ♗xc6 13 ♕c2 ♘xd4 14 cxd4 b6 15 cxb6 ♕xb6 16 0-0 with a clear advantage to White.

| 12 | ♘bd2 | ♖h6 |
| 13 | 0-0-0 | g4 (103) |

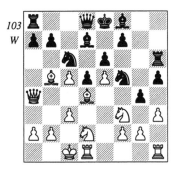

103
W

14 ♘e1!

It is wise to resist 14 hxg4 hxg4 15 ♖xh6 ♗xh6 16 ♘e1 when Black has relieved the pressure by exchanging the dormant rook. After the text White has the benefit of choosing the right moment for hxg4, while Black would have trouble justifying ...gxh3 which allows White to double rooks on the h-file.

14	...	a6
15	♗xc6	♗xc6
16	♕c2	♕c7

Black's wretched position is rather passive. The main concern is to restore material equality by capturing on c5.

| 17 | ♘d3 | ♗b5 |
| 18 | ♘f4 | 0-0-0 |

If Black plays 18...♗xc5, White gains material by 19 ♘xd5 exd5 20 ♗xc5.

| 19 | g3! | ♔b8 |

The same idea to the previous note applies: 19...♗xc5 20 ♗xc5 ♕xc5 21 hxg4 hxg4 22 ♖xh6 ♘xh6 23 ♕h7 ±.

20	♘b3	♗e7
21	hxg4	hxg4
22	♖xh6	♘xh6
23	♔b1	

The situation has clarified. White has firmly secured c5 and Black has few prospects of counterplay.

23	...	♘f5
24	♖h1	♗g5
25	♘g2!	

With this manoeuvre, White starts an infiltration on the kingside.

25	...	♕c8
26	♖h5	♖g8
27	♕d1	♗e7
28	♘e3	

A logical reaction to trade the knight which covers the pivotal square d4.

28	...	♘xe3
29	♗xe3	♗e8
30	♔a1	♔a8
31	♕d4!	(104)

In view of the intended c6 to threaten mate, Black is obliged to go further on the defensive.

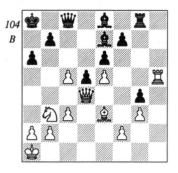

31	...	♗d8
32	♖h7	♕c6
33	♘c1	

White's superiority is such that there is plenty of time to relocate the knight to d3, as the central role allows it to protect c5 and threaten ♘b4.

33	...	a5
34	♘d3	♗e7
35	b3	♔b8
36	♔b2	

The king slightly improves its position in preparation for an eventual b4.

36	...	♕a6
37	a4	♔c8
38	♔c2	♗d8
39	♔d2	f6?!
40	exf6	♗g6
41	♖g7	1-0

7 Kupreichik Variation

The system that is signified by 5 ♗e3 is known as the Kupreichik Variation. For a long time it has been regarded as a doubtful continuation, with Lewis in 1835 suggesting 5...♕b6, ...♗d7 and ...♖c8 as the antidote. In modern tournament practice the Byelorussian is predestined to add his name to the line, due to his large number of games that have proved it to be a viable weapon. The primary idea is to avoid the main lines by delaying the development of the king's knight.

Game 35
Kupreichik-Farago
Passau 1993

1	e4	e6
2	d4	d5
3	e5	c5
4	c3	♘c6

5 ♗e3 *(105)*

A committal but solid continuation. It looks rather simplistic to over-protect d4 with the bishop but there is no clear way for Black to take advantage of the situation. Now Black is obliged to enter relatively

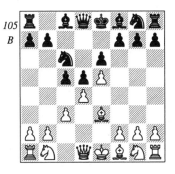

unknown territory as early as move five.

The other rare moves should be quite harmless:

a) 5 f4 cxd4 (5...♕b6 6 ♘f3 ♘h6! 7 b3 cxd4 8 cxd4 ♗b4+ 9 ♔f2 ♘f5 10 ♗b2 h5 ∓ Cohnen-Harberditz, 1940) 6 cxd4 ♕b6 7 ♘f3 ♗d7 8 ♘c3 ♖c8 9 ♖b1 ♗b4 10 ♕d3 a6 11 a3 ♗e7 12 b4 ♘a6 13 ♗e3 ♘f5 14 ♗f2 ♘a7 15 g4 ♘b5? 16 ♘a4 +− Capablanca-Paredes, Havana 1901.

b) 5 ♕g4 cxd4 6 cxd4 ♕b6 7 ♘f3 ♘h6 8 ♕f4 ♘f5 9 ♗d3 ♘cxd4 −+ Weiss-Haberditz and Kellner, corr. 1933.

c) 5 ♘e2 f6 6 f4 fxe5 7 dxe5 ♘h6 8 ♘g3 ♗d7 9 ♗e2 ♕b6 10 0-0 0-0-0 11 c4?! ♘d4 12 f5 ♘hxf5 13 ♘xf5

exf5 14 cxd5 ♗a4 15 b3 (15 ♕xa4
♘xe2+ 16 ♔h1 ♘xc1 17 ♖xc1 ♖xd5
–+) 15...♘xe2+ 16 ♕xe2 ♗b5 17
♕f3 ♗xf1 18 ♔xf1 ♕b5+ 19 ♔f2
♕b4 20 ♗e3 f4! 21 ♕g4+ ♖d7 22
♗xf4 h5 23 ♕f3 ♖f7 0-1 Romero
Holmes-Korchnoi, Pamplona 1990.

5	...	♕b6
6	♕d2	cxd4

The backbone of the variation
rests on its ability to deal with the
flexible 6...♗d7. Kupreichik has for-
mulated a way to handle the situation
by making the most of the deployment of the queen and bishop. After
7 ♘f3 play might proceed:

a) 7...♖c8 8 dxc5 ♗xc5 9 ♗xc5
♕xc5 10 ♕g5 ♘ge7!? (10...♔f8 ±)
11 ♘bd2 (11 ♕xg7?! ♖g8 12 ♕xh7
d4! ∓) 11...0-0 12 ♗d3 ♕b6!?
(12...f6? 13 exf6 ♖xf6 14 ♘e4 ±;
12...h6 13 ♕g3 ±) 13 ♗xh7+ ♔xh7
14 ♕h5+ ♔g8 15 ♘g5 ♖fe8! 16
♕f7+ ♔h8 17 ♕h5+ ♔g8 18 ♘df3
(18 0-0 ♘xe5!) 18...♕b5! (18...♕xb2
19 ♕h7+ ♔f8 20 0-0 with unclear
play) 19 0-0-0 (19 ♖d1 d4! 20 cxd4
♘b4!; 19 ♕h7+ ♔f8 20 ♕h8+ ♘g8
21 ♕h5 ♘h6 22 ♘h7+ ♔e7 23
♕h4+ ♔f7 24 ♘f6 ♘f5! with unclear play) 19...♕c4! 20 g3 ♕a2 =
Kupreichik-Dolmatov, Yugoslavia
1992.

b) 7...cxd4 8 ♗xd4!? (8 ♘xd4
♘xe5 9 ♘b5 ♗c5; 8 cxd4 ♗b4
{8...♖c8 9 a3? ♘a5 10 ♖a2 ♕b3 11
♘c3 ♖xc3! 12 bxc3 ♕b1+ –+ Mor-
ris-Schaffner, Bern 1991} 9 ♘c3

♘a5 10 ♖c1 ♖c8 is unclear) 8...♘xd4
9 ♘xd4 ♘e7 10 ♗d3 ♘c6 11 ♘f3
with unclear play.

c) 7...f6 8 ♗d3 fxe5 9 ♘xe5 (9
dxe5?! ♘h6 10-0-0 ♘f7 11 ♗f4 ♗e7
12 ♖e1 0-0-0 ∓ Westerinen-Ulybin,
Benidorm 1993) 9...♘f6 10 0-0 ♗d6
11 f4 0-0 and the position is equal
according to Ulybin and Lysenko.

7	cxd4	♘ge7
8	♗d3	♘f5

Staking a claim to central territory
and simultaneously putting pressure
on d4.

9	♘c3	♗b4
10	♘ge2	

White now reveals his intention to
plant the knight on e2 rather than the
usual f3. This has the benefit of supporting c3 and introduces the possibility of advancing the kingside
pawns.

10	...	♗d7
11	0-0	♘ce7

Not 11...0-0 12 ♗xf5 exf5 13
♘xd5 ♗xd2 14 ♘xb6 ♗xe3 15
♘xd7 +–.

12 a3

With his development completed
White undertakes action to put pressure on Black, initially by forcing
the trade of the bishop.

12	...	♗xc3
13	bxc3	0-0
14	♖ab1	♕c7
15	♗g5	

This is the type of position White
was aiming for with 5 ♗e3. Unlike

other Advance positions, the knight on e2 opens up different possibilities, while Black has already made a limited concession by transferring the queen's knight to the kingside as an extra defensive measure. The transparent threat of 16 g4 is sufficient to start a strong initiative on the flank.

15	...	h6
16	♗f4	♘g6
17	♗xf5	exf5 *(106)*

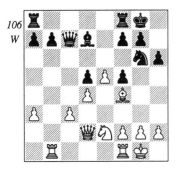

18 ♗xh6!

In a seemingly peaceful position White decides to lash out with a bold sacrifice. The reasoning is that the lack of co-ordination amongst Black's pieces allows the slow ♘g3-h5 to be a powerful menace to the exposed king.

18	...	gxh6
19	♕xh6	♕c6
20	♕g5	

The immediate 20 ♘g3 fails to 20...♘xe5, so a more restrained response is required, which also introduces the prospect of h4.

20	...	♔h7
21	♘g3	b6

After 21...f6!? 22 exf6 ♖xf6 23 ♘h5 (23 ♖xb7 ♕xb7 24 ♕xf6 ♖f8 is unclear) 23...♖f7 24 f4 ♖g8 25 ♖f3 ♘e7 the position is unclear according to Kupreichik.

22	♘h5	♖h8
23	h4	

With this move White shows that, although he has no immediate mate threat, Black is paralysed to the extent that the attack can at least restore material equality.

23 ♕f6 is refuted by 23...♔h6!.

23	...	♗e6
24	♖bc1	♕c4
25	♖fe1	♕d3
26	♖e3	♕d2
27	♖f1	

A necessary precaution to prevent Black's queen becoming a nuisance.

27	...	♖ac8
28	♘f6+	♔g7
29	h5	♖h6

Unfortunately for Black, 29...♖xc3 allows 30 hxg6 fxg6 31 ♘g4! fxg4 32 ♕f6+ ♔h7 33 ♕xe6 ♖xe3 34 ♕f7+ ♔h6 35 ♕f4+ g5 36 ♕f6+ ♔h7 37 ♕f7+ ♔h6 38 fxe3 which Kupreichik assesses as winning for White.

30	hxg6	♖xg6
31	♘h5+	♔f8
32	♕h4	

The situation has become much clearer. White enjoys a superior pawn structure, an extra pawn and the attack is still raging. Black has to contend with sheltering the exposed king while trying to maximize the value of his active queen.

32	...	♖g4
33	♕f6	♖g6
34	♕h4	♖g4
35	♕h2	

Having conducted a little dance with the queen for the benefit of the clock, White is obliged temporarily to retreat.

35	...	♖e4
36	♖xe4	

There is a more precise way to preserve the initiative: 36 ♘f4!? ♖xe3 37 ♘xe6+ fxe6! 38 ♕h8+ ♔e7 39 ♕xc8 ♖xc3 40 ♕b7+ ♔f8 41 ♕b8+ ♔g7 42 ♕xa7+ ♔f8 43 ♕xb6 ♖c1 44 ♕d8+ ♔g7 45 ♕f6+ ♔h7 46 ♕h4+ ± Kupreichik.

36	...	fxe4
37	♘f4	♖c6

Kupreichik points out that Black can put up a stout defence by means of 37...♖xc3! (37...e3 38 ♘e6 ±) 38 ♕h8+ ♔e7 39 ♕f6+ ♔d7 40 ♘xe6 (40 ♘xd5 ♗xd5 41 ♕d6+ ♔e8! 42 ♕xd5 e3! =) 40...fxe6 41 ♕f7+ ♔d8 42 ♕xe6 ♕xd4 43 ♕d6+ ♔c8 44 e6 e3 with an unclear position.

38	♕h4	♔e8

It is necessary to avoid the deadly 39 ♕d8+ ♔g7 40 ♕g5+ ♔h7 41

♘xe6 with a discovered attack on the queen.

39	♘h5	♔d7
40	♘f6+	♔c7
41	♘e8+	♔b7
42	♕e7+	♔a6
43	♘d6	♖xd6
44	exd6	e3 *(107)*

White's extra exchange gives him a clear advantage. A forlorn gesture to prolong the game by a series of checks is Black's best chance, but faced with a strong passed pawn the prospects for a draw are bleak. The game concluded as follows: 45 fxe3 ♕xe3+ 46 ♔h2 ♕h6+ 47 ♔g3 ♕g6+ 48 ♔f2 ♕c2+ 49 ♔g1 ♕xc3 50 ♕h4 ♕xa3 51 ♕f4 ♕a4 52 ♖c1 ♔b5 53 ♕f1+ ♔b4 54 ♕e1+ ♔b5 55 ♕e2+ ♔a5 56 ♕b2 ♕b4 57 ♖a1+ ♔b5 58 ♕xb4+ ♔xb4 59 ♖xa7 ♔c4 60 d7 1-0.

8 White Deviations on Move Four

It was Nimzowitsch who first proposed the daring sortie 4 ♕g4 in an effort to disrupt Black's development by attacking g7. The drawback is that the queen can become a target and the pawn chain to support e5 is broken.

The intention of 4 ♘f3 is to develop rapidly while preserving e5 in an effort to restrict the activity of the opposing forces. It has been adopted by a number of players who have a penchant for aggressive off-beat lines such as Hodgson and Velimirović.

With 4 dxc5 White conjures up an ambitious attacking scheme. It was originally promoted by Steinitz and attracted the attention of Keres and Reshevsky.

These three options are usually employed as surprise weapons.

Game 36
Hector-King
London 1991

1	e4	e6
2	d4	d5
3	e5	c5

4 ♕g4   ♘c6

The immediate 4...cxd4 tends to transpose to the game, although there is an independent line: 5 ♘f3 f5!? 6 ♕g3 ♘c6 7 ♗d3 ♗d7 8 0-0 ♕c7 9 ♖e1 (9 a3 intending b4 is a suggestion by *ECO*) 9...♘ge7 10 a3 0-0-0 11 b4 h6 12 h4 g6? 13 ♘bd2 ♔b8 14 ♘b3 ± Basman-van Seters, Bognor Regis 1964.

5 ♘f3   cxd4

The unusual move 5...♕a5+ has been tested: 6 c3 cxd4 7 ♘xd4 f5 (7...♘xe5 8 ♕g3! intending ♗f4 and ♘b5) 8 ♕d1 ♘xd4 9 ♕xd4 ♘e7 10 ♗f4 ♘c6 11 ♕d2 ♗e7 12 ♗d3 0-0 13 0-0 ♗d7 14 ♕e2 ♕c7 15 ♖e1 ♖f7 16 ♗c1 f4 17 ♘d2 g5 18 b4 ♖g7 19 ♘b3 ♖f8 20 f3 ♗e8 21 ♗b2 a6 22 a4 ♗g6 23 ♗xg6 ♖xg6 24 b5 ♘a5 25 ♘xa5 ♕xa5 ½-½ Hector-Dokhoian, Copenhagen 1991.

The decision to exchange knights on d4 also offers Black no advantage: 5...♘ge7 6 ♗d3 ♘xd4 7 ♘xd4 cxd4 8 0-0 ♘c6 9 ♖e1 ♕c7 10 ♗f4 ♕b6 11 ♘d2 ♘b4 12 a3 ♘xd3 13 cxd3 ♗d7 14 ♖ec1 ♗b5 15 ♕g3 ♕a6 16 ♘b3 ± Turci-Bukal, Reggio Emilia 1987/88.

6 &d3 *(108)*

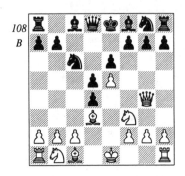

6 ... g6?!

A rather passive continuation, allowing White to support the strong-point of e5. The idea of the text is to blunt an attack against g7 while making room for the bishop to put pressure on e5. The whole process is too slow and compromises the king-side pawn structure.

There are a number of options available, but the critical line is to instigate immediate threats to e5:

a) 6...&ge7 7 0-0 &g6 8 &e1 &c7 9 &g3 &c5 10 h4 ± Nimzo-witsch-Szekely, Kecskemet 1927.

b) 6...f5 7 &g3 and now:

b1) 7...&ge7 8 0-0 &g6 9 h4 &c7 10 &e1 &d7 11 a3 0-0-0 12 b4 a6 13 h5 &ge7 14 &d2 h6 15 a4 g5 16 b5 f4 17 &g4 &b8 18 c3 &e8 19 cxd4 &d8 20 &c1 &b6 21 a5 &a7 22 b6 &a8 23 &c7 &f5 24 &c3! &e7 25 &xd5 &xd4 26 &xd4 exd5 27 &xd7+! 1-0 Nimzowitsch-Håkansson, Kristianstad 1922.

b2) 7...&d7 8 0-0 &ge7 9 h4 &c7 10 &e1 h6 11 &bd2 0-0-0 12 &b3 a6 13 &d2 &b8 14 &c5 &c8 15 &xd7+ &xd7 16 &ab1 &b6 17 b4 &c4 18 b5 axb5 19 &xb5 &f7 20 &eb1 &d7 21 &c1 &e7 22 &b2 g5 23 &xc4 gxh4 24 &h3 dxc4 25 &xd4 &xd4 26 &xd4 &g8 27 &f3 &f8 28 &e3 &g7 29 &a5 &g6 30 &a7+ &c8 31 &c5 &d5 32 &a8+ 1-0 Trapl-Backwinkel, Bundesliga 1992.

c) 6...&c7! 7 0-0 (7 &f4 &b4 8 &xd4 &xd3+ 9 cxd3 &b6! 10 &b3? &b4+ 11 &1d2 g5! 0-1 Smolkin-Matiukhin, corr. 1988) 7...&xe5 8 &xe5 &xe5 9 &f4 &f6!? (9...&f6 10 &g5 &e5 11 &d2 with unclear play according to Short) and now:

c1) 10 &xe5 &xg4 11 &xd4 &d6 ∓.

c2) 10 &g3 &h5 ∓.

c3) 10 &b5+ &d7 11 &xd7+ &xd7 12 &g3 &f5! intending ...&h5 gives Black a clear advantage.

7 0-0 f5

It is now clear that the simple &e1 and &f4 will safeguard e5, so Black decides to try to limit the scope of the queen.

8 &g3 &b6

Black is keen to lend support to the extra pawn. However, White is in no hurry to restore material equality, but instead intends to complete development and further compromise the opposing kingside with the thrust h4.

9	a3	a5
10	c3 *(109)*	

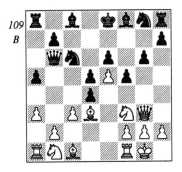

Now that Black has been induced to play 9...a5, White is eager to post a knight on b5 as ...a6 is not an option. Also, the threat to invade on d6 would disrupt Black's efforts to employ his dormant kingside pieces.

10	...	♗d7
11	h4	

A familiar feature of the Advance Variation is this pawn thrust, which seeks to add pressure to the attack by keeping open the option of h5.

11	...	♘h6
12	a4	♘g4
13	♘a3	♗g7
14	♗f4	

The plan for White is relatively straightforward with the knight heading for b5 and a desire to oust the intruding knight on g4. The main theme is to secure e5, which will act as a pivot for the rest of White's forces. Black has to rely on the extra pawn as compensation for the lack of co-ordination amongst his forces, which is largely due to the lack of space to manoeuvre.

14	...	0-0

The pawn is taboo because after 14...♕xb2? the reply 15 ♘b5 0-0 16 ♖fb1 picks up the queen.

15	♘b5	dxc3
16	bxc3	♕c5 *(110)*

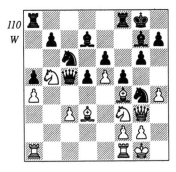

17	♖fe1	

The e-pawn requires extra reinforcements because the king's knight must move to facilitate f3, which would further force Black on to the defensive.

17	...	♘d8
18	♘fd4	♘f7
19	♖ac1	♖ae8
20	f3	♘gxe5?

A more prudent try is 20...♘gh6, although Black remains congested with little chance of counterplay.

21	♖xe5	♘xe5
22	♗xe5	f4
23	♕e1	♖e7
24	♗d6	1-0

Game 37
Short-Bareev
Tilburg 1991

1	e4	e6
2	d4	d5
3	e5	c5
4	♘f3	cxd4
5	♗d3	*(111)*

White can also follow a different path:

a) 5 ♘xd4 ♘c6 6 ♘f3 ♘ge7 7 ♗d3 ♘g6 which is assessed as equal by Pachman.

b) 5 ♕xd4 ♘c6 6 ♕f4 and now:

b1) 6...f5 7 ♗d3 ♘ge7 8 0-0 ♘g6 9 ♕g3 ♗e7 10 ♖e1 0-0 11 a3 ♘b8?! 12 ♘bd2 a5 13 ♘b3 ♘a6 (Keres-Euwe, Zanvoort 1936) 14 ♗xa6 ♖xa6 15 ♗g5 ±.

b2) 6...♕c7 7 ♘c3 a6 8 ♗d3 ♘ge7 9 0-0 ♘g6 10 ♕g3 ♘gxe5 11 ♘xe5 ♘xe5 12 ♖e1 f6 13 ♘xd5! exd5 14 f4 ♗c5+ 15 ♔h1 ♗e6 16 fxe5 f5 17 ♗e3 with a small advantage for White; Velimirović-Kholmov, Yugoslavia-USSR 1975.

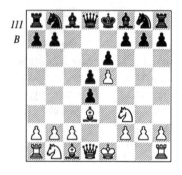

5 ...   ♘e7

This is an unusual move which prepares 6...♕b6 as a strong reply to 6 ♗f4, when it would not be so easy for White to justify jettisoning the b-pawn. The move-order difference is important because, compared to normal lines, it is more difficult for White to develop swiftly:

a) 5...♘c6 6 0-0 and now:

a1) 6...♘ge7 7 ♗f4 ♘g6 8 ♗g3 (8 ♗xg6!?) 8...♗e7 9 ♘bd2 (9...0-0 10 ♘b3 ♖e8 11 ♖e1 ♕b6 12 h4 ♘b4 13 ♗f1 d3 14 cxd3 ♗d7 15 h5 ♘f8 16 a3 ♘c6 17 d4 ± Heyken-Geveke, Bundesliga 1992) 9...f5 with a further division:

a11) 10 exf6 gxf6 11 ♘h4! ♘ge5 12 ♕h5+ ♔d7 13 ♗b5! ♕e8 14 ♕e2 a6 15 ♗xc6+ ♘xc6 16 c4! dxc3 17 bxc3 ♕f7 18 ♖ad1 ♖d8 19 ♘c4 ♗c5 20 ♘e3 ♘e7 21 ♔h1 ♔e8 22 c4 with an edge for White; Spraggett-M.Gurevich, Havana 1986.

a12) 10 h3 0-0 11 ♖e1 ♘h4 12 ♗xh4 ♗xh4 13 ♘b3 ♗d7 14 ♘xh4 ♕xh4 15 ♗b5 ♖ac8 16 ♗xc6 ♖xc6 17 ♘xd4 ♖c4 18 c3 b5 19 a3 a5 20 ♕d3 ♖fc8? 21 ♘xf5 1-0 Hodgson-Ree, Wijk aan Zee 1986.

a2) 6...f6 7 ♕e2 fxe5 (7...♕c7 8 ♗f4?! {8 ♗b5!?} 8...g5! 9 ♗g3 g4 10 ♘h4 f5 11 f3 ♘h6 12 ♘d2 ♗g7 ∓ Bryson-Züger, Manila OL 1992; 7...f5 8 ♘bd2 ♘ge7 9 ♘b3 ±) 8 ♘xe5 ♘xe5 9 ♕xe5 ♘f6 10 ♗f4 ♗c5 11 ♗b5+ ♔f7 12 ♘d2 ♗d7 13 ♗d3 g6 14 ♘f3 ♖e8 15 ♕g5 ♘h5 16

♗xg6+ hxg6 17 ♘e5+ ♔g8 18
♕xg6+ ♘g7 19 ♕f7+ ♔h8 20 ♗h6
♖g8 21 ♘xd7 ♗e7 22 ♘e5 ♗f6 23
♖fe1 1-0 Bator-Ottenklev, Stockholm 1986.

a3) 6...f5 7 ♘bd2 ♘ge7 (7...♗c5
8 a3 a5 9 ♘b3 ♗b6 10 ♗b5 ♗d7 11
a4 ♘ge7 12 ♘bxd4 = Trapl-Müller,
Bundesliga 1991/92) 8 ♘b3 ♘g6 9
♘bxd4 (Keres suggested that 9 ♖e1
♗e7 10 ♘bxd4 0-0 11 c4 is slightly
better for White) 9...♗e7 10 ♗b5
♗d7 11 c4 a6 12 cxd5 axb5 13 dxc6
bxc6 14 ♕b3 ♕c8 15 ♗g5 h6 16
♗xe7 ♔xe7 17 ♖fc1 ♕b7 18 h4
♖hc8 19 h5 ♘f4 20 ♘xf5+ exf5 21
♕b4+ c5 22 ♕xf4 ± Binham-Hajek,
Vienna 1991.

a4) 6...g6 7 a3 ♗g7 8 ♗f4 ♘ge7
9 ♕c1 0-0 10 b4 a6 11 ♖e1 f6 12
exf6 ♗xf6 13 ♘bd2 ♕e8 14 ♘b3
♕f7 15 ♕d2 ♖e8 16 ♖e2 ♕g7 17
♖ae1 b6 18 ♗g5 with a slight plus
for White; Kobelev-Lobach, USSR
1988.

a5) 6...♗c5 7 ♗f4 (7 ♘bd2 ♘ge7
8 ♘b3 ♗b6 9 ♗f4 ♘g6 10 ♗g3 intending 11 h4 is slightly better for
White according to Keres) 7...♘ge7
8 ♘bd2 ♘g6!? 9 ♗g3 ♗d7 10 ♘b3
♕b6 11 ♖e1 ♖c8 12 h4 ± Spraggett-
I.Ivanov, Canada 1986.

a6) 6...♕b6 7 ♖e1 ♘ge7 8 a3
♘g6 9 h4 f6 10 exf6 gxf6 11 c4
dxc4 12 ♗xc4 e5 13 h5 ♘ge7 14
♘bd2 ♘f5 15 ♘e4 ♗e7 16 b4 ♗d7
with unclear play in the game Kin-
lay-Formanek, London 1977.

a7) 6...♗d7 7 ♗f4 (White can
follow the same plan as in the illustrative game, so Kogan-Djurhuus,
Oakham 1992 continued 7 ♖e1
♘ge7 8 a3 ♘g6 9 b4 ♕c7 10 ♕e2 f6
11 exf6 gxf6 12 b5 ♘ce7 13 ♘xd4
e5 14 ♕h5 0-0-0 15 ♘b3 ♔b8 16 a4
♖g8 17 a5 with an unclear position)
7...♖c8 8 ♘bd2 ♗b4 9 ♘b3 ♘xd3
10 ♕xd3 h6 11 ♘fxd4 a6 12 c3 ♘e7
13 ♗d2 ♘c6 14 f4 ♕b6 15 ♗e3 ♕c7
16 ♖ae1 ± Heur-Tonningen, Germany 1992.

b) 5...♕b6 6 0-0 and now:

b1) 6...♘d7 7 ♘bd2 ♘e7 8 ♘b3
♘c6 9 ♖e1 g6 10 ♗f4 ♗g7 11 ♕d2
0-0 12 h4!? ♕c7 (12...f6?! 13 exf6
♘xf6 14 ♗d6 ♖e8 15 ♗c5 ±) 13
♕e2 f6!? 14 exf6 ♕xf4 15 ♕xe6+
♖f7 16 fxg7 ♘de5!? 17 ♕e8+ ♔xg7
18 ♖xe5 ♗h3? (18...♖f8 19 ♕xf8+!
♔xf8 20 ♖xd5 was judged by Keres
to be better for White; 18...♗g4! 19
♕xa8 ♘xe5 20 ♘xe5 ♕xf2+ 21
♔h1 ♕xh4+ ½-½ Strauss-Müller,
West Germany 1964) 19 ♕xa8 ♘xe5
(19...♗xg2 20 ♖f5!) 20 ♕e8 ♘c6 21
♕xf7+ ♔xf7 22 ♘g5+ ♔f6 23
♘xh3 ♕xh4 24 ♖e1 g5 25 ♘d2 ♕h6
26 ♘f3 f4 27 ♘fg5 ♕h5 28 ♘xh7
♔g7 29 ♘f4 ♕h6 30 ♘g5 ♕d6 31
♘h5+ ♔f8 32 ♖e6 ♕b4 33 ♗g6
♘e7 34 ♖f6+ ♔g8 35 ♗h7+ 1-0
Keres-Ståhlberg, Warsaw 1935.

b2) 6...♘c6 7 a3 ♘ge7 8 b4 ♘g6
9 ♖e1 ♗e7 10 ♗b2 a5?! 11 b5 a4 12
♘bd2 ♘a7 13 ♗xd4 ♗c5 14 ♗xc5
♕xc5 15 c4 dxc4 16 ♘e4! ♕d5 17

♘d6+ ♔e7 18 ♘xc4 ♕c5 19 ♗xg6 hxg6 (19...♕xc4 20 ♕d6+ ♔e8 21 ♖ad1 fxg6 22 ♕d8+) 20 ♕d6+ ♕xd6 21 exd6+ 1-0 Nimzowitsch-Leonhardt, San Sebastian 1912.

6   0-0

White can also follow another course: 6 ♗f4 ♘d7 (as noted above, 6...♕b6 is logical) 7 0-0 ♘c6 8 ♘bd2 ♘c5 9 ♘b3 ♘xd3 10 ♕xd3 ♗e7 11 ♘fxd4 0-0 12 ♕g3 with equal chances; Heyken-Luther, Bundesliga 1990/91.

6   ...   ♘g6
7   ♖e1

Short has suggested 7 ♗xg6 hxg6 8 ♕xd4 ♘c6 9 ♕f4 as a way to obtain equal chances.

7   ...   ♘c6
8   a3?!

The start of a dubious plan to advance the queenside pawns and molest Black's queen's knight, in order to lessen the pressure on e5 and allow the d4 pawn to be captured.

A better scheme of action is 8 ♘bd2 and ♕e2.

8   ...   ♗d7
9   b4   ♕c7

There is no immediate concern about the effect of b5, so Black is content to pile up the pressure on e5.

10   ♕e2   ♗e7
11   b5   ♘a5
12   ♗g5?!

A distinctly ambitious attempt to instigate play on the kingside. It would be more sensible to keep faith

with the original plan by 12 ♘xd4, when Black would be only slightly better.

12   ...   ♘c4?!

Black misses a chance to fully exploit White's mistake. The critical reply is 12...♗xg5 13 ♘xg5 ♘c4 when another pawn leaves the board, giving Black a clear advantage.

13   ♗xe7   ♔xe7 *(112)*

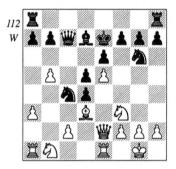

It is feasible to give up the right to castle in this position as the king is under no immediate danger and can seek sanctuary on f8 as soon as the king's rook has become centralized.

14   g3!

In his analysis to the game (upon which these notes are based) Short demonstrates the problems that arise after 14 ♗xc4 ♕xc4 15 ♕xc4 dxc4 16 ♘xd4 ♖hc8 17 a4 ♖c5 18 ♘f3 a6!; this is in Black's favour because of White's vulnerable queenside pawns.

14   ...   ♗xb5
15   h4

A more exact line is 15 ♘bd2! ♖hc8 (15...♘xd2 16 ♕xd2 ♗xd3 17 ♕b4+! with unclear play) 16 ♘xd4 ♗a6 17 ♘2f3 when Black has only slightly the better chances.

15 ... ♖hc8!
16 ♘bd2

After 16 h5, Black has a tactical reply available: 16...♘gxe5 17 ♘xe5 ♕xe5 18 ♗xc4 (18 ♕xe5 ♘xe5 19 ♖xe5 ♗xd3 20 cxd3 ♖c1+ 21 ♔g2 ♖ac8 −+) 18...♕xe2 19 ♗xe2 ♗a4! 20 ♘d2 ♗xc2 −+.

A superior try is 16 ♘xd4 ♗a6 17 f4 although Black still has an edge.

16 ... ♘xd2
17 ♕xd2 ♗xd3
18 cxd3 ♕c3

To a large extent Black has managed to snuff out White's resistance by exchanging pieces in an attempt to capitalize on the extra pawns. The White strategy is now to try to confuse matters with a kingside lunge.

19 ♕g5+ ♔f8
20 h5 h6!

The most precise way to fend off the attack; alternatively 20...♘e7? 21 h6 gives White good prospects against the exposed king.

21 ♕g4 ♘e7
22 ♘xd4 ♘c6
23 ♘b5 ♕xd3
24 ♘d6 ♖c7
25 ♖ad1 ♕a6
26 ♖xd5!? ♖d8

It is not advisable to snatch the rook due to 27 ♘f5 with mating

threats, but 26...♘xe5! seals White's fate. For example: 27 ♖exe5 exd5 28 ♘f5 ♕f6 or 27 ♖dxe5 ♕xd6 and in both cases the attack has fizzled out, leaving Black with a devastating pawn advantage.

27 ♖dd1 ♘xe5??

A remarkable move. Black overlooks a crafty response, so his whole game collapses.

The quieter 27...♖cd7 28 f4 ♕xa3 would have reaped greater dividends.

28 ♘f5! *(113)* **1-0**

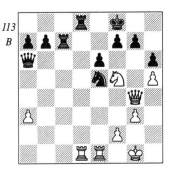

113
B

Bareev capitulates immediately; the finish would have been 28....exf5 (28...♘xg4 29 ♖xd8#) 29 ♖xd8+ ♔e7 30 ♕xg7 ♔xd8 31 ♕xe5 and White wins.

Game 38
J.Littlewood-Brooks
Manchester 1985

1 e4 e6
2 d4 d5

3 e5	c5
4 dxc5	♘c6 *(114)*

A necessary preliminary measure as other paths allow White the initiative:

a) After 4...♗xc5 5 ♕g4 ♘e7 6 b4 ♗b6 7 ♕xg7 Keres felt that Black had no compensation for the pawn.

b) 4...♘d7 5 ♘f3 ♗xc5 6 ♗d3 ♘e7 (after 6...f6?! Reshevsky analysed 7 exf6 ♘gxf6 8 ♕e2 ♕e7 9 ♗f4 0-0 10 0-0 with play on the e-file) 7 0-0 ♘c6 8 ♗f4 ♕c7 (8...0-0? 9 ♗xh7+ +−) 9 ♘c3 a6 10 ♖e1 ♕b6 11 ♗g3 ♕xb2 12 ♘xd5! exd5 13 ♖b1 ♕a3 14 e6 ♘f6 15 exf7+ ♔xf7 16 ♗h4 ± Reshevsky-Vasconcellos, Boston 1944.

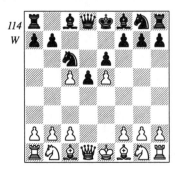

114
W

5 ♘f3

If 5 ♗f4 ♗xc5 6 ♗d3, 6...♘ge7 transposes to the illustrative game, but Harding pointed out a big improvement: 6...♕b6! 7 ♘c3 ♕xb2 8 ♘ge2 (8 ♘b5 ♘xe5! 9 ♘c7+ ♔d8 10 ♘xa8 ♘xd3+ wins for Black)

8...♕b6 9 ♖b1 ♕d8 10 0-0 and Black is better.

5 ...	♗xc5
6 ♗d3	♘ge7!?

Other possibilities are:

a) 6...f5 7 0-0 ♘ge7 8 a3 intending b4 and ♗b2 which is slightly better for White according to Keres.

b) 6...f6 7 ♕e2 fxe5 8 ♘xe5 and now:

b1) 8...♘f6 9 ♗f4 0-0 10 0-0 ♘e4 11 ♘xc6 bxc6 12 ♗e3 ♗xe3 13 ♕xe3 ♘f6 14 ♘d2 (Becker-Maroczy, Karlovy Vary 1929) 14...♕b6! 15 ♕e5 ♘g4 16 ♕h5 ♘f6 with equality (Becker).

b2) 8...♘xe5 9 ♕xe5 ♘f6?! (9...♕f6 = *BCO*) 10 ♗b5+ ♔f7 11 0-0 ♕b6 12 ♘c3 ± Nimzowitsch-Bogoljubow, Stockholm 1920.

7 ♗f4   ♗d7

Black has also attempted to wrest an initiative from the alternatives:

a) 7...♘g6 8 ♗g3 0-0 9 0-0 f5 10 exf6 ♕xf6 11 ♘c3 ♔h8 12 ♘e2 ♗b6 13 ♗xg6 ♕xg6 14 ♘f4 ♕g4 15 ♘d3 ♗d7 16 a4 ♗e8 17 ♘fe5 ♕f5 18 ♘xc6 bxc6 19 a5 ♗d8 20 ♖e1 ± Todorčević-van Setters, Nice OL 1974.

b) 7...♕b6 8 0-0 and now:

b1) 8...♕xb2 9 ♘bd2 ♕b6 10 c4 h6 (10...0-0? 11 ♗xh7+) 11 ♕c1 (intending 12 cxd5 exd5 13 ♖b1) 11...♘b4 12 ♗e2 ♗d7 13 a3 ♘a6 14 ♖b1 ♕c6 15 ♗g3! ♘f5?! 16 cxd5 exd5 16 e6! fxe6 18 ♘e5 ♘xg3 19 hxg3 ♕c7 20 ♘xd7 ♔xd7 21 ♕b2

♗b6 (21...♖hg8 22 ♖fc1! ♕b6 23 ♕c2 ♗xf2+ 24 ♔f1) 22 ♕xg7+ ♔d6 23 ♘c4+ dxc4 24 ♖fd1+ 1-0 Keres-Alexandrescu, Munich 1936.

b2) 8...♘g6 9 ♗g3 (Keres assessed the position after 9 ♕c1 ♘xf4 10 ♕xf4 ♕xb2 11 ♘bd2 as reasonable for White) 9...♕xb2 10 ♘bd2 ♘gxe5! 11 ♘xe5 ♘xe5 12 ♖b1 ♕c3 13 ♖b3 ♕d4 14 ♗b5+ ♘d7 15 ♗xd7 ♗xd7 16 ♖xb7 is unclear (Pachman).

	8	0-0	♘g6
	9	♗g3	♘b4
	10	♗e2	

The light-squared bishop is worth preserving for a future attack whereas the knight is soon ousted from its active post.

	10	...	♖c8
	11	♘c3	

White takes advantage of the omission of c3 to play the knight to a central post.

There was a still a chance to opt for a more usual set-up: 11 c3 ♘c6 12 ♗d3 0-0 14 ♘bd2 with a slight plus for White.

	11	...	♕b6
	12	a3	♘a6
	13	♗d3	♕xb2?! *(115)*

The moment of crisis has arisen. Black has followed a regular theme in this line by taking on b2. The problem is that White is already developed and an initiative can be gained by hounding the queen.

| | 14 | ♘b5! | |

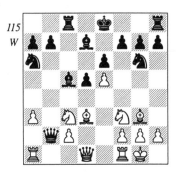

This is the point. To give his queen flight squares, Black must give up the right to castle.

	14	...	♗xb5
	15	♖b1	♕xa3
	16	♗xb5+	♔f8
	17	♘g5	♗e7

Black's pieces are too disorganized to present any coherent defence, for example 17...h6 18 ♘xe6+! fxe6 19 ♕g4 ♘e7 (19...♔f7 20 ♖b3 ♕a5 21 ♖f3+ ♔g8 22 ♕xe6+ ♔h7 23 ♗d3 +−) 20 ♖b3 ♕a5 21 ♕xe6 and ♖f3 wins.

	18	♖b3	♕c5
	19	♘xe6+!	fxe6
	20	♕g4	♖c6
	21	♖fb1	♔g8
	22	h4	

There is no hurry to start recovering the material deficit, so the h-pawn is used as a battering-ram to create further weaknesses.

	22	...	♘f8
	23	♖f3	h5
	24	♕f4	♘g6
	25	♕f7+	1-0

9 Wade Variation

It was Bob Wade in his match against Lothar Schmid in 1950 who introduced the manoeuvre 4...♕b6 and 5...♗d7 to exchange bishops. It has since had fluctuating periods of popularity with Karpov and Beliavsky being the most eminent players who have adopted it for occasional use. The most common reply is 6 ♗e2 intending to meet 6...♗b5 with the sharp 7 c4. A simpler method is explored in the game Kupreichik-Molner which examines a more positional approach.

Game 39
J.Wolf-Gerbić
Corr 1988

1	e4	e6
2	d4	d5
3	e5	c5
4	c3	♕b6
5	♘f3	♗d7
6	♗e2	♗b5

Psakhis has recommended the exchange 6...cxd4 to avoid the forthcoming complications. This method severely reduces Black's options and the best he can hope for is a drawish middlegame. After 7 cxd4 play might proceed:

a) 7...♗b5 and now:

a1) 8 0-0 ♗xe2 9 ♕xe2 ♘c6 (9...♕a6!? 10 ♕d1 ♘c6 11 ♗e3 h6 12 ♘bd2 ♘ge7 13 ♘b3 ♘f5 = Szitkey-Styblo, Czechoslovakia 1988) 10 ♗e3 ♘ge7 11 a3 ♘a5 12 b4 ♘c4 13 ♘bd2 ± Pietzsch-Czerniak, Varna OL 1962.

a2) 8 ♗xb5 ♕xb5 9 ♘c3 ♕a6 (9...♗b4 10 ♗d2 ♕d3 11 ♕a4 ♘c6 with unclear play; Kupreichik-Eingorn, USSR 1977) 10 ♘e2 ♗b4 11 ♗d2 ♗xd2 12 ♕xd2 ♘e7 13 0-0 0-0 14 ♖fc1 ♘bc6 15 ♘f4 ± Kupreichik-Kapengut, Minsk 1979.

b) 7...♗b4+ 8 ♘c3 ♗b5 9 0-0 ♗xe2 10 ♘xe2 ♘c6 11 ♕d3 h6 12 a3 ♗f8 13 b4 ± Hübner-Debarnot, Las Palmas 1976.

7 c4 *(116)*

It was Zaitsev who first advocated this move as a way for White to wrest the initiative.

7 ...   ♗xc4

This move has been accepted as the norm for years, since the other possibilities can cause Black problems:

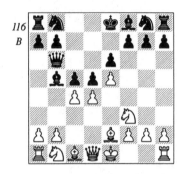

a) 7...♗c6 8 0-0 ♘d7 9 ♘c3 ♘e7 10 dxc5 ♗xc5 11 ♕c2 dxc4 12 ♘d2 ♘f5 13 ♘xc4 ♕d8 14 ♖d1 ♕h4 15 b4 ♘e4 16 ♘xe4 ♕xe4 17 ♕xe4 ♗xe4 18 a3 ♖d8 19 ♗g5 ± Yanovsky-Rohlmann, Moscow 1991.

b) 7...dxc4 8 ♘c3 (or 8 d5!?) 8...♘c6 9 d5 exd5 10 ♘xb5 ♕xb5 11 ♕xd5 ♘e7 12 ♕xc4 ± Nikolenko-Shaboian, Pula 1990.

8 ♗xc4   ♕b4+!

A refinement designed to improve on the old system that has scored heavily in White's favour. Play might instead continue 8...dxc4 9 d5 and now:

a) 9...exd5 10 ♕xd5 and now:

a1) 10...♕c6 11 ♕xc4 ♕a6 12 ♘a3 ♕xc4 13 ♘xc4 ♘c6 14 ♗f4 0-0-0 15 0-0 ♗e7 16 ♖fd1 ± Edelman-Bicknell, Los Angeles 1991.

a2) 10...♘e7 11 ♕e4 (11 ♕xc4 ♕b4+ 12 ♘bd2 ♕xc4 13 ♘xc4 ♘ec6 14 ♗e3 ♘b4 15 ♔e2 = I.Horvath-Hetenyi, Hungary 1992) and now:

a21) 11...♘d7 12 0-0 ♕c6 13

♕xc4 ♘b6 14 ♕e2 ♘ed5 15 a4! ± Zaitsev-Doda, Riga 1968.

a22) 11...♕c6 12 ♕xc4 ♕a6 13 ♘a3 ♕xc4 14 ♘xc4 ♘f5 (14...♘ec6 15 ♗f4 ♘d4!? with unclear play) 15 b3 ♘c6 16 ♗b2 ♗e7 17 0-0-0 0-0 18 g4 ♘h4 19 ♘xh4 ♗xh4 20 ♖hf1 f5 21 gxf5 ♖xf5 22 ♖d7 ± Zlotnik-Scherbakov, Moscow 1968.

b) 9...♘e7 10 dxe6 fxe6 11 0-0 ♕c6 12 ♕e2 ♘f5 13 ♕xc4 ♗e7 14 ♘c3 0-0 15 ♗g5 ♕a6 16 ♘b5 ♗xg5 17 ♘xg5 ♘d4 18 ♕xc5 ♘xb5 19 a4 ♘d7 20 ♕xb5 ♕xb5 21 axb5 ♘xe5 22 ♘xe6 ♖f6 23 ♘c7 ♖d8 24 ♖xa7 and White wins; Zaitsev–Bonch-Osmolovsky, USSR 1968.

9 ♘bd2   dxc4
10 a3

Not obligatory, as there have been experiments with 10 0-0:

a) 10...cxd4 11 ♘xd4 ♘d7 12 ♕h5! ♕b6 13 ♘4f3 ♕c6 14 ♖e1 ♘e7 15 ♖e4 ± Afek-Ghinda, Netanya 1987.

b) 10...♘c6 11 dxc5 ♗xc5 12 ♕e2 ♘ge7 13 ♘xc4 0-0 14 b3 ♕b5 = Malaniuk-Vaiser, Tashkent 1987.

10   ...   ♕a5 *(117)*

At this juncture the major alternative 10...♕b5 deserves attention:

a) 11 0-0 ♘c6 12 dxc5 ♗xc5 13 ♕e2 ♘ge7 and now:

a1) 14 ♕xc4 (14 b4?! ♘d4! with an edge for Black; Stean-Forintos, Moscow 1975) 14...♕xc4 15 ♘xc4 b5 16 ♗e3 bxc4 17 ♗xc5 ± Meshkov-Moroz, Podolsk 1990.

a2) 14 ♘xc4 ♘f5 15 b4 ♘cd4 16 ♘xd4 ♗xd4 17 ♖a2 0-0 18 ♗f4 ♖fd8 19 g4 ♘e7 20 ♘d6 ♕xe2 21 ♖xe2 ♘d5 22 ♗g3 ♖db8 23 ♖d2 ♗b6 24 ♖c1 a5 25 b5 a4 26 ♖c4 ♔f8 27 ♖d3 ♔e7 28 g5 ♖a5 29 ♖f3 ♖f8 30 ♖c8 ♗d8 31 ♖xd8! 1-0 Galdunts-Gavrilov, USSR 1988.

b) 11 ♕e2 cxd4 (11...♘c6?! 12 ♘xc4 ♕a4 13 dxc5 ♗xc5 14 ♕e4! with a clear plus for White; Boey-Berta, corr. 1980) and now:

b1) 12 ♘xc4 ♕d5 13 b3 ♘c6 14 ♗b2 b5 15 ♘cd2 ♘ge7 16 a4 d3 with unclear play; M.Horvath-Rozkovec, Prague 1987.

b2) 12 ♘xd4 ♕d5 13 ♘4f3! (13 ♘2f3?! ♗c5 14 ♗e3 ♗xd4 15 ♗xd4 ♘c6 16 0-0-0 ♘ge7 17 h4 0-0 18 ♗c3 ♕b5 19 ♘g5 ∓ Ivell-Beliavsky, London 1985) 13...♘d7 14 ♘xc4 ♖c8 15 ♘e3 ♕e4 16 b4! ♘xe5 (16...♘e7!? 17 ♗b2 ♘d5 = Howell-Mestel, British Ch 1987) 17 ♘xe5 ♕xe5 18 ♗b2 ♕e4 19 0-0 ♘e7 20 ♖ac1 ± Pinter-Ornstein, Budapest 1977.

117
W

| 11 | 0-0 | ♘c6 |
| 12 | ♘xc4 | ♕a6 |

Zlotnik considers the position to be equal, but the evidence suggests otherwise.

13	♘d6+!?	♗xd6
14	exd6	cxd4
15	d7+!	♔e7

White could meet 15...♔xd7 by 16 ♘xd4 ♔e7 17 ♗d2 with advantage.

| 16 | ♘xd4 | ♘f6 *(118)* |

118
W

| 17 | ♘f5+! |

A brilliant tactical stroke. White invests a piece to expose the king, so the rest of the forces can use the influence of the d7 pawn to stage a daring attack.

| 17 | ... | exf5 |
| 18 | ♖e1+ | ♔d8 |

Black can fare no better with a different retreat, according to Wolf; 18...♔f8?! 19 ♕d6+ ♔g8 20 ♗h6! and now:

a) 20...♖f8 21 ♕xf6! gxf6 22 ♖e8 +–.

b) 20...♘e4 21 ♖xe4! fxe4 22 ♕g3 ♔f8 23 ♕xg7+ ♔e7 24 ♖d1 ♕d3 25 ♗g5+ ♔xd7 26 ♕xf7+ ♔d6 27 ♗f4+ ♔c5 28 ♖c1+ ♔b6 29 ♕c7+ ♔a6 30 ♖xc6+ bxc6 31 ♕xc6+ ♔a5 32 ♗c7#.

c) 20...♘xd7 21 ♕g3 g6 22 ♕c3 ♘6e5 23 ♖xe5 ♕f6 24 ♖ae1 ♘xe5 25 ♕xe5 ♕xe5 26 ♖xe5 +−.

19 ♗f4   ♘e7

The ploy of blocking the d-file appears to be strong but Black has an improvement on the text: 19...♕b6!? (19...♘xd7? 20 ♕d5 ♖e8 21 ♕xf7 +−) 20 ♕e2 ♕d4 (20...♔xd7? 21 ♕d3+ wins for White) 21 ♗g5 with unclear play.

20 ♖c1   ♘fd5

After 20...♘ed5 21 ♗g5 ♕d6 22 ♕b3 ♕xd7 23 ♗xf6+ gxf6 24 ♖c5 intending ♖d1 wins material.

21 ♖xe7!   ♘xf4

Of course, 21...♘xe7 allows 22 ♗c7#.

22 ♕e1   ♕d6

Wolf points out that there is no respite whatever obstacles Black constructs:

a) 22...♘g6 23 ♖e8+ ♔xd7 24 ♖e2 +−.

b) 22...♘e6 23 ♖xf7 ♕d6 (or 23...♕b6 24 ♕e5 h5 25 ♖e1 ♖h6 26 ♖f8+!) 24 ♖d1 ♕c6 25 ♕b4 ♕c5 26 ♕h4+ g5 27 ♕h6 ♕e5 28 f4! +−.

23 ♖xf7   ♕e6

The prospects for Black are bleak in every line:

a) 23...♘d3 24 ♕a5+ b6 (or 24...♕b6 25 ♕xf5 ♘xc1 26 ♕g5+ +−) 25 ♕xa7! ♖b8 26 ♖c8 ♖xc8 27 dxc8♕+! ♔xc8 28 ♕a6+ +−.

b) 23...♘g6 24 ♕a5+ ♕b6 25 ♕xf5 ♘e7 26 ♖c8+! +−.

c) 23...♖f8 24 ♕a5+ b6 25 ♖xf8+ ♕xf8 26 ♕e5 ♔xd7 27 ♖c7+ +−.

d) 23...b6 24 ♖c6! +−.

24 ♕a5+   b6 (119)

The swarming pieces cannot be rebuffed, for example 24...♕b6 25 ♕xf5 ♘e2+ 26 ♔f1 ♘xc1 27 ♕g5+ +−.

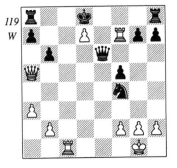

25	**♕xa7!**	**♕e1+**
26	**♖xe1**	**♖xa7**
27	**♖e8+**	**♖xe8**
28	**dxe8♕+**	**♔xe8**
29	**♖xa7**	**1-0**

Game 40
Kupreichik-Molnar
Gemer 1990

1	**e4**	**e6**
2	**d4**	**d5**

3 e5   c5
4 c3   ♕b6
5 ♘f3   ♗d7
6 ♗e2 *(120)*

The alternative treatments are useful as surprise weapons:

a) 6 a3 ♗b5 and now:

a1) 7 c4 ♗xc4 (7...♗c6?! 8 b4! cxb4 9 c5 ♕a5 10 ♗d2 ♗a4 11 ♕c1 ♗b5 12 axb4 ♕xa1 13 ♗xb5+ ♘c6 14 ♕c2 1-0 Fruteau-Roumegous, Paris 1993) 8 ♗xc4 dxc4 9 ♘bd2 ♕a6 10 ♕e2 cxd4 11 ♘xd4 ♗c5 12 ♘4f3 c3 13 ♘e4 ♕xe2+ 14 ♔xe2 cxb2 15 ♗xb2 ♘a6 16 ♖hd1 ♘e7 17 ♖ac1 b6 18 ♘d6+ ♔f8 19 ♘g5 h6 20 ♘gxf7 ± Sveshnikov-Ehlvest, Leningrad 1984.

a2) 7 ♗d3 ♗xd3 (7...♕a6?! 8 ♗c2 ♘d7 9 a4 ± Ciocaltea-Wade, Bucharest 1954) 8 ♕xd3 ♕a6 9 ♕xa6 ♘xa6 with equality; Toran-Heidenfeld, Venice 1953.

a3) 7 ♗xb5+ ♕xb5 8 dxc5 (8 ♕e2!?) 8...♗xc5 9 ♘bd2 ♘e7 10 c4 dxc4 11 ♕e2 ♘bc6 12 ♕xc4 ♕xc4 13 ♘xc4 ♘g6! 14 b4 b5 15 bxc5 bxc4 16 0-0 0-0 17 ♗e3 ♖fd8! 18 ♖fc1 ♘a5 ∓ Witkowski-Portisch, Munich 1958.

b) 6 ♘a3 and now:

b1) 6...♘c6 7 ♗e2 cxd4 8 cxd4 ♗b4+ 9 ♔f1 f6 (9...♘h6!? 10 ♘c2 ♗e7 11 ♗xh6 gxh6 12 ♖b1 f6 = Clarke-Heidenfeld, Ilford 1953) 10 ♘c2 fxe5 11 ♘xb4 ♘xb4 12 dxe5 ♗b5 13 a3 ♘c6 14 ♗e3 ♕a6 15 ♗xb5 ♕xb5+ 16 ♔g1 ♘ge7 17 b4

b6 18 ♘g5 ♘d8 19 ♖c1 ♕d7? 20 ♕h5+ g6 21 ♘xh7! +− Schmid-Wade, England (9) 1950.

b2) 6...cxd4 7 cxd4 ♗b4+ 8 ♗d2 ♘c6 9 ♘c2 a5 10 ♗d3 ♗xd2+ 11 ♕xd2 ♘b4 12 ♘xb4 ♕xb4 13 ♕xb4 axb4 14 ♔d2 ♘e7 = Kupreichik-Zlotnik, Cheliabinsk 1975.

c) 6 ♗d3 cxd4 and now:

c1) 7 cxd4 ♗b5 8 0-0 ♗xd3 (8...♕a6! =) 9 ♕xd3 ♘c6 10 ♘c3 ♘ge7 11 ♗d2 ± Natapov-Kolker, USSR 1968.

c2) 7 ♘xd4 ♘c6 8 ♘xc6 (8 ♘f3 f6! ∓) 8...bxc6 9 0-0 ♘e7 10 ♘d2 ♘g6 11 ♘f3 ♗e7 12 ♕e2 ♕c7 13 ♖e1 0-0 14 ♘g5 (15 h4 f5 ∓ Koch-Schmid, corr. 1951) 14...♗xg5 15 ♗xg5 ♕xe5 16 ♕xe5 ♘xe5 17 ♖xe5 f6 18 ♗xf6 gxf6 19 ♖h5 ♖f7 20 f4 ♖e8 21 ♖e1 ♖8e7 intending ...♗e8 and ...♖g7 with a slight advantage to Black according to Schmid.

d) 6 a4 ♘c6 7 ♗e2 c4 = Messere-Tarnovsky, London 1960.

e) 6 ♕b3?! ♘c6 7 ♗e3 cxd4 (7...♕xb3!) 8 ♕xb6 axb6 (Babrikowski-Espig, East German Ch 1976) 9 ♘xd4! with the idea 10 ♘b5 gives White the better game.

6 ...   ♗b5
7 dxc5

White abandons the pawn chain in order to gain space and strive for the initiative. Other paths are available:

a) 7 0-0 and now:

a1) 7...♘c6?! 8 ♗xb5 ♕xb5 9 a4

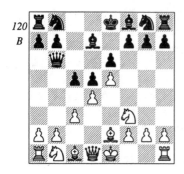

120
B

♕b6 10 dxc5 ♗xc5 11 b4 ♗f8 12
♖e1 ♘ge7 13 a5 ♕c7 14 ♕a4 ±
Pietzsch-Uhlmann, East Germany
1958.

a2) 7...♗xe2 8 ♕xe2 ♕a6 9 ♕d1
(9 ♕c2 ♘d7 10 ♗e3 ♖c8 11 ♘bd2
h6 12 a3 ♘e7 13 h4 ♘c6 14 ♖fe1
♗e7 15 ♘f1 0-0 16 ♕d2 ± Santana-
Turner, Pinar del Rio 1990) 9...c4
(after 9...♘d7, 10 ♘a3 ♘e7 11 dxc5
♘xc5 12 ♘d4 ♘c6 = was Netusil-
Alster, Czechoslovakia 1988, but
White can try for more with 10
dxc5!? ♘xc5 11 b4 ♘d3 12 ♗e3
♘b2 13 ♕b3 ♘c4 14 ♘bd2! ♘xe3
15 fxe3 ± Kaidanov-Zlotnik, Moscow 1979) 10 ♖e1 ♘c6 11 ♘bd2
0-0-0 12 ♘f1 ♖d7 13 ♗f4!? ♘ge7!
14 h4 h5 15 ♘g3 ♘g6 16 ♗g5 ♗e7
17 ♕d2 ♕b6 18 ♗xe7 ♖xe7 19 ♖e2
♕d8 20 ♘f1 f6 21 ♘1h2 fxe5 22
♘xe5 (Hecht-Karpov, Bath 1973)
22...♘gxe5 23 de ♖d7 =.

b) 7 ♘bd2!? ♗xe2 8 ♕xe2 cxd4
9 ♘xd4 ♘c6 10 ♘2f3 ♘xd4 11
♘xd4 ♗c5 12 ♘c2 ♕c6 13 ♕g4
♘e7 14 ♕xg7 0-0-0 15 ♗e3 ♘f5

16 ♕xf7 ♖d7 17 ♕h5 ♖g8 18 0-0-0
♗xe3+ 19 fxe3 ♖xg2 20 ♕f3 ♖dg7
21 ♖d2 ♖xd2 22 ♔xd2 ♕b5 23 ♔c1
with a slight plus for White; Braun-
Muhl, Bundesliga 1986/87.

c) 7 ♗e3!? ♗xe2 8 ♕xe2 ♘c6 9
dxc5 ♗xc5 10 ♗xc5 ♕xc5 11 ♘bd2
♘ge7 12 ♘b3 ♕b6 13 ♘bd4 0-0 14
0-0 ♖ae8 15 ♖ad1 = Pilgaard-Jo-
hansson, Lyngby 1988.

7   ...   ♗xc5
8   0-0

It used to be the accepted practice
to continue with the committal 8 b4,
which creates dynamic positions:

a) 8...♗f8 9 0-0 ♘d7 10 ♘a3
♗xe2 11 ♕xe2 a6 12 c4 ♘e7 13 ♗d2
± Widenmann-Berge, corr. 1983.

b) 8...♗e7 9 0-0 (9 ♗e3 ♕a6 10
♗xb5+ ♕xb5 11 ♘a3 ♕d7 12 0-0
h5 13 ♘d4! ♘c6 14 ♘ab5 a6 15
♘xc6 bxc6 16 ♘d4 c5 17 bxc5
♗xc5 18 ♖b1 ± Gonsior-Alster,
Czechoslovakia 1988) 9...♗xe2 10
♕xe2 ♘h6 11 a4 ♘f5 12 g4 (12
♘bd2!?) 12...♘h6 13 h3 ♘c6 14
♗f4 ♘g8 15 ♘bd2 h5 16 ♘b3 hxg4
17 hxg4 ♘h6 18 ♘fd2 ♖c8 19 ♖fc1
♕d8 20 b5 ♘b8 21 c4 dxc4 22 ♘xc4
♘d7 = Mestel-Small, Haifa 1976.

c) However, Black has found
new nuances to cause White difficul-
ties: 8...♗xf2+!? 9 ♔f1 ♗c6! (it was
formerly thought that the dark-
squared bishop would be trapped but
there is no forced win) and now:

c1) 10 c4?! dxc4 11 ♘a3 ♗d5 12
♘xc4 ♗xc4 13 ♗xc4 ♘c6 14 ♕e2

♗d4 15 ♖b1 ♘ge7 ∓ Nederkoorn-Kahn, corr. 1982.

c2) 10 ♕d2 d4! 11 ♔xf2 d3+ 12 ♕e3 ♕xe3+ 13 ♗xe3 dxe2 and Black is slightly better.

c3) 10 ♕d3 ♘e7 11 a4 a5 12 b5 ♗d7 with unclear play; Vanka-Matoušek, Prague 1986.

8	...	♗xe2
9	♕xe2	♕a6
10	♕c2	

The ending offers equal chances, so White prefers to avoid an exchange of queens in the hope of obtaining attacking chances with a queenside advance.

10	...	♘d7
11	a4	♖c8
12	a5	

Of course 12 b4? is refuted by 12...♗xb4 due to the pin on the c-file.

12	...	♕c6 *(121)*

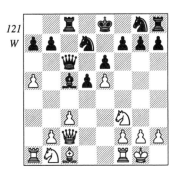

13 ♕e2

White's strategy is proceeding smoothly. He has expanded on the queenside to stifle the opposition, and the plan is to develop behind the pawn mass before striking out with a further advance. In the meantime, it is difficult for Black to create counterplay against such a solid pawn structure and instead he must concentrate on getting the rest of his forces into play.

13	...	a6
14	b4	♗a7
15	♘a3	♘e7

It is too risky to snatch the pawn. For example: 15...♕xc3?! 16 ♗d2 ♕c7 (16...♕b3? 17 ♖fb1 ♕a4 18 ♘c4 +−) 17 b5 ♗c5 18 bxa6 bxa6 19 ♕xa6 with a formidable passed pawn.

16	b5	axb5
17	♘xb5	♗c5
18	a6!	

A neat trick which takes advantage of the opposing king being left in the centre. Now after 18...bxa6 19 ♖xa6 ♕b7 (19...♕xa6 20 ♘c7+ +−) 21 ♗e3 White has the better chances.

18	...	0-0
19	a7	♖a8
20	♘fd4	

This manoeuvre spells trouble for Black. The knight is transferred to the queenside in an effort to exchange a defensive piece, which would increase the likelihood of making use of the mighty pawn on the seventh rank.

20	...	♕b6

| 21 | ♘b3 | ♘c6 |
| 22 | ♘xc5 | ♘xc5 (122) |

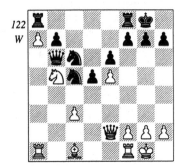

23 ♗a3

Astute tactical awareness. The a-pawn is jettisoned in order to unleash a winning combination based on the vulnerability of the pinned knight.

23	...	♘xa7
24	♕e3	♖fc8
25	♘d6	♖c7
26	♖fb1	♕c6

Black is overloaded with defensive duties and this can inevitably be exploited.

27	♗xc5	♕xc5
28	♕xc5	♖xc5
29	♖xb7	♖xc3
30	♔f1	1-0

10 Systems with ...b6

The choice of 3...b6 is a popular way of avoiding the main lines. It prepares to exchange Black's light-squared bishop, which normally has a restricted rôle in the French. This inevitably results in Black's development being retarded while the process is carried out, which can cause problems. With 3...♘e7 and 4...b6 Black is trying to avoid certain lines. The original idea was that the closed nature of the position would allow Black to activate the pieces at a later stage, but the current trends indicate that White gains too much territory to justify Black's passive opening.

Game 41
Anand-Rogers
Manila IZ 1990

1	e4	e6
2	d4	d5
3	e5	b6
4	♗b5+	(123)

A recent concept. The check is intended to disrupt Black's slow manoeuvring game.

| 4 | ... | ♗d7 |

123
B

At this juncture Black has experimented with 4...c6 5 ♗a4! when White has used his space advantage to maximum effect:

a) 5...a5 6 c3 and now:

a1) 6...♗a6 7 ♘e2 h5 8 ♘d2 ♘h6 9 ♘f3 ♘f5 10 ♗g5 ♗e7 11 h4 ♗xg5 12 hxg5 ♗xe2 13 ♕xe2 g6 14 ♗c2 0-0 15 0-0-0 c5 16 ♗xf5 exf5 17 e6! ♘c6 18 dxc5 bxc5 19 exf7 ♔xf7 20 ♕b5 1-0 Murey–Brinck-Claussen, Copenhagen 1986.

a2) 6...b5 7 ♗c2 c5 8 ♘f3 ♘c6 9 0-0 c4 10 ♖e1 h6 11 ♘bd2 ♘ge7 12 ♘f1 ♗d7 13 ♘e3 ♘c8 14 b3 cxb3 15 axb3 ♘b6 16 ♗d3 b4 17 c4 ♘e7 18 ♗d2 ♗c6 19 c5 ♘d7 20 ♖a2 ± Lein-Gonzales, Saint John 1988.

b) 5...♘e7 and now:

b1) 6 ♘e2 ♘f5 7 0-0 ♗e7 8 c3 ♗a6 9 ♖e1 ♔f8 10 ♘d2 c5 11 ♘f1 cxd4 12 cxd4 ♗xe2 13 ♖xe2 ♘a6 14 ♘e3 ♘xe3 15 ♗xe3 ♘c7 16 ♖c1 a6 17 ♖ec2 ♖a7 18 ♖c6 b5 19 ♕c2 ♘e8 20 ♖c8 ♕b6 21 ♗b3 h6 22 ♕c6 ♕xc6 23 ♖1xc6 ♗b4 24 ♖xe8+! 1-0 Marić-Mitrović, Belgrade 1989.

b2) 6 c3 ♘f5 7 ♘d2 ♗e7 8 ♘df3 ♗d7 9 ♗c2 ♘a6 10 h4 ♘c7 11 ♗g5 ♗c8 12 ♕d2 ♗a6 13 ♘e2 h6 14 ♗xe7 ♘xe7 15 h5 ♕d7 16 ♕f4 c5 17 ♘g3 ♖g8 18 0-0-0 0-0-0 19 dxc5! bxc5 20 ♘e4 ♕c6 21 ♘d6+ ♔b8 22 ♕xf7 and wins; Lein-Blees, Belgrade 1988.

5	♗d3	c5
6	c3	♘c6
7	♘f3	

As usual, the knight belongs on f3 to support d4.

7	...	f6

This is the only way to put pressure on White's position because the pawn on b6 has reduced Black's options.

8	0-0	fxe5
9	dxe5	

The most exact reply is 9 ♘xe5! ♘xe5 10 dxe5 when the threat of 11 ♕h5+ ensures that Black must compromise his kingside.

9	...	♕c7
10	♖e1	♘h6 *(124)*

After 11 ♗xh6 Black gains compensation for the doubled pawns because the open g-file is available for the rooks to start an attack.

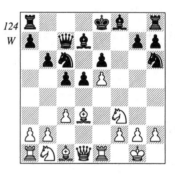

The natural continuation 10...♘e7 lands Black in dire straits: 11 ♘a3 a6 (11...♘c8 ±) 12 ♗xa6! ♖xa6 13 ♘b5 ♕b8 14 ♘d6+ ♔d8 15 ♘f7+ ♔e8 16 ♘xh8 +−.

11	c4	d4
12	♘a3	

In his analysis of the game (upon which these notes are based) Anand prefers a more forceful continuation: 12 ♗xh6 gxh6 13 ♘bd2 0-0-0 (not 13...♗g7 14 ♕e2 0-0? 14 ♕e4 +−) 14 a3 ±.

12	...	a6
13	♗e4	0-0-0

There is nothing to be gained from a delay in whisking the king to safety. For example: 13...♗e7 (13...♘f7 14 ♘g5!) 14 ♗xh6 gxh6 15 b4 cxb4 16 ♘b5! ±.

14	♘c2	♘f7
15	♗f4	

White proceeds in an acceptable manner by securing e5 – by now a familiar theme. However, the different circumstances that are apparent due to queenside castling suggest another approach: 15 b4 cxb4 16 a3 with unclear play.

15	...	♗e7
16	b4	g5
17	♗g3	g4?!

This is the logical conclusion of a brash plan to snatch e5, despite the deployment of White's forces in an attacking stance.

If Black had been more alert to the danger, then a way to deflect the on-slaught could have been pursued: 17...h5! 18 bxc5 bxc5! (18...h4 19 cxb6 ♕xb6 20 ♖b1 with unclear play) 19 h3 ♖dg8 intending 20...g4 21 hxg4 hxg4 22 ♘h2 ♗h4 when White is forced to embark upon defensive measures.

| 18 | ♘d2 | ♘cxe5 |
| 19 | a4! | (125) |

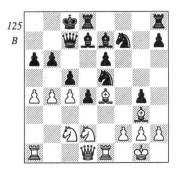

125
B

While Black is temporarily caught up in avoiding tactics based on the pinned knight, White reveals his true intentions. Now there is a concerted effort to disrupt the defensive pawn barrier.

| 19 | ... | cxb4 |

After 19...a5 20 bxa5 bxa5 21 ♖b1 the rook invades into the heart of Black's camp.

| 20 | a5! | bxa5 |
| 21 | ♘xd4 | |

With the pair of bishops bearing down on the queenside White is in the ascendancy. Anand prefers an even more stylish continuation to take advantage of the vulnerable knight on e5: 21 c5! ♗b5 (21...♗xc5 22 ♘c4 +–) 22 ♘b3 a4 23 ♘xb4! a5 24 ♘d3 ♗xd3 25 ♗xd3 axb3 26 ♗a6+ ♔d7 (26...♔b8 27 ♖xe5! +–) 27 ♗b5+ ♔c8 28 ♕xb3 ±.

21	...	♗c5
22	♘4b3	a4
23	♘xc5	♕xc5
24	♗c2	a5

Anand supplies the following variations to demonstrate White's superiority:

a) 24...a3 25 ♘e4 ♕c7 26 c5 ♗c6 27 ♘d6+ ♘xd6 28 cxd6 ♖xd6 29 ♕e2 +–.

b) 24...b3 25 ♗xb3 (25 ♘e4?! ♕b4 with unclear play) 25...axb3 26 ♘xb3! (26 ♕xb3 ♗c6) 26...♕xc4! (26...♕c7 27 ♖xa6 ♗c6 28 ♕a1 ♗b7 29 ♖a5 ±) 27 ♗xe5 (27 ♖c1 ♗c6) 27...♘xe5 28 ♖xe5 ♗a4 29 ♕e1 ♕xb3 (29...♗xb3 30 ♖c1 ♗c2 31 ♖e2!) 30 ♖c5+ ♔d7 31 ♖b1 ♕a2! 32 ♖a5 ♕c2 (32...♔e8? 33 ♖xa4!; 32...♔e7 33 ♕b4+; 32...♖b8 33 ♖a1 ±) 33 ♖xa6 ±.

| 25 | ♘e4 | ♕c7 |

26	♗xa4	♗c6
27	♕c2	♗b7
28	c5	♖d5

The demands on the defender are enormous. The text is designed to re-inforce e5, while 28...♔b8 fails to 29 ♘g5!.

29	♗b3	♖hd8
30	♖ac1!	

After 30 ♗xd5 ♖xd5 31 ♖ac1 ♕c6 Black can struggle on. The pre-ferred move-order will extinguish any lingering hopes for a revival.

30	...	♕c6
31	♗a4	♕c7
32	♘d6+	♖8xd6
33	cxd6	♕xc2
34	♖xc2+	♔b8
35	♗b3	♖xd6
36	♖xe5!	1-0

Game 42
Ivanović-Gonzales
Saint John 1988

1	e4	e6
2	d4	d5
3	e5	b6
4	c3	

Other moves are relatively in-nocuous:

a) 4 ♘h3 ♕d7 5 a4 ♗a6 6 ♗xa6 ♘xa6 7 ♗e3 ♘e7 8 0-0 ♘b8 9 a5 ♘bc6 10 axb6 cxb6 11 c3 ♘a5! 12 ♘a3 ♖c8 13 ♘c2 = Velimirović-Marić, Yugoslavia 1966.

b) 4 f4 ♘e7 5 ♘d2 ♕d7 6 ♘df3 ♗a6 7 ♗xa6 ♘xa6 8 c3 c5!? 9 ♕d3

♘b8 10 ♘e2 ♘bc6 11 0-0 h5 12 ♗d2 ♘f5 13 ♘g3 ♘ce7 14 ♘e2 c4 15 ♕c2 0-0-0 16 b3 f6 = Castro-Orn-stein, Budapest 1977.

c) 4 c4!? dxc4 5 ♗xc4 ♗b7 6 ♘f3 ♘e7 7 ♘c3 ♕d7 8 0-0 h6 9 ♕e2 ♘bc6 10 a3 ♘a5 11 ♗a2 ♘d5 12 ♗d2 ♘xc3 13 bxc3 c5 14 ♖ad1 c4 15 ♘e1 ♕d5 16 f4 g6 17 ♘c2 ± Zait-sev-Kärner, Sochi 1977.

d) 4 ♘f3 ♕d7 5 c4 ♗b4+?! 6 ♘c3 ♘e7 7 a3 ♗xc3+ 8 bxc3 dxc4 9 ♗xc4 ♗a6 10 ♘xa6 ♘xa6 11 0-0 c5 12 ♘g5 ♕d5? and 1-0 Hodgson-Ka-linin, Bath Z 1987.

4	...	♕d7

A necessary precaution in view of the elementary mistake 3...♗a6? 4 ♗xa6 ♘xa6 5 ♕a4+ which picks up a piece.

| 5 | h4 *(126)* | |

White prefers to expand rapidly on the kingside to take advantage of Black's slow manoeuvring game. Other possibilities are:

a) 5 f4 and now:

a1) 5...♗a6 6 ♗xa6 ♘xa6 7 ♕d3 ♘b8 8 ♘e2 g6 9 0-0 ♘e7 10 b3 h5 11 ♗a3 ♘f5 12 ♗xf8 ♔xf8 = Witkowski-Raisman, USSR 1958.

a2) 5...h5 6 f5?! exf5 7 ♘h3 c6 8 ♗d3 g6 9 0-0 ♗h6 10 ♘d2 ♘a6 11 ♘f3 ♘c7 12 c4 ♘e7 13 ♗xh6 ♖xh6 14 ♕d2 ♖h8 15 b4 dxc4 16 ♗xc4 ♕d8 17 ♘hg5 ♗e6 18 ♖ac1 ♗xc4 19 ♖xc4 ♕d5 20 ♖fc1 ♘e6 ∓ Py-hälä-Nei, Helsinki 1989.

a3) 5...c5 6 ♘d2 cxd4 7 cxd4

♘h6 8 ♘df3 ♗a6 9 ♗xa6 ♘xa6 10 ♘e2 ♗b4+ 11 ♔f2 ♘g4+ 12 ♔g1 h5 13 h3 ♘h6 14 g3 0-0-0 15 ♕d3 ♔b7 16 ♗e3 = Chekhov-Kengis, Gausdal 1991.

b) 5 ♘h3 c5 6 ♘a3 cxd4 7 cxd4 ♗a6 8 ♗xa6 ♘xa6 9 0-0 ♗xa3 10 bxa3 ♘e7 = Mohrlok-Ivkov, Vrnjačka Banja 1967.

c) 5 ♗d3 ♗a6 and now:

c1) 6 ♗c2 c5 7 ♘e2 ♘c6 8 ♗a4 ♘ge7 9 0-0 ♘f5 10 ♖e1 ♖c8 11 dxc5 bxc5 12 ♘d2 ♗e7 13 ♘f4 0-0 14 ♘f3 ♖fd8 15 ♗c2 d4 ½-½ Calvo-Andersson, Las Palmas 1972.

c2) 6 ♗xa6 ♘xa6 7 ♘e2 c5 8 0-0 ♘c7 9 a4 ♘e7 10 ♘g3 ♘c6 11 ♗e3 c4 12 ♘d2 ♘a5 13 ♘h5 0-0-0 14 b3 cxb3 15 ♘xb3 ♘c4 = Kontić-Nikolić, Vrnjačka Banja 1989.

d) 5 ♗e3 ♘e7 6 f4 h5 7 ♘d2 ♘f5 8 ♗f2 ♗a6 9 ♗xa6 ♘xa6 10 ♘e2 g6 11 ♘f3 ♗e7 12 ♕d3 ♘b8 13 0-0 c5 14 c4 ♘c6 15 dxc5 bxc5 16 cxd5 ♘b4 = Kupreichik-Vaganian, USSR Ch 1976.

e) 5 a4!? and now:

e1) 5...a5 6 ♘f3 ♘e7 7 ♗d3 ♗a6 8 0-0 ♗xd3 9 ♕xd3 ♘f5 10 ♘a3 ♗e7 11 b3 ♘a6 12 g4 ♗xa3 13 ♗xa3 ♘e7 14 ♘g5 c5 15 f4! ♘c6 16 f5 ♕d8 17 h4 h6 18 fxe6 hxg5 19 ♖xf7 1-0 Eley–MacDonald-Ross, Glasgow 1975.

e2) 5...♗a6 6 ♗xa6 ♘xa6 7 a5 b5 8 b4 ♘e7 9 ♘f3 f6 10 h4 ♘c6 11 ♗f4 fxe5 12 ♘xe5 ♘xe5 13 ♗xe5 ♗d6 14 ♘d2 (14 ♕e2!?) 14...♘b8

15 ♕h5+ ♕f7 16 ♕xf7+ ♔xf7 18 ♘f3 ± Grosar-Siegal, Geneva 1991.

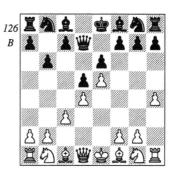

126
B

5 ...   ♘e7

Black is reluctant to impede the pawn's progress with 5...h5 as it makes it easier for a knight or bishop to be established on g5. White obtained a winning attack in the game Galdunts-Paris, St. Ingbert 1992, after 5...c5 6 h5 f5 7 ♘d2 cxd4 8 cxd4 ♗a6 9 ♘e2 ♘c6 10 ♘f3 ♗b4+ 11 ♗d2 ♘h6 12 ♘f4 ♗xf1 13 ♔xf1 ♘f7 14 ♖h3! 0-0-0 15 ♕a4 ♗xd2 16 ♘xd2 ♔b7 17 ♖a3 g5 18 18 ♖c1! gxf4 19 ♖xc6 ♕xc6 20 ♕xa7+ ♔c8 21 ♖c3 +-.

6	**h5**	**h6**
7	**♘d2**	**c5**
8	**♘h3**	

The knight is heading for f4, where it will also lend support to h5 if there is a need for kingside castling.

8	**...**	**♗a6**
9	**♗xa6**	**♘xa6**
10	**♘f4**	**0-0-0**

This is where the king belongs as Black can now form a long-term plan based upon closing the queen-side and eventually advancing on the kingside to create a counter-attack.

11	a3	♔b7
12	b4	cxd4
13	cxd4	♖c8 *(127)*

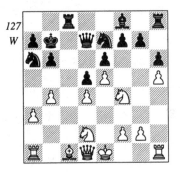

14   ♖h3!

Inaugurating a lightning attack by swinging the rook across to the queenside. This is a regular feature of lines with an early h4 as the closed centre means that the white king can sometimes safely stay in the centre.

14	...	♘b8
15	♘d3	f6
16	♗b2	♘bc6
17	♘b3	

The strategy of building up the forces on the queenside is simple but effective. Black is obliged to adopt a dour defensive set-up as the cramped nature of the position presents little opportunity for counterplay.

17	...	♘d8

Of course, 18 ♘c5+ has to be ruled out.

18	a4	♘ec6
19	♗a3	♔a8
20	b5	

The pawns advance to ensure the retreat of Black's last active piece. Now the game enters the final phase, which sees White in hot pursuit of Black's king.

20	...	♗xa3
21	♖xa3	♘e7
22	♕a1	♖c7
23	a5	♕xb5

Good or bad, the queen is obliged to capture the pawn to avoid instant calamity, thus opening up another path for the rooks.

24	axb6	♕xb6
25	♘bc5	♘ec6
26	♖e3	fxe5 *(128)*

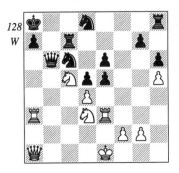

27   ♖e2!

At first sight, it appears that White has intended to shore up e5 but the real purpose of the manoeuvre is now revealed.

27	...	♘b4
28	♖b2	♘xd3+
29	♖xd3	♕d6
30	♕a3	♘f7
31	♖db3	♖hc8
32	♖b7	1-0

Game 43
Kupreichik-Vaganian
USSR 1980

1	e4	e6
2	d4	d5
3	e5	♘e7

The introduction of 3...♘e7 is closely linked to lines with 3...b6. The move-order is designed to avoid various continuations by feigning a desire to transpose to the main lines. There are no benefits to be found from immediately undermining the pawn formation: 3...f6?! 4 ♗d3! (intending 5 ♕h5+) 4...g6 5 ♘f3 ♘c6 6 exf6 ♘xf6 7 0-0 ♗g7 8 ♗g5 0-0 9 ♕d2 ± Weiss-Blackburne, Hamburg 1885.

4	♘f3	b6
5	c4 *(129)*	

A popular way to confront the system is to open up the game as soon as possible. Once again, gaining territory on the kingside is also a viable alternative:

a) 5 c3 ♕d7 6 h4 h5 7 a4 ♗a6 8 ♗xa6 ♘xa6 9 a5 ♘b8 10 axb6 cxb6 11 ♘bd2 ♘bc6 12 ♘f1 ♘f5 13 ♘g3 ♘xg3 14 fxg3 ♗e7 15 0-0 f6 16 exf6 gxf6 17 ♕e2 ♗d6 18 ♗f4 0-0-0 19

b4 ♖de8 20 ♕a6+ ♔c7 21 b5 +− Romero Holmes-Purgimon, Andorra 1987.

b) 5 h4 ♕d7 6 h5 h6 7 ♘c3 ♗a6 8 ♗xa6 ♘xa6 9 ♘e2 c5 10 c3 ♖c8 11 0-0 ♘c6 12 ♘h2 ♘c7 13 ♘g4 ± Fedorowicz-Prié, Paris 1989.

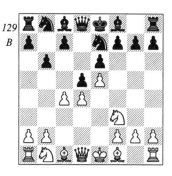

5	...	♗b7

After 5...♗a6 the simple reply 6 b3 avoids the trade of bishops.

6	♘c3	♕d7
7	cxd5	

The prospect of opening up the a8-h1 diagonal is of little concern as it is difficult to exploit, while White can quickly develop without distraction.

White soon had an advantage in the game Sax-Short, London 1980, after 7 ♗e2 ♘bc6 8 0-0 dxc4 9 ♗xc4 ♘a5?! (9...0-0-0!?) 10 ♗b5 ♗c6 11 ♗d3 ♘d5 12 ♗d2 ♗e7 13 ♘e4 ♗b4 14 ♖c1 ♗b5 15 ♗xb4 ♗xd3 16 ♕xd3 ♘xb4 17 ♕d2 ♘d5 18 ♕g5! ♔f8 (18...0-0? 19 ♘f6+ gxf6 20 exf6 g6 21 ♕h6 +−) 19 ♘c3 ±.

7	...	♘xd5
8	♗d3	c5
9	0-0	

There is no problem adjusting to the situation after 9...cxd4 10 ♘xd4 as Black remains congested, while in certain positions the white queen is able to roam on the kingside via g4 or h5.

9	...	♘xc3
10	bxc3	cxd4

If Black seeks to add pressure to d4 the situation can be brought under control: 10...♘c6 11 dxc5 ♗xc5 12 ♕e2 ♖d8 13 ♗c2 ±.

11   ♘xd4 *(130)*

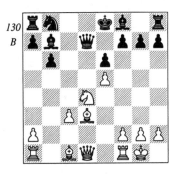

130
B

In Kupreichik's opinion this is the best way to maintain the initiative. Black's basic idea to earn equality would be evident after 11 cxd4 ♘c6 12 ♗e4 ♖d8 (12...♘e7 13 ♗xb7 ♕xb7 14 ♗a3! ±) 13 ♗g5?! (13 ♗e3 ♘e7 =) 13...♗e7 14 ♗xe7 ♘xe7 15 ♘g5 ♗xe4! (15...h6 16 ♘xf7!) 16 ♘xe4 0-0 17 ♘d6 ♘c8 with good chances against the d-pawn.

11	...	♘c6
12	♖b1	

With a series of exchanges White can exploit the opposing king being in the centre: 12 ♗b5 a6 13 ♗xc6 ♗xc6 14 ♘xc6 ♕xc6 15 ♕d3! ♗e7 16 ♕g3 ±.

12	...	♗c5
13	♗e3	0-0-0
14	♗b5	♗xd4?!

The chance for equality is lost. Much better is to activate the queen immediately: 14...♕d5! 15 ♘xc6 (15 c4?! ♕e4) 15...♗xc6 16 ♕xd5 ♗xd5 17 ♗xc5 bxc5 =.

15	♗xd4	♕d5
16	♗xc6	♗xc6

Little is gained from 16...♕xc6 17 f3 ♖d5 18 ♖b4, intending a4 with a promising attack.

17   f3

A simple but effective remedy, which blunts the power of controlling the diagonal.

17	...	h5
18	a4	♔b7
19	♕e2	

The first step towards a decisive infiltration. Now Black must be beware of the likelihood of opening up the a-file for the rook: 20 a5 ♕xa5 21 ♖a1 ♕b5 22 c4 ♕b4 23 ♖fb1 ♕e7 24 ♖xa7+! ♔xa7 25 ♗xb6+ +-. It would be premature to advance the pawn too rapidly: 19 a5?! ♕xa5 and now 20 ♕e2 ♕a6! 21 ♕e3 ♖d5 ∓ or 20 ♖a1 ♕d5 21 ♕e2 ♗b5 ∓.

19	...	♕a5

20	♖b4	♖d5
21	♖fb1	♖hd8
22	h4	♔a8
23	♔h2	♗xa4?! *(131)*

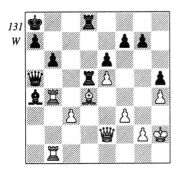

131
W

Black's patience finally cracks. Vaganian hopes that the deadlock can be broken in a positive way by stealing the a-pawn.

24 ♗xb6!

A sparkling sacrifice that will launch a formidable onslaught based on the might of the rooks.

24	...	axb6
25	♖xb6	♔a7
26	♖b7+	♔a8
27	♕b2	♖8d7

The attempt to neutralize the attack with 27...♖b5 results in a lost ending: 28 ♖xb5 ♕xb5 29 ♕xb5 ♗xb5 30 ♖xb5 +–.

28 ♖xd7?!

All lines lead to victory, but checkmate would be more impressive: 28 ♖b8+ ♔a7 29 ♖a8+! ♔xa8 30 ♕b8#.

28	...	♖b5
29	♕e2	♖xe5
30	♖d8+	1-0

11 3...♗d7

The desire to exchange White's light-squared bishop has resulted in an unusual opening strategy. It involves the simplistic 3...♗d7 and 4...a6 to support the outpost b5. The idea is to tempt White into trading pieces, which has the drawback of doubling the b-pawns, but offers dynamic compensation in the form of the open a-file. It has been occasionally adopted by a number of players who wish to seek an unbalanced position. However, Bronstein's model example of how to deal with the situation casts doubt on the viability of Black's variation.

Game 44
Bronstein-Kärner
Tallinn 1981

1	e4	e6
2	d4	d5
3	e5	♗d7
4	♘f3	a6!?

An ambitious and controversial idea. It paves the way for Black to relieve the traditional problem of the dormant 'French' bishop by exchanging it for White's more active light-squared bishop.

5 ♗g5 *(132)*

Black achieves the aim of reaching an uncharted position after the alternatives:

a) 5 ♘bd2 c5 6 dxc5 ♗xc5 7 ♗d3 ♘e7 8 ♘b3 ♗b6 9 ♗f4 ♘bc6 10 0-0 ♘g6 11 ♗g3 0-0 12 ♗xg6 hxg6 13 ♖e1 ♘e7 14 ♘bd4 ± Renet-Mellado, Palma de Mallorca 1989.

b) 5 c4!? dxc4 6 ♗xc4 ♗c6 7 0-0 ♘e7 with unclear play; Lau-Benjamin, New York 1985.

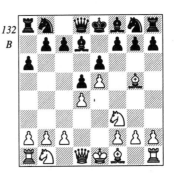

132
B

5 ...　　　♕c8?!

Black responds timidly to White's aggressive plan, wishing to preserve his dark-squared bishop from exchange; in that case d6 would act like a beacon to a white knight after a future ...c5. The ...♗b5 idea is unconvincing when the dark-squared bishop is not available to support the pawn thrust ...b4 to undouble the pawns.

A more acceptable line is available: 5...♘e7 6 ♘c3 c5 7 dxc5 ♕a5 8 a3 ♕xc5 9 ♗d3 ♘g6 ± Borngässer-Basman, Birmingham 1972.

6 c4

White is keen to open up the position to facilitate a rapid deployment of his forces. This has added appeal due to Black's cumbersome opening and especially now that the queen is misplaced.

6	...	h6
7	♗e3	dxc4
8	♗xc4	♘e7
9	♘c3	♗c6

It is a hollow victory to have activated the bishop at last, as the rest of the queenside remains congested.

10	0-0	♕d7
11	♖c1	

The rook moves to the most active square and further limits the options at Black's disposal.

11 ... a5 (133)

The necessity to make space for the queen's knight has resulted in an admission that the initial opening scheme has proved to be a failure. There is no respite if the bishop is given up to clear c6: 11...♗xf3 12 ♕xf3 ♘c6 (12...c6 13 ♘e4 with an edge for White) 13 ♖fd1 (intending

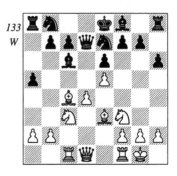

♕e4 and d5) 13...♖ad8 14 ♕g4 ♘d5 15 ♘e4 ±.

12 d5!

An ingenious sacrifice of a pawn to keep a grip on the position, which is energetically executed. Against the capture 12...♘xd5, White claims a clear advantage with 13 ♗xd5 ♗xd5 (13...exd5 14 e6 ♕xe6 15 ♖e1 ±) 14 ♘xd5 exd5 15 e6 ♕xe6 17 ♖xc7 ±.

12	...	exd5
13	♗d3	

A calm response that gives Black plenty of opportunities to go wrong. White holds the pawn-push e5-e6 in reserve, intending ♖e1 and ♗d4. In the meantime, Black faces a crisis in deploying his pieces before the attack gathers momentum.

13	...	♘a6
14	a3	g6
15	e6!	

Another clever device which quickly opens a direct avenue to the king. The e-file will be accessible to the rook and Black's kingside can be compromised by staking a claim for control of the a1-h8 diagonal.

15	...	♕xe6
16	♗d4	f6 *(134)*

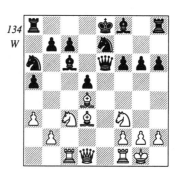

If the rook takes evasive action it makes little difference to Black's bleak prospects in Bronstein's opinion: 16...♖g8 17 ♖e1 ♕d6 18 ♘e5 ♗g7 19 ♘b5 ♕d8 20 ♖xc6! ♗xe5 21 ♖xa6 bxa6 22 ♖xe5 axb5 23 ♗xb5+ ♔f8 24 ♗c5 +–.

17	♗xg6+	♔d8	20	♖e6	♕d7
18	♖e1	♕d6	21	♗xf6	♗xf6
19	♗f7	♗g7	22	♖xf6	1-0

Index of Variations